BUS

P9-DKD-728

Designing & Building Your
Own Home

designing &building
your own home

Martin Cummins

The Crowood Press

First published in 2002 by
The Crowood Press Ltd
Ramsbury, Marlborough
Wiltshire SN8 2HR

www.crowood.com

British Library Cataloguing-in-Publication Data
A catalogue record for this book is available from the British Library.

ISBN 1 86126 535 2

Acknowledgements
Many thanks to: my friends and colleagues at Quad Architects for supplying me with source material, drawings and photographs (and generally putting up with me); Roger Newhall at Infields Solicitors for checking my legal section; and Joanna Burt for general photography including the frontispiece.

Illustration Credits
Bushey House, Bushey, by Quad Architects.
Capel-y-Nant, North Wales, by Quad Homes (perspective drawing by the author).
Clubhouse, Strawberry Hill, designed by Quad Architects.
The Fisheries, North Wales, by Quad Architects.
Flats in Putney, by Quad Architects.
'House of the Future', Acton, for Dr Saroj Patel and Dr Alan Warr, by Quad Architects.
Jersey Road, Isleworth, by Quad Architects.
Regatta Point, Brentford, by the author.
System-Built House by Huf Haus Ltd.
The Octagon, Chelsea, by Quad Architects.
The Quadhouse, Twickenham, by Quad Architects.
Timber-Framed House by Border Oak Design and Construction Ltd.

Typeset by Jean Cussons Typesetting, Diss, Norfolk

Printed and bound in Malaysia by Times Offset (M) Sdn. Bhd.

Contents

Introduction

Well! some people talk of morality, and some of religion, but give me a little snug property.
(Maria Edgeworth *The Absentee*)

The design and self-build of your own home may seem, at first, to be a somewhat daunting project to undertake, but it should be realized that the basic issues, although quite complex, are easy to grasp and that the whole process of designing and building your own home is not only an exciting and interesting process, but is also an affordable and realistic option.

There are many reasons why a person may opt to design and build their own home; perhaps it is for reasons of economy, geography or purely the wish to create something that is uniquely theirs. Whatever the reason may be, the self-build industry's existence in all its varied and myriad forms is a result of the fact that the existing housing stock is not catering for the needs of a large (and growing) section of the population.

Record numbers of homeowners want to design and build their own homes; in 1978 only 2,000 new homes were self-built, but current figures indicate that at least 15,000 people are now doing this, and the number is steadily growing. A study from the Joseph Rowntree Foundation predicts that self-builders will be creating 20,000 new homes by the year 2010, which will equate to approximately 10 per cent of all houses built.

Most self-builders will achieve their goal by choosing a plot, and commissioning an architect and builder(s) to work to their requirements but, whatever the means, what they will all have in common at the end of the process is a home that is to their own specification and design. The vast majority will also have achieved a property that is significantly more valuable than the cost of the land and the build cost added together. 'BuildStore', a specialist agency in the self-build sector, say self-builders can save 40 per cent on the price of a four-bedroom house if bought on the open market, with Bedfordshire, Somerset, Glamorgan, Aberdeenshire and Essex being the most cost-effective, and with West Midlands, Kent and Lancashire lagging behind somewhat.

Given the obvious advantages in designing and building your own personally tailored home, the first question that comes to mind is why on earth do not more people do this? After all, 15,000 is a drop in the ocean when compared to the huge number of domestic property transactions that are made every year. The answer to that question is that it is not easy to do; there is huge competition for sites, a slow and unwieldy planning system and a good deal of technical know-how required. After all, there is a large professional body (many of whom train for years) dedicated to the building industry, and some of the processes need specialized and in-depth knowledge. However, there is no magic at work in the house-building industry (although there is the occasional professional secret, shrouded in mystery) and with a little application you can gain the proper knowledge and the skills you need. That is where this book comes in.

This book is designed to be a 'how to' manual of the processes involved in getting a project up and running. It will lead you through the selection of ways of achieving your dream, finding a site, obtaining finance, navigating your way through the planning and building regulations processes, constructing the building and, most important of all, achieving a building that you will be happy with and proud of.

There is a limit to what you can get into one book and this volume does not pretend to have all the answers, but it does provide a route map through the self-build jungle, a travel guide so that you can enjoy your trip, a guide to finding a way around or through the obstacles you will encounter, and pointers to other places you can go if you get lost.

With a positive attitude and a willingness to get to grips with the issues, designing and building your own home will be a life-enhancing experience, both from the point of view of the excitement and interest involved in the process, and the long-term benefit of living in something that you have created to your own design and specification.

CHAPTER 1

Getting Started

… and the winds blew, and beat upon that house; and it fell not:
for it was founded upon a rock.
(Matthew 7:25)

It is important in the process of designing and building your own home to have a clear and concise framework that you can use as a guide to each of the steps along the way. To extend the building analogy, it is vital to ensure that the framework is built on firm foundations. It is important, therefore, to make the fundamental decisions and set in motion the correct procedures right at the beginning. If you do this you will find that things follow on naturally later on and you are less likely to go up blind alleys.

This chapter is intended to help you to set up a template for the type of home you want, can afford and is practical. It will assist you in asking yourself the fundamental questions as to what exactly it is that you want to achieve and, having done that, it will go on to guide you into asking the right questions of others to ensure that your home can be built. In short, what this chapter will do is help you to create a *feasibility study* for your project; this can then be used to check progress later on and to ensure that you are not straying away from your fundamental aims.

LOCATION

It may seem to be rather banal to be asking yourself where you want to live, but the old estate agent's adage that the three most important things when buying a property are location, location and location also holds true with the self-build market when you come to resell. In addition, plots for new dwellings are often a scarce commodity, especially in popular areas, and it is important to decide how far you are prepared to cast your net when looking for a site. The actual mechanics of selecting a site are covered in Chapter 2, but the first thing you need to ask yourself is where exactly you would like to be. Is it as wide as a whole county; is it a particular town or village; or does it have to be a specific area within a town or city? Whatever you do, the more you narrow your choice down, the more difficult it will be to find a plot. If you can decide what it is you are looking for as early as possible, when the right site does come along, you will be ready to act and indecision on your part will not waste the opportunity.

TYPE OF PROPERTY

Having decided where you want to live, the next step is deciding what you would like to live in. Again this may appear to be a slightly obvious question, but by asking yourself the right questions you will ensure that, at the end of the process, you will be happy with your new home. The type of property question breaks down into three sub-categories: they are accommodation, form and style.

Accommodation and Size

The obvious place to start with is what sort of accommodation you want or, possibly more simplistically, how many and what type of rooms you want. It is important when answering this question to cross-check your answer against the budget section of your *feasibility study*. It is easy when planning a project to aim too high – this can mean that the build costs will be excessive.

Listing the number of room types may be a little simplistic for your tastes; after all, open plan living is quite fashionable these days and might be more what you have in mind, if so for 'rooms' read 'space' in this section.

Rooms do not necessarily have to be dedicated to a single purpose, the issue of flexible space is dealt with in a later chapter, but it is worth considering at this stage which rooms could be multi-functional. Could you combine a study and guest room? Could a dining room also serve as an activities or music room? The answer does not have to be yes, but if it is maybe, then you can have a fall-back position if your budget is under pressure.

It is also worth, at this point, beginning to think about how you might use space and what your requirements for that space might be. In this way you can begin to assemble an *accommodation schedule.* This will be dealt with in greater depth in a later chapter, but it is an essential part of the feasibility stage to know approximately what you expect your new house to supply.

At the same time as assembling the accommodation schedule you can begin to estimate the size of your new house; this will be invaluable in setting the budget and also in creating a *footprint* that will allow you to assess whether a site is adequate for your needs. The table below gives you a shopping list of sizes, which will allow you to calculate the floor area of your new home. Bear in mind that this only needs to be very approximate for feasibility and the best way to express your calculation is by putting in a range of size; for example, 150–200sq m (1615–2150sq ft).

When using this table it should be remembered that the minimum dimension is fairly fixed, but the maximum dimension only reflects what you would regard as the 'normal' upper limit. In practice the sky is the limit (I do not think the designer of the banqueting hall at Windsor Castle would agree with my assessment of the upper limit for a dining room) so it rather depends on whether you want (or can afford) to live in a palace or a normal house. You can help yourself to decide where in the range you want to be by cross-checking against your present house or flat. This can be done by measuring a familiar room with a measuring tape or by pacing (one good pace is about a metre or three feet); when you have measured the room you can decide whether you would like your new room to be bigger or smaller.

Typical Room Sizes

	Size (square metres)	Size (square feet)
Living Room	15–40	160–430
Dining Room	12–35	130–175
Kitchen (without dining)	7–15	75–160
Kitchen (with dining)	12–21	130–225
Downstairs Hall	4–15	43–160
Study	10–20	107–214
Downstairs Cloakroom/WC	2–5	22–54
Stairs (per floor)	3.5–7	38–75
Downstairs Store	1–3	11–33
Utility Room	2.5–8	27–86
Garage (single)	14–18	151–194
Garage (double)	33–36	355–388
Master Bedroom	15–30	161–323
Other Bedroom (single)	8–14	86–150
Other Bedroom (double)	14–30	151–323
En-Suite Shower/Bathroom	2.5–4.5	27–48
Family Bathroom	3.5–7	38–75
Upstairs Store (Linen)	1–3	11–33
Upstairs Hall	5–15	53–160

Once you have established the size of your home you can decide what the footprint will be. This is best done, at this stage, in a very simplistic manner – just take your overall size and divide it by the number of storeys. Thus a bungalow will have the same footprint as the overall area for a two-storey house divided by two, for a three storey house divided by three and so on. This will obviously be very approximate since storeys are not necessarily the same size, but it will still be a useful guide.

Form

There are, as we all know, a great many forms that a home can take. Which one you select will be largely dependent on your choice of location. It is unlikely that you would want to build a four-storey town house in an area of bungalows; it is equally unlikely that you would get planning permission for such a house.

By making an early decision about the form of your new home, you can avoid wasting time looking at unsuitable plots. If you would like to live in a bungalow, for instance, it may be a waste of time to look for a plot in a highly developed urban area since the site is likely to be worth more to someone who wants to build several floors of development.

Similarly there are certain special forms of development that you might have considered but written off as not being part of the self-build arena, such as conversion or flatted development where, if you look in the right place, you can find something perfectly suitable. Again this will be dealt with in more detail in later chapters.

Style

An interest in what your home looks like is often one of the prime reasons for wanting to build your own home, since it might be impossible to find your ideal amongst the readily available building stock. If you start to consider at this stage what you would like your home to look like, both internally and externally, you will be ready and able to embark straight into the design stage when the time comes.

If you already have a very clear idea of what you want your home to look like then this is great, but you still will need to impart your ideas to various people along the way – from planners to designers to builders to suppliers. If you are not sure what you want your home to look like, you need to start formulating your ideas. Whichever way, the best thing to do is to start collecting images of buildings that interest you inside and outside.

Source material – the only limit is your imagination.

Good source material for this process is plentiful; there are numerous magazines linked to the building process and there is also a plethora of books on houses, interiors, decorating and so on. All images can be useful, they do not have to be specific; an image that sums up the spirit of what you are after can be as simple as a photograph of a single object. You do not have to be limited by realism when assembling your file.

In general, a good building should be strongly connected to the site in which it sits and, indeed, the planning process is designed to ensure that this is the case. Despite this, however, it can be useful to start categorizing what you are after in terms of style – are you looking for a building that reproduces the architecture of a bygone era but with all the modern conveniences, or would you like something more modern?

A starting point for setting the style of your house is to remind yourself that the style you choose will say the same things about you that your choice of clothes or car do. Mass house-builders generally opt for a traditional feel for their houses, on the basis that it is likely that this approach will be the one that suits the greatest number of potential clients; even then however, they will opt for more modern style in areas that they believe to be more fashionable.

You may find that this book will provide a source of the look you are after, but if not there are plenty of other sources of inspiration.

In all probability none of the images you will collect will sum up exactly the way you feel about your new project, or perhaps a combination of several of them will. Whichever is the case, if you start collecting an album of images that appeal to you, you will be able to start focussing in on what you want.

OPTIONS

The next thing to start thinking about is how you would like to achieve your aims. This will depend to some extent on the reason for you deciding to design and build your own home. If your primary reason is an economic one then it may lead you into doing things differently than if you are looking to fulfil a dream. Listed below are some of the options, with some of the pros and cons associated with them.

Group Self-Build

This once popular form is now rare, but it may rise again and is worth a brief mention.

Group self-build is the process by which a group of people who are trying to achieve the same aims band together and, by pooling resources and talents, are able to build more cheaply than with any other method.

The idea is that joint-purchasing power gives a greater edge to finance the project, and you contribute whatever you can to the communal effort, from professional acumen if you have a useful skill, through to unskilled labour. In addition, the monetary 'punch' of the group allows advantageous finance to be arranged.

In the past there were some instances of group self-build organizations being formed by like-minded individuals without a particularly formal structure, but mostly they were dominated by commercial operations who could arrange finance through the banks or building societies.

The problem with this system was that, during the deep recession of the late 1980s/early 1990s, the

---

Group Self-Build

Advantages:

- Cost effectiveness.
- Making the most of individual abilities.
- Fosters a ready-made feeling of community.

Disadvantages:

- Currently almost impossible to achieve finance.
- Cannot guarantee that all members will pull their weight.
- Since most of the schemes rely on a group planning approval you do not get a great deal of say in what the building looks like externally.

group nature of these organizations worked against them since, almost without fail, individuals within the group would default as a result of the spiralling-repayments/falling-equity trap, houses would be left unsold or incomplete and this would destabilize the whole organization.

This then caused the building societies and banks to reconsider their position on offering finance for group projects, and it is now very difficult to fund group self build schemes.

Community Self-Build

This is a variant of the group self-build; again the emphasis is on a group of like-minded individuals using mutual cooperation to achieve their objectives, but in this case the controlling organization is in the public sector, either a local authority or a housing association.

This form of building is part of the effort to provide low-cost housing for people within a community who are in housing need and are struggling to source suitable accommodation through any other means.

Community Self-Build breaks down into three sub-categories:

Outright Ownership

This form is based on a combination of private borrowing and loans from the Housing Corporation. The Housing Corporation loan can be up to 49 per cent of the development cost and acts as seed capital, with the private-sector finance clicking in when that money is expended. When the building is finished the Housing Corporation loan must be repaid and the members of the scheme must finance their own mortgage.

The scheme generally gets underway when the Community Self-Build Agency identifies a suitable site for a self-build project. It will then advertise for people who are interested in becoming part of the scheme, who must then apply to become members. The selection process is very stringent and there is a hefty fall-out rate. Members have to demonstrate that they have a genuine need for this kind of scheme and also have the abilities to make a useful contribution. Members then have to dedicate 2–3 days a week to the project,

with their input being based on their particular skills.

On completion, the members retain full ownership of their property subject to their financing arrangements, but have to sign a legal agreement (which is appended to the deeds of the property) that they will only sell to people who meet the qualifying requirements that they themselves had to meet (excepting the self-build skills), and also that they will sell at only 80 per cent of the open-market value of the property. This means that the property is maintained in perpetuity as affordable housing.

Shared Ownership

This type of scheme is similar to the above, but is for those who would like to take advantage of the self-build process and whose income is not adequate to raise a loan for the whole property when the building process is complete.

This will be based on a 50/50 ownership, with the government providing a Social Housing Grant that is controlled via a Housing Association. These schemes usually include a buy-out provision, whereby the Member can increase his ownership to 100 per cent within a certain period.

Community Self-Build

Advantages:

- Cost effectiveness
- Making the most of individual abilities.
- Fosters a ready-made feeling of community.
- Puts self-build into the grasp of those who might not normally be able to afford it.

Disadvantages:

- The selection process is very stringent.
- Cannot guarantee that all members will pull their weight.
- Since most of the schemes rely on a group planning approval you do not get a great deal of say in what the building looks like externally.

Rented Schemes

This form is for people on very low incomes or the unemployed and relies on Social Housing Grants being provided via a Housing Association. It is basically a way of rewarding self-builders with accommodation at much lower rates than equivalent accommodation built under a conventional process.

Developer-Led Self-Build

This is essentially when a developer has control of an area of land and gains planning permission for its sub-division into a number of different building plots. The developer will then advertise, normally in a self-build magazine or on a web-site, for suitable self-builders. When a purchaser is found they will be offered limited scope for influencing the design and materials of construction of the house, and the developer will then go ahead and construct the property on their behalf, with payment being made by the purchaser in tranches, based on the developer's assessment of the value of the work carried out at each valuation point.

The advantage of this method is that the self-builder can find themselves moving into their new home much more quickly than with other methods, albeit at the cost of being obliged to conform to the existing designs.

When assessing the disadvantages of this method you should ask yourself one simple question: why has the developer chosen this way of selling? Developers are not generally associated with altruism and philanthropy, and there will be a profit motive or a force-of-circumstances motive to their selection of this method.

It is possible that the developer does not have the available cash to build out the whole site at one time and is using the drip-feed of cash available from a self-build arrangement to finance the work as he proceeds. In this case you should make careful enquiries into the financial state of the company you are buying from and you should ensure that the developers are not getting ahead of themselves in the valuation of work completed. Care must also be taken to ensure that you are adequately protected in the case of insolvency of the developer – that is to say, that it is clear that the ownership of the plot belongs to you, that there is no third party with a second

charge over it, and that the purchaser has the right to employ his own builder to complete the plot. It is important, therefore, to ensure that you engage the services of a good solicitor to advise on the form of building contract and on the transfer of the property, and the services of a surveyor or architect to ensure that interim payments properly reflect the amount of work completed on-site.

Another reason for developers opting for this method may be that they do not have the confidence in the site or design to sell them out if they were to build them all at once. They may not be in a particularly good area or they may suffer from an unfortunate aspect that would make them less attractive when actually built. You should, therefore, take a good long look at the site, ask yourself if you really want to be there and try to envisage what the house and its neighbours will look like when it is built. Again, it is worth paying for a few hours of an architect's time to advise on whether the building is likely to be a good one.

Yet another reason for this method might be that the developers believe that, by opting for this way of doing things, they can get more money out of the purchaser on the basis that they think that they are getting a special bespoke-building tailored to their individual needs rather than an off-the-shelf arrangement. This may be true, but there is a limit to how much extra a buyer should pay for this service and it

---

Developer-Led Self-Build

Advantages:

- A good way of getting to completion in quick time.

Disadvantages:

- Can be risky financially.
- Can result in a disappointing home in terms of siting, design or aspect.
- Can be expensive.
- May not suit those who want to be involved in the actual construction.

is prudent to check out the price of houses of a similar size and specification in the area before committing to this kind of arrangement. After all, if and when you sell on, the fact that the house has been tailor-made for you will have no bearing on the next potential resident's feelings.

Shell-and-Core

This is variant of the 'developer-led' type of scheme and is a relative newcomer to the table. It is a reaction to the increasing popularity of 'loft'-type developments and the high design input that goes into this type of scheme. Some developers have recognized that this sort of property attracts those who want a high-design 'trendy' type of flat and also that this is not the format for neat compartmentation into conventional rooms – open-plan living is almost the norm.

A typical development will involve the developer providing the basic weather-tight building and the communal facilities, such as reception, staircases, lifts and sometimes leisure facilities such as sauna, gym or swimming pool. Each flat will have its front door provided, but inside you will just find an open, empty space, without partitions, sanitary ware, kitchen or any internal finishes. It is then up to the purchaser to design and construct the interior of their apartment.

This method of construction once again has advantages in terms of speedy access to the new home and can result in very interesting design arrangements. It is subject, however, to the same potential problems as any developer-led scheme and can also be prone to a couple of additional difficulties. It is fairly common practice to allow the purchaser access to the flat while work is still going on in the communal areas, on the basis that it is better to get work in the individual flats over before there are any finishes in the communal areas to be damaged by the purchasers' building process. It is not uncommon for this process to be going on between legal exchange and completion, and in the event of insolvency on the part of the developer the purchasers might find themselves in a vulnerable position.

The other thing to watch out for in this type of deal is that, once again, you should ask yourself why the developers are doing it this way. It may be that the building is simply more saleable when the purchaser is given the flexibility in design, but these sort of developments are often in converted warehouses and may be quite 'deep' in plan with a long distance from the windows to the more remote sections of the apartment – this space may not achieve the value for a developer if supplied finished rather than on a cost-per-square-metre basis. This can be quite problematic when it comes to sub-dividing

Shell and Core – *the developer provides the shell – you fit it out.*

15

> ### Shell and Core
>
> Advantages:
>
> - A good way of getting to completion in quick time.
> - Can result in a very attractive 'high design' type of property.
>
> Disadvantages:
>
> - Can be risky financially.
> - Can be expensive.
> - Can result in compromises in design.

the space, and you would be well advised to do (or have done) a sketch design for the flat before committing yourself to the purchase.

System Building

There are a number of companies who advertise in the self-build publications and on the Internet who provide system-built or 'kit' buildings. These are based around a pattern-book approach whereby the company provides a catalogue of pattern-book designs that the client can choose from.

Very often the 'system-built' approach will be similar to that of the developer-led self-build scheme, in that when you ring up you will be offered plots that already have planning permission or that the system builder has control over.

Typically if you already have your own plot then the system-builder will offer a design service to obtain the various required permissions before building commences.

System building can vary in type from the fairly flexible, such as timber-frame construction where a basic timber frame can be clad with a material that suits the location, the planners and the purchaser, through to the more rigid, such as the 'chalet'-type accommodation that is increasingly being imported from Scandinavia, which has a distinctive style – not always to the taste of everyone (and the planners). There is also a growing market in the supply of the more esoteric type of system building, such as 'traditional' oak frame.

The advantage of system building is that it is often quick to build and can be a fast way of getting a finished product. It is also, quite often, a realistic alternative in terms of value for money to traditional methods (although care should be taken, as with developer-led schemes when the system builder controls the land, that the finished product is not excessively more expensive than similar-sized properties in

Kit of Parts houses can be traditional (Border Oak timber-frame house) …

… or more radical (Huf Haus prefabricated house)

the area). The purchaser should bring the same scrutiny to the valuation and contract arrangements as suggested for the developer-led methods.

How good the system-built format is for you rather depends on your view of context; a good building is generally one that respects and enhances its location. If you go for a building designed 'off-site'

it can feel inappropriate to the area – so have a good look at the site and ask yourself, does it fit in?

Conventional Procedure

This form of self-build is probably the most common and, if you have the time, the best.

It involves getting control of a plot of land (in one of the ways described in Chapter 2) then designing, or having designed, a house to your precise requirement, then arranging for the construction of the building. The exact procedure is analysed in more detail later in this book.

The advantage of this method is that you should get a building more exactly tailored to your needs than can be supplied by any other of the methods listed, something that is unique, and something that you can tailor to give yourself the exact level of involvement you want during the construction.

The problem with doing it this way is that it can be much more involved than the others and can take a great deal of time. You are subject to the whims of local authorities, designers and builders; you can be more exposed due to the various different contractual arrangements; and you must be careful to ensure that you are not at risk when purchasing the plot of land. Again this will all be dealt with in more detail in Chapter 2.

System Building

Advantages.

- Can be a quick cost-effective way of getting the desired product.

Disadvantages:

- Is prone to inflexibility.
- May lead to a product not to everyone's taste.
- Can be subject to the same contractual and economic difficulties as developer-led schemes.
- May not suit those who want to be involved in the actual construction.

Conventional procedure – more flexibility.

COST

The next and, in many ways, most important factor in the feasibility study stage of the whole self-build process is setting a proper budget for the project; ensuring that the finance is achievable and that the money is ready as soon as you need to press the button to start the process.

Budget

The cost of self building tends to come in six distinct categories: these are set-up costs, land costs, build costs, finance costs, tax and fees. It is well worth, at this stage, doing an estimate of each of these categories so that a realistic budget can be set.

Set-Up Costs

Set-up costs are usually fairly minimal in terms of actual money, since they are basically any costs associated with making the initial enquiries and getting everything in place, and most advisers and companies involved in the self-build business will not charge for initial consultation, since they will be looking for your business. The aspiring self-builder will be involved in a fair amount of travel, which is a cost, also in buying publications, photocopying and so on, which are very minor costs in the great scheme of things. The real cost at this stage, however, is time. You must be prepared to invest a lot of time; failure to do so means that the foundations for the whole project are not properly laid. The amount of calendar time that is required is dealt with in the 'Programme' section of this chapter.

Land Costs

It is important to put in a realistic cost for land at the feasibility stage, since it makes up a substantial part of the budget. However, land costs can vary greatly and until you actually settle on a plot it will be an unknown cost – all you can do is make an informed guess.

The best way of slotting a land cost into the equation is to make enquiries into similar sites in areas similar to where the development will eventually be. This should not be time wasted, since initial enquiries will get the ball rolling to find the plot in any case.

If this is too time consuming and you are just engaged in a back-of-the-envelope exercise to see if the whole thing is worth doing, there is an easier method involving opening the property section of the local paper and looking for houses (preferably newly built) of a similar size and in a similar area to the eventual finished product, and compiling a list of their prices. The land cost of a housing project tends to be between 20 and 40 per cent of the sales price of the finished product, so it is possible to get a 'broad brush' land cost by multiplying the sales price of the properties by this figure. Generally speaking, the better the area the higher the percentage of the sales cost made up by the land cost will be.

Build Cost

It is likely that the build cost will be the most expensive single item in the equation and it is, again, of prime importance to make a realistic estimate of this cost.

Again there are various different ways, with various different degrees of accuracy, to estimate build cost. There is a whole profession, that of Quantity Surveying, dedicated to estimating the cost of buildings before they are constructed and even they tend to be out by a significant margin when they are calculating build cost prior to the design of a building, so it should be realized that at this stage all one can do is to get an approximate cost.

Obviously the most accurate way of getting a build cost is to hire a Quantity Surveyor, but that would be expensive at the feasibility stage and would not necessarily be particularly accurate without a design to work from.

Perhaps the best way of estimating the cost for feasibility study purposes is to refer back to the 'Accommodation and Size' part of this chapter; this will give a preferred area for the prepared house (this must be the full area, not the footprint) in square metres or square feet. A cost per square foot or metre can then be attached to the area. It would be foolish to give any detailed guidance on build costs in this book, since the cost varies with means of construction, time, quality and location, so it is better to refer to one of the guide lists that are being constantly being updated. Suffice it to say, build costs can vary between £450 and £1,200 per square metre (£42–£111 per square foot) with most costs appearing in the median range.

There are a number of price guides for the industry, such as 'Spons' – the bible of the Quantity

Surveyor – but these can be quite specialized and expensive. Better sources are the self-build publications, which will give costs per square metre of recent case histories, but again these are only approximate pending a full design. Websites by system builders that purport to give price guidance can be used to get a rough guide, but they will generally only relate to their own particular product and can be misleading in ignoring significant costs such as landscaping, road and drain construction, and the like.

If you are planning to do a lot of your own construction work, you need to factor in a percentage for your efforts; a simple rule of thumb in this process (and assuming that the self-builder is not a skilled builder) is to multiply the amount of time that can be devoted to the project by the current minimum wage, over the projected timescale for the project, and then deduct this from the overall cost of the building.

Not withstanding the above the scale of costs will equate to the chosen method of procurement of the building contract as shown in the table below.

Finance Costs

It is more likely than not that you will be borrowing at least part of the cost of the project and that expense

Procurement Method – Table of Cost	
Most Expensive	Built by an established NHBC-registered contractor working from their own offices.
	Built by a small builder working from home.
	Built by a small builder to 'shell' stage then turned over to you for finishing.
Least Expensive	Built by yourself using subcontractors to complete the processes you cannot manage yourself.
NOTE: The items in this table can change in their ranking depending on how successful the process is and how hard a bargain you have driven with the parties involved!	

will start as soon as the first tranche is borrowed. Since these costs are not disguised as living costs, like an ordinary mortgage, they should be factored into the projected overall budget. Costs will vary according to what method of finance is chosen (see below). Both arrangement fees (where appropriate) and interest should be calculated.

Fees

There will inevitably be a number of fee costs associated with the project, and this will vary according to the method of self-build chosen. At its simplest the only cost will be for a solicitor, but for more complex projects fees for the planning application, building regulations application, architect, structural engineer, party-wall surveyor, planning supervisor and NHBC should all be added in. The next chapter will give guidance as to what, if any, of these disciplines will be needed.

Tax

There are three main types of tax to consider when setting off in the self-build process; these are VAT, Capital Gains and Stamp Duty. Normally the only tax which you will have to bear is Stamp Duty, but there are situations where the other taxes may apply and you should be aware of these so that they can be slotted into the equation where appropriate.

VAT is normally zero rated on new-build domestic properties, but there are certain situations where VAT will be chargeable. Conversions, for instance, will be standard rated unless they involve a change of use from commercial to residential or if they are listed buildings (in which case only the work which requires planning permission is zero rated). Also, when the self-builder does most of the work they need to either set up a VAT-registered company themselves or issue the appropriate certificate to any contractors they do use. In addition there are certain items on which VAT cannot be reclaimed; these tend to be fittings as opposed to fixtures, for instance furniture, carpets and curtains. If in any doubt, the local VAT office can be contacted and they will give guidance. Her Majesty's Stationary Office produce a helpful publication entitled 'VAT Refunds for Do-It-Yourself Builders and Converters'

that can generally also be obtained at the local VAT office.

Capital Gains Tax can be applied, but only when it can be demonstrated that the self-builder is building for profit rather than for their own use. There is obviously not an issue if the self-build process is a conventional one, but care should be taken when more than one property is owned or the new property is sold very quickly after completion. In such circumstances it is wise to consult a taxation accountant before going too far.

After the bad news there is also good; you are entitled to reclaim interest on the first £30,000 of any loan given to buy a plot as MIRAS relief – your accountant will, again, advise you on this.

Finance

It is clearly necessary to ensure that finance is available throughout the project, that there is sufficient cash flow and that it has been checked that the finance is possible before you commit to any real expense.

There is a plethora of options available for raising finance, and more appearing all the time. So volatile is the market that it is not possible to give a complete guide in a book such as this, since it is quite possible that any advice will be superseded quite quickly. The principles are fairly constant, however, and they will be dealt with here.

The problem facing the self-builder is that the conventional way of buying a house is to arrange for a mortgage whereby the purchaser completes on the sale of their old property and the purchase of their new one on the same day, so that at no time are they paying for two houses at once. The self-builder, however, has to pay for the property where they are living at the same time as finding the finance on the property they are building. This can obviously place a burden on cash flow and should be factored into the cost of self-building, but in practice it is usual to arrange a means of finance by which there is no burden of repayment until the new property is complete.

Some of the options for financing the self-build process are set out below but it is well worth consulting an accountant or independent mortgage consultant before making the final decision.

Sale of Existing Property

For those fortunate enough to wholly or partially own their own house, one option is obviously to sell the property and use the equity to finance, to whatever degree, the new venture. Although this might be less daunting in terms of commitment than financing two properties at the same time, in practice it tends to be expensive, in that temporary accommodation must be paid for and, in addition, you will lose out on any house-price inflation that you would have enjoyed had you retained your existing property.

Bank Loan

Many banks will provide venture capital on a commercial basis. They will look at the scheme from the point of view of a business proposal and will base their decision as to whether to provide finance on what level of equity the self-builder is providing, what the proportion of finance against eventual value is likely to be and what the borrower's credentials are. Typically, a banker will not lend money for a venture such as this unless the borrower puts up at least 30 per cent of the cost and on the basis that the total amount lent does not exceed 70 per cent of the value of the finished product. Bank lenders often take a more progressive view than mortgagers and will lend money when the borrower is already quite highly geared on the basis of the individual deal, but the cost of a bank loan tends to be relatively high when compared to a mortgage, with two or three points over the bank base rate commonly being charged and an arrangement fee and interest being rolled up into the loan. There is then the problem at the end of the process of arranging a mortgage and paying off the loan.

Self-Build Mortgage

There are quite a lot of institutional lenders prepared to lend money to self builders. At the time of writing and depending on the lender, you can borrow up to 95 per cent of the value of the building plot, and then up to 95 per cent of the value of the completed house (BuildStore Accelerator Mortgage, Bradford & Bingley, Britannia, Lloyds TSB Scotland, Mortgage Express and Skipton). This will depend on their view of how much the plot and the completed building will be worth, regardless of how much you paid for

them. Mortgagers will also take into account your complete financial position, including what you are paying for your existing accommodation, what other financial commitments you have, and what your asset base and income is.

When seeking finance you will need to make a convincing presentation of your project to the lender; this will need to include projected cash-flow, cost and details of the proposal. A well thought out, convincing presentation will considerably increase your chances of obtaining finance.

PROGRAMME

The final part of the equation when conducting your feasibility study is to consider the programme for realizing your aims. The building industry is not the fastest moving operation in the world and a realistic idea of the time involved will ensure that you take the right decision when opting for the self-build process, and also avoid frustration at a later date.

The best way of setting up a programme for your project is to create a bar chart with each square representing a week and then write out the major processes involved in the right-hand column.

There are several major processes involved, these are:

- Inception and feasibility.
- Selecting a site.
- Design (including planning).
- Detail design and production information.
- Construction.

You will find that these processes correspond broadly with the sections in this book, and that (depending on the mode of self-build selected) some of these processes can be ignored completely. Each category is dealt with in greater depth later on, but a brief synopsis is given here for the purposes of forming a realistic programme.

Inception

For this stage, as described in this chapter, the amount of time taken rather depends on how much you throw yourself into it. But since you are unlikely to prepare a programme until you have made up your

33 ACACIA AVENUE
PRELIMINARY PROGRAMME

MONTH	SEPT	OCT	NOV	DEC	JAN	FEB	MARCH	APRIL	MAY	JUNE	JULY	AUG	SEPT	OCT	NOV	DEC	JAN	FEB
WEEK COMMENCING	1 8 15 22 29	6 13 20 27	3 10 17 24	1 8 15 22 29	5 12 19 24	2 9 16 23	1 8 15 22 29	5 12 19 26	3 10 17 24 31	7 14 21 28	5 12 19 26	2 9 16 23	30 6 13 20 27	4 11 18 25	1 8 15 22 29	6 13 20 27	3 10 17 24 31	7 14 21 28

Tasks:

- SITE FINDING
- SITE ACQUISITION
- FEASIBILITY
- RAISING FINANCE
- DESIGN
- PRE-APPLICATION PLANNING MEETING
- SUBMISSION OF PLANNING APPLICATION
- CONSIDERATION OF PLANNING APPLICATION
- BUILDING REGULATIONS APPLICATION
- BUILDING REGULATIONS CONSIDERATION
- DETAIL DESIGN AND PRODUCTION INFORMATION
- MAIN CONTRACT TENDER
- MOBILISATION
- SITE OPERATIONS
- SNAGGING AND CLEANING
- MOVE IN

CHRISTMAS / NEW YEAR HOLIDAY

CHRISTMAS / NEW YEAR HOLIDAY

A preliminary project programme.

mind about a lot of the other key items, inception might not feature in the programme.

Selecting a Site

This is a bit like 'How long is a piece of string?' You may be lucky and find the right opportunity straight away or it may take months or even years to do it. Whichever, it is important to be realistic and thus avoid disappointment or frustration. My later example shows three months to find a site and another month to secure it. This is optimistic and it would need luck and application on the part of the self-builder to achieve it.

Design and Planning

If you opt for one of the community, developer or system-built self-build schemes you may not need to factor in this item. If, however, you are going down the more conventional route, you should allow for a couple of months to design the building and two to three months for planning. Again, this is a moveable feast since time for the planning authorities to consider your scheme can vary greatly depending on whether or not the scheme is controversial or in a sensitive area.

Detail Design and Production Information

This is the process of producing the drawings and documents in detail for constructing your home. Again, it is possible to cut this time out of the loop if you are using the community or developer-led options. A typical time for this process is eight to ten weeks and then if you are taking the scheme out for competitive prices to a number of contractors you should allow them four weeks to get a proper tender together.

Construction

Again, this time can vary greatly according to the complication of the building, what time you build it (digging foundations and building walls in freezing or rainy weather can take twice as long) and what method you use to build it (if you build it yourself you are unlikely to be as efficient or as quick in time as a normal contractor). A realistic time, as you will see from the example is between six and twelve months.

Holidays

As you will see from the example, it is a good idea to factor in holiday periods – yours if you are managing the site and other people's when you are employing tradesmen to do the work.

If you have worked through all the stages above you should now have an idea of what you want to build, where you want to build it, how you want to build it, how much you want to spend and how long it will take you. If this hasn't put you off you are ready for the next step, so read on to the 'Finding a Site' section.

CHAPTER 2

Finding a Site

Castles in the air – they are so easy to take refuge in. And easy to build, too.
(Henrik Ibsen *The Master Builder*)

So, having gone through everything described in the last chapter you have found that designing and building your own home is now a feasible option, but there is just one small detail remaining – finding somewhere to design and build it. So far, however serious you are, the exercise has been an imaginary one – building castles in the air; now begins the process of building the castle on the ground. This chapter is intended as a guide to clearing this next hurdle both in terms of finding a suitable site and then, having done so, of avoiding the various possible pitfalls.

At first sight it might seem quite easy to find a site – everywhere one looks there are sites that could hold a new house. What must be born in mind, however, are the United Kingdom's stringent planning laws, probably the toughest in the world, and the competition from others (BuildStore currently has a register of 10,000 plot-seekers). So although you might find somewhere where you *could* build a house it doesn't mean you will be allowed to.

Up until the beginning of the last century there was a cheerful anarchy about the way development occurred, the basic premise being that if you owned the land you could do with it what you wanted. The only controls tended to be legal provisions or restrictive covenants attached by the vendor to a site so that the purchaser could only do certain things with it (this will be dealt with in more detail later on in this chapter).

Planning law, as we know it, developed initially as sets of byelaws varying from area to area that controlled to some extent the location you could build in and what you could actually build there.

These laws varied from relaxed to draconian, depending on the local personalities involved.

From the Industrial Revolution onwards, the sprawling urban and suburban estates that were appended to cities and most towns of any size gradually began to eat into the surrounding countryside and led to the development of super cities or 'conurbations', whereby adjacent towns were joined together by infill development and lost their individuality. This effect was especially apparent in the southeast and northwest but, to some extent, went on everywhere. In addition, zoning was indiscriminate in that it was the norm to mix residential and industrial uses, with discomfort and health problems being the inevitable result. Also, in many places, there was little amenity area in the form of open spaces and gardens.

It was gradually recognized that national policy was the only way to address these problems and this led to the development of what is now known as planning law. At the heart of planning law are two principles: that new development should be neighbourly to existing adjacent properties, and that areas and suburban sprawl should be checked.

This has evolved into the stringent and far-reaching set of rules that we now have to deal with. It has made the UK a very controlled and cohesive place visually – certainly when compared with the sprawling development in other countries. But it has also meant that there is intense pressure on the sites that are available and it is not easy to gain control of one.

Despite all the aforesaid, however, the sites are there and it is only a matter of knowing where to look.

SITE FINDING

If you have followed the advice laid out in the previous chapter you will by now know where you want to search and what kind of plot you are searching for. As far as the method of building is concerned, if you are opting for the community self-build or for the developer-led option then these will come with a site attached. You will be well-advised to still bring to those sites the scrutiny that is suggested in the 'Site Analysis' section of this chapter, but you may want to skip the 'Site Finding' section entirely.

There are a number of different ways of sourcing a site and, as an aspiring self-builder, it would be prudent to start off by exploring them all.

Estate Agents

In any area there are developers of property – people who make a living from buying, selling and developing pieces of land that come onto the market. They will have an established reputation in the area as people who get things done. They will have an established relationship with local estate agents, be on their books on a permanent basis and will be a preferred option when a site comes on the market, since they will be less trouble and more likely to perform than an unknown. It is these people, therefore, who you will have to compete against when trying to purchase a site from estate agents. With that said, however, most agents work on a percentage of the cost of the property they are trying to sell and, providing you can convince the agent of your seriousness and commitment, your ability to perform and can come up with the right deal, you are in with a proper chance.

It is wise when initially approaching an agent not just to drift in off the street and ask if there are any sites they know of in the area, although you can be lucky this way. If you do cold-call, you need to be properly prepared so that the agent will remember you and bear you in mind if anything does come up.

Try to see someone in the most senior position you can. It is well worth a telephone call before you visit in order to find out who the manager or assistant manager of the agency is – they are more likely to deal with sites since they often go to their more important repeat customers. Also take a résumé of

what you are actually looking for with you so that you can leave it with them. This document should state clearly the size of site you would like, what you would like to put on it and what you are willing to pay. Make sure it has your name and address on it, and also a telephone number where you can be reached at any time of the day; good sites can provoke a feeding frenzy when they appear on the market and you can lose out if you are not immediately contactable. It is also a good idea to include your financial status and stress your ability to perform.

Your time can often be better spent contacting estate agents by writing to them with a letter of introduction, addressed to the manager and again including the resume.

You may be told that the particular agency you approach rarely or never gets building plots for sale, but do not be put off. All agencies get building plots sooner or later and very often they will get plots with houses on them that are suitable for development. How to spot these properties is dealt with later on.

Once you have made initial contact with the estate agents in the area you want to be, do not let them forget you. Follow up your initial visit/letter with a telephone call to make sure that your particulars have been placed on file. Try to strike up a relationship with a particular person so that you do not get shuffled from one person to another when you call subsequently. Then keep on calling intermittently so that you are always in the back of their mind. Persistence will convince them of your seriousness.

Other Professionals

Estate agents do not have a monopoly when it comes to having the contacts to source sites. Most plots of land that have the potential for becoming house-building plots will go through the hands of other professionals at some time. These tend to be architects, surveyors and solicitors.

It is common for a vendor to engage the services of an architect to gain planning permission in order to maximize the value of a site that they are about to sell, to employ a solicitor to arrange for conveyancing and sometimes a surveyor to ascertain the condition of a structure already on site. So it is quite possible that a professional working in the area will know of a site that the vendor can sell directly to you and thus avoid paying an estate agent's fees. It is even possible that you might get a bargain, although usually this will work the other way and produce a slightly inflated figure, since the price has not been set by market forces.

In order to get to the right professionals the best way is simply to telephone their offices and ask them if they ever get this kind of property on their books and, if so, would they mind if you wrote to them registering your interest (if they discourage you then it is worth asking them if they know anyone in the area who they think does handle this kind of site). It is then simply a matter of writing, again with your resume, and then following up with reminder calls every couple of weeks. As an incentive it is usual that you would offer to retain the professional when you purchased the site (although in the case of an architect you should be careful to employ the 'Selection of an Architect' procedure described later on in this book). As an alternative it is also common practice to offer a 'finders fee' of about 1–2 per cent of the land value.

Auctions

Another possible way of sourcing building plots is the property auction. In most areas there are periodic property auctions where houses and plots are auctioned off to the highest bidder. This process attracts those who want to realize the liquid value of their asset in a hurry and is commonly used by building societies and banks who have had to repossess the property because of a default on a loan, people who find they need short-term money due to cash-flow difficulties and (here's the crunch) those who want to get rid of a property because there is something wrong with it. However, using this system it is possible to get a genuine bargain if you keep your wits about you.

You can find out about property auctions in your area by consulting the *Estates Gazette* magazine, keeping your eye on the local papers and entering property+auction+uk into a search engine on the Internet.

The problem with auctions is that they are generally 'sold as seen', in that you cannot make the offer subject to surveys or planning – the essence of this system is speed and, for that reason, you must satisfy yourself that what you are buying is viable. In the case of building plots, do not buy plots with 'development potential' without first consulting the planners about what their potential might be and always run through the list of potential pitfalls listed in this chapter before committing. The price of a site is a lot of money to gamble and you should ensure that any risk is cut down to the minimum. This will be very time-consuming and your success rate may be very low (especially if sealed bids are used). You should also ensure that you set a realistic budget for the site based on the cost of similar sites in the area or by using the formula of site-to-sales value set out in the previous chapter and, having set this budget, do not exceed it. If you are serious about a site it may even be worth paying an architect to have a look at it and assess the value of the site on your behalf.

Planning Applications

In the UK it is a matter of democracy to give the public access to details of new developments so that, if they feel uncomfortable or threatened by a proposal, they can make their feelings felt.

All local government authorities have planning departments that are responsible for development control and to which any potential developer must apply when he or she wants to build a new building. These departments keep detailed records of planning applications, past and present. These documents are a matter of public record and are open for your scrutiny; all you have to do is ask.

Clearly, people have many different motives for making a planning application. Often it is for a building that they specifically want for their own uses, such as an extension or a new commercial building or house. Another primary reason for making a planning application is simply to realize the full value of a plot of land that they own or have control of. Applying for planning approval is relatively clean and risk free, and there are many owners of land who, having obtained planning approval, are quite happy to realize the value of their new asset by selling it on straight away for a quick profit. It is worth, therefore, putting yourself forward as a potential purchaser who can buy the site from them without them having the expense of advertising it for sale or of paying an estate agent.

The way to go about finding what new developments there are in your preferred area is to simply go to the Local Government Office in the area that you would like to live, ask to be directed to the department of planning and development control and ask for a list of current planning applications and approvals. A quick scan should be able to tell you if there is anything useful in there, since the description of the proposed development has to be quite straightforward. Do not be afraid to consider ones that might sound a little inappropriate, such as applications for multiple or mixed development, since an applicant may be primarily, for instance, a developer of shops, but has found themselves in the position of having to include an element of housing in a scheme that they may not want to develop themselves. When you have got a list of applications that you feel might be appropriate then ask the desk clerk for the files.

Any application will come in the form of drawings, a letter of support and a completed planning application form. Of most importance when you want to have a quick skim-through are the site plan and the individual floor plans, of secondary importance are the elevations, which show how the building will look from the outside.

The site plan will tell you how the building(s) sit on the site and how it (they) relate to surrounding buildings. If you feel that there is sufficient room around the site for your needs then move on to the actual floor plans; these will tell you how many floors and rooms there are. The number of rooms is of no particular importance – you can always change that later – but it is important to ensure that there is enough space for what you need. You can also check the planning forms, which will tell you what the gross floor area of the proposed development is – you can check this back against the schedule of accommodation you prepared at feasibility stage to see whether there is sufficient space.

The elevations will tell you what the building will look like from the outside; if you like the look, fine, but if you do not then there is always the possibility of making minor changes by agreement with the planners, or major changes by making a fresh application for planning approval. The look of the building might have been something that was negotiated with the planning authorities, in which case it is fairly immovable, or it may be something that was just the whim of the applicant, in which case you can alter it to something you like more. Usually, letters in the file will tell you if the look has been a matter of negotiation or not, or you can simply get the name of the planner who is in charge of the case from the letters in the file and ring and ask them yourself.

When you have got a list of possible applications, copy down the name of both the *Agent* and the *Applicant* from the head of the planning form. It is common for the person who owns the site to employ an architect or surveyor to deal with the application for them, but also always write to the applicant themselves since their agents might not (for whatever reason) pass your letter on.

It is then simply a matter of writing your letter of introduction. In this case it is better not to include your resume, since if it does not match the specification of the property they are dealing with they may be put off. A simple letter stressing your seriousness and your ability to perform should be enough, and if you like the design an indication that you would like to keep the architect on may be appropriate. Also do not forget to stress that, even if this site is not available, you are in the market for something similar.

Again, do not forget to follow up your letter with a telephone call, which should be directed at the person who has been signing the letters. In the case of an agent, ask them if they have passed your letter on and check with them who the actual applicant is, and get, if possible, a contact name for the applicant.

Publications, Journals and Websites

There are a number of different organizations that deal with land or where self builders can register their interest in finding a plot. Typical of these are BuildStore, Landbank and Plotfinder. You may also find advertisements in *Build It*, *Self Build*, or one of the other house-design and lifestyle magazines.

Most vendors will keep the advert fairly simple to save money, but will, on request, send you details such as architects' drawings and site plans. Be wary of sites that are sold as 'having development potential' and always work through the list of possible pitfalls before committing yourself.

Keeping Your Eyes Open

It is surprising how many potential building plots there are that just haven't been discovered yet. As was mentioned at the beginning of the chapter, planning laws have been designed in part to prevent the sprawling of towns and villages into the surrounding green areas, and this has led to urban and suburban areas being looked at increasingly as a resource for new housing. Finding this kind of site relies on resourcefulness; you need to keep your eyes open, looking at the local newspapers, getting any potential site sent to you by estate agents and sometimes just driving or walking around your chosen areas looking.

A new building can often be tucked into the existing urban fabric – this one was built in an old access into a rear courtyard.

A lot of supply for this new housing land comes from, what is known in planning terms, 'brown field' sites; this is where, due to the changing nature of the UK's commercial base, industrial or commercial premises have become surplus to requirements and more suitable for residential use. These sites are generally keenly contested by the mass house-builders and are of little use to the self-builder. There are, however, a number of these sites in miniature; an older residential area (one that grew up before the sweeping suburban estates of the thirties) will often contain small commercial premises now typically occupied by small garages and the like. These are often located in positions that are not commercially viable, off main streets tucked away where they cannot benefit from 'passing trade', and can sometimes be picked up at a reasonable price. Getting planning permission on sites such as these can be a bit tricky. Although national government policy encourages the conversion of redundant commercial premises to residential, you may have to prove the redundancy of the site (usually done by showing a long period with no occupancy or a high turnover rate of businesses). It is also important to point out the site's unsuitability for the area and its lack of neighbourliness (if such is the case).

Another way of sourcing a site in a built-up area is by taking a look at the density of development. Before the advent of planning laws it was generally much easier and cheaper to buy development land, so the efficient use of land was not so much of an issue; a servant culture led to much bigger gardens and the use of horses sometimes led to stables being built on-site at the bigger houses. It is not uncommon to have rural buildings with adjacent outbuildings or even barns absorbed into suburban areas. An area can, therefore, contain development potential in the form of hiving off the bottom of a garden. Planners are quite likely to resist applications that change the character of a very uniformly developed area and will also resist giving permission to something that will create, in their eyes, a dangerous precedent, which will lead to a flood of similar applications. But these sites are there to be found.

Corner plots can also provide a potential site, although you may have to negotiate the purchase of two (or more) gardens.

Another, and increasingly common, way of sourcing a site is to consider the building stock already on the site. You might see a site with a perfectly viable building on it, but which is an inefficient use of the site itself. For instance, a single small bungalow may occupy a site that could quite happily contain two reasonably sized houses and it might make perfect commercial sense to demolish the bungalow if you can get planning approval. This method of procurement will not generally work when to demolish and redevelop would produce an arrangement out of keeping with the area, so it is better to look for a site where the existing building is something of an anomaly when compared with surrounding, bigger buildings.

You may also find a site where there is enough room beside the existing building to build another house – my own experience of this was in 1993 when I bought a house on a large plot and then built another house beside it.

As to purchasing these infill sites, that is easy when the site is up for sale, although if it needs a change of use from commercial to residential you may need to do a 'subject to planning' deal (explained later on in this chapter). If you notice a potential site in the form of redundant out-buildings or a long garden on a corner plot you could try dropping a letter into the house explaining your position and what you are trying to achieve, they can only say no. In your letter you should be as friendly and open as possible; remember you will be their new neighbour and if you can convince them you will be a good one you are more likely to be able to strike a deal. Any deal you make should, again, be subject to planning.

SITE ANALYSIS

When you have found a site (or a number of sites) that seem to be viable, but before you buy, you need to make sure that the site is actually practical for your purposes; there is a quite extensive checklist procedure to go through before you should take the plunge. Set out below is a step-by-step guide to the various points you should consider before going for it. The order these are set out in is intentional, it is far better to deal with the big items first, then gradually narrow your field of search to items that are of interest, but are not fundamental to the success of the project.

Cost

However good a site may be, you still need to ensure that you are paying a reasonable price for it. Certainly if it is the site of your dreams you should be prepared to pay slightly over the odds for it, but not at the expense of making the whole project non-viable.

There are two types of costs associated with any site; these break down into the *direct* costs and the *hidden* costs. The direct costs are (or should be) transparent – how much does the vendor want for the site? The hidden costs tend to be site-specific items that may impact on the building cost. Hidden costs are dealt with below in greater detail.

By now you should, as part of the feasibility stage, have built up a quite detailed financial model of the project – what your budget is and how much you can afford. You should now ensure that the proposed site falls within the parameters you have set yourself. To some extent the cost of the site is related to the area it falls within. The more desirable the location, the more a site will cost but, on the other hand, the more the property will be worth. It is important, therefore, to work through the process described in chapter 1 under 'Site Cost'. Look at similar properties to the one you are planning to build in the area, deduct your projected build-cost, fees and all other likely costs, and then see whether the net figure is more or less than the asking price for the site. Try to allow yourself a margin of error of between 10 and 15 per cent. If the site cost is in excess of what the figures say you should be paying, you can always try to renegotiate with the vendor. Failing that, it is up to you to decide whether to go for it or not, but do bear in mind that if the site cost is part of a finance package then the bank or building society will value it at slightly less than market value on the assumption of getting a quick sale.

If the site you have chosen is in a good area you might find that the figures add up very nicely, but that the end result will be a mortgage that you will find difficult to pay, so it is worth keeping the final cost in mind and not getting carried away.

You can find a site with an unusually large garden.

Planning Status

It might seem a little premature to be worrying about planning at an early stage like this, but the fact is that nothing will scupper a project quicker than not being able to get planning permission for it. On seeing a potential site it is important that you establish its planning status as quickly as possible.

The first port-of-call in establishing a site's planning status is to ask the vendor for details of any planning approvals, applications and negotiations. If the site has planning approval for something close to what you want this is ideal, but have a look at the *conditions of approval*, which form a list attached to the planning approval. These generally relate to materials of construction and landscaping, but can be more onerous, forcing the developer to carry out works to highways or limiting the type of occupant,

for instance by age. If you are uncertain about what any of the conditions mean consult a solicitor or architect. If you wish to vary the permission, the best thing to do is go and meet the planning officer. You can arrange a meeting by telephoning quoting the planning reference number and explaining your situation, if you can speak to the planning officer who dealt with the original application this will be the best idea. Try and explain as clearly and succinctly as possible what you would like to do, including sketches if at all possible; even though you are unlikely to get a definitive answer you should get a fairly good idea as to whether or not what you are proposing is viable.

If the site does not have the benefit of a planning approval at all then it is paramount that you see the planners as soon as possible. Try to ensure that the

Where a building plot can be fitted in without detriment to existing properties.

planner you talk to is part of the team dealing with the area within which the site is situated. Again, you should get some good pointers as to whether or not what you are looking at is feasible.

The problem with all planning consultations is that they are not definitive and the ultimate test of what you are proposing is putting in a planning application. You are, therefore, taking a risk if you buy a site without planning approval even if your initial negotiations seem to indicate that there should not be a problem. The common way to ensure that you do not get into difficulty is to negotiate a sale *subject to planning* – literally, the sale only goes through if you successfully get planning permission. There are a couple of different ways these contracts can be set up. The best is a straightforward contract that allows you to exchange immediately, thereby giving you the security of controlling the site, with completion only occurring when you actually attain planning approval. A variation is for you to give the vendor a non-returnable deposit so that they have a reward for taking the property off the market while you get your planning approval. A further variation is the delayed completion, whereby you exchange with a completion date set in, say, twelve week's time and an option for you to bail out of the deal at any time prior to completion – if you haven't got your approval when completion approaches you can either re-negotiate, drop out or take the risk; you should have a good idea whether or not you will get approval by then.

Legal Status

It seems rather obvious to say that the legal status of

Long gardens on a corner plot can be a rich source of potential building plots …

the site is of prime importance when purchasing a site, but the legal position is one of the items that are of such fundamental importance that it can break a deal, so it is important that you consider it as soon as possible. The best way of doing this is to get a solicitor on board at the earliest opportunity and to give them a clear brief that you need to know four things as soon as possible. These are *ownership*, *charges*, *easements* and *covenants*.

Ownership

Again, it is obvious to the point of triteness that you need to establish that the vendor enjoys ownership of the site, but it is surprising how often this is not the case. Quite often a site will be in joint names, such as when a couple buy a site in tandem, or a property is purchased as a business or in the name of a company. There is also a quite common situation

when someone has died and left a property to another party, but full probate has not yet been obtained. It is also possible (but unusual) that a party who believes they have a right to a property can register that right on the deed, making it effectively impossible to sell the property until that problem is discharged. If any of these circumstances prevail then the prospective purchaser should beware; it can take a lot of time to sort out ownership difficulties, and you should steer clear if you are in a hurry.

In addition, a property may be leasehold, that is to say held under a lease for a limited number of years and then reverting to the freeholder on expiry of the lease. It is important, in this case, to ensure that the lease has long enough to run so that your ownership is not jeopardized and also to consider how long the lease will run when (and if) you come to sell the

… which can be slotted in over two (or three) garden widths

property, since this may impact significantly on its value. If in doubt then it is worth negotiating to extend the lease, but this can take time.

The terms of a lease may also contain restrictions preventing development, or making it difficult to undertake. Such restrictions can be lifted by agreement with the freeholder, but this can take time and money.

Charges
It is important that you should ensure that the title to the land is 'unencumbered' – it is common practice to use land as surety against loans and other business or personal transactions. In such cases it may be that the person who is giving the loan has taken out a charge against the site such that they have first call against the monies raised from its sale. In most

cases this is fairly straightforward – as the sale goes through the outstanding money is paid to the person who has the charge. If the charge is against a number of plots then the sale of each plot will reduce the amount of the loan until the full debt is discharged. Whatever way, if the sale of the land is done with the full knowledge and approval of the person who has the charge there should not be a problem.

A difficulty may arise when a charge has been taken out over a property for some transaction that has been forgotten or not discharged. This sort of charge can be very old and also for a very minor amount. It is also possible that the person who has taken the charge is no longer alive and their descendants are untraceable; in this case you must make a decision based on the likelihood of the person with

33

Existing Bungalow

Bungalows can be an inefficient use of good building land.

the charge on your property emerging from the woodwork in the future, since technically you may be responsible for the debt. This scenario is quite rare and extremely unlikely.

When the property is leasehold, it is also worth ensuring that any ground rent that has accrued is paid off or deposited in a solicitor's escrow account to allow for payment if the freeholder cannot be found.

Easements

An easement is created when a third party enjoys and has enjoyed a right over a property for a number of years. This can be as simple as an overhanging gutter through to rights of light, support, drainage and rights of way. These rights are created by usage rather than by legal agreement and may not show up on the title. Your solicitor will ask the vendor whether they are aware of any rights or easements, but they may not know of them so this is not foolproof. Thus it is well worth visiting the site and checking it thoroughly before you commit.

If there is an established right of way across the property then you will have to allow access for the person who enjoys that right. This can belong to an adjoining owner so that they can maintain and repair their property where they cannot get to it from their side of the boundary, or it may belong to an adjoining owner to gain access to part of their property; it may belong to a service provider (gas, electricity, water) so that they can provide and maintain a service; or it may be a public right of way such as a footpath or bridleway. None of this may be a problem but you should be aware, so look out for

You may even be able to get two plots from the site of an existing bungalow.

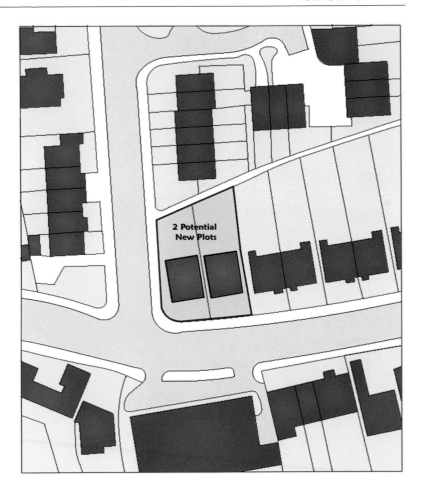

2 Potential
New Plots

gates leading on and off the property and for signs of regular foot traffic. If it does appear that there is some possible use ask the person who seems to be using it how long they have enjoyed the right. Similarly, write to all the service providers for details of their services – this will come in handy later anyway. If a right of way seems to cross a place where it is likely you will want to build this is not necessarily a problem, as a right of way can be diverted or extinguished by agreement with the person who owns that right.

It is also common for an adjoining property to enjoy rights of drainage through a site. This can range from a rainwater pipe through to a sewer or even a stream. Whatever, it is the responsibility of the person who owns the land to maintain the right of drainage. The owner of the land does not necessarily have to maintain the drain in exactly the same place,

but they will have to ensure that the right is upheld and this can prove to be an expense. When you visit the site look for rainwater pipes coming down onto the land from adjoining buildings, also manhole covers, culverts and the like; try to establish where they are coming from and where they are going to, and check with your solicitor if you are in any doubt.

Surprisingly, an adjoining owner may have rights of air over a property if they have enjoyed it for long enough. The most common instance of this is when a gutter or eaves overhang the site. There is no right to remove such overhangs even if they get in the way of where you want to build, although there is a right to alter and adapt them as part of the Party Wall Act, which will be dealt with later. Again, consult your solicitor if you observe any material encroachment of the property. In the case of limbs of plants and trees

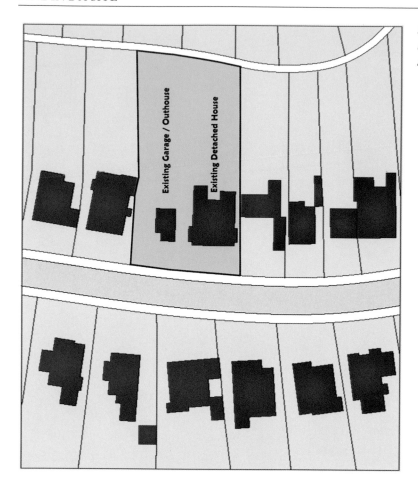

Sometimes an existing house can make inefficient use of an existing plot ...

that overhang the property, you have the right to lop or remove these providing that that you return the lopped branches to the property where the tree is growing from. You should take care, however, that the tree concerned is not listed or in a Conservation Area; if it is you will need permission from the Local Authority before you lop or prune. You can find out by ringing and asking to talk to the relevant council officer.

You may also find that an adjoining property is enjoying support from the site and, again, this must be maintained. A common example of this is with terraced housing, where neighbouring properties help each other stand up. If you remove such support you will need to replace it and if in doubt you should consult a structural engineer.

Another easement you should look out for is a right of light. It can be that an adjoining property has a window that faces directly onto your property and is the only source of light for a particular room. If that window has been there long enough to create an easement you cannot block the light by building directly in front of it. It is more than likely, in any case, that the planning authorities will not let you do this. You should be aware, therefore, that your new property will have to be designed in such a way as to avoid blocking the window or, if this is not possible, you should negotiate with the adjoining owner such that any loss of amenity in terms of loss of light is agreed and you have settled a sum or action as a compensation.

Covenants
When selling a site, it is common practice for a

... and you can insert another house beside it.

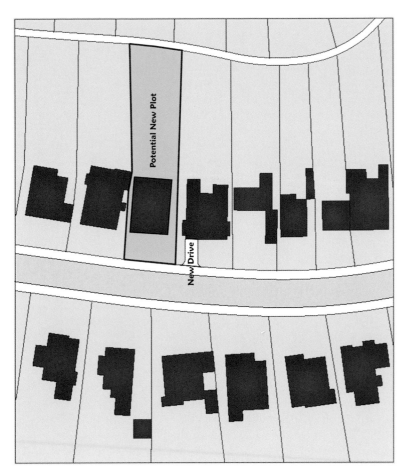

vendor, who may be concerned about other adjacent land they own, to put conditions on the future use of the site. This is called a restrictive covenant.

A restrictive covenant can vary from conditions about the nature of what is done on the site (for example, residential plots often have a covenant to prevent the future business use of the plot) through to conditions about the number of buildings a plot can contain. In some cases you can find moral covenants attached to a property, for instance, properties that have passed through Quaker hands sometimes have covenants restricting the consumption or sale of alcohol on the premises.

It is important to establish what, if any, restrictive covenants apply to the property you are considering, in case they prevent you from carrying out your building. If a restrictive covenant does, on the face of it, prevent you from carrying out what you wish to

do, this doesn't necessarily mean that you can't go ahead. The way a restrictive covenant works is that there is generally a named party who enjoys the benefit of it, either an individual or a company. If the individual or the company can be traced they may be open to persuasion to release the property from the restrictive covenant. It is very often the case that a restrictive covenant is very old and the beneficiary of it may be a long-defunct company or an untraceable individual. In such cases you can take the view that it is most unlikely that you will ever be pursued for breaking the terms of the covenant. Sometimes it is possible to obtain a declaration that the covenant is so old that it can no longer be enforced. Alternatively, it is possible to take out insurance against anyone ever pursuing you for damages for breaking the terms of a restrictive covenant. Your solicitor will be able to advise you on a current insurance scheme.

It is also possible that there will be a condition attached to the title by which you covenant to carry out something. This is commonly in the form of a legal agreement to do something in return for a past or future gain. For instance planning approvals are sometimes awarded subject to a 'Section 106' agreement, whereby if you want to go ahead with the scheme you must do something in return, perhaps carry out road improvement works at the site entrance or give part of the frontage of the site to footpath widening. If an approval contains such a condition you should make sure you are, first, happy with having to do this and, second, have built the expense into your cost plan.

Site Size

It may be stating the obvious but, when buying a site, you should ensure that the building you are proposing actually would fit on the site. This is a difficult issue and the only real way of ensuring that you are covered is to do (or have done) a sketch of the proposed footprint on the site plan.

If you can afford it at this stage you can get an architect to do the sketch for you, but if you are trying to keep costs under control until you have secured the site you could do this yourself.

The first step is to obtain a plan of the property and any adjoining properties. You can use the title plan for this but it is unwise, since they are often inaccurate in both size and detail. A better way is to obtain an ordnance survey map at the largest scale possible. These can be obtained from specialist shops such as the National Map Centre of London or you can try the library that is closest to the property, which will often have ordnance survey maps of the locality. An ordnance survey map will generally be at a scale of 1:1250 or 1:2500 and will show the property itself, its boundaries and any other adjoining properties.

There is no guarantee that the property or adjoining properties will not have changed since the map you are working from was produced, so walk the site and mark on any changes. For instance, are adjoining properties correct? Have any extensions been added? Having done this you can now sketch on a rough footprint of what you think your property will be, using the rule-of-thumb method described in

the first chapter. If the footprint sits happily on the site with masses of space all round it then fine, but if it is a lot tighter do be aware of a few items that you will need to respect:

Rights of Light

As mentioned in the previous section, if there are windows facing out onto your site try to ensure that your proposed building does not overshadow them.

Overlooking

In a similar vein, if you are likely to get direct window-to-window overlooking between a window on your proposed building and a window on a neighbouring property then you need to consider the issue of privacy. Try to keep the minimum distance to 21m (69ft) at the back of the property and the general overlooking conditions in the street or road at the front.

Building Line

When an area is built up (as opposed to being in a rural area) you will notice that the buildings will generally be roughly equal in distance from the road and will often be roughly in line at the rear. This line is known as the *building line* and it is likely that the planners will resist any attempt to come significantly further forward than this line at the front of the property, or further back at the rear. So on your site plan, try to project these imaginary lines across your site and try to keep within them.

Building Height

It is unlikely that the planners will allow your building to be significantly different in scale from adjoining buildings, so look at them and draw your footprint to conform roughly in height. This doesn't mean necessarily that you have to have the same number of storeys. Older buildings often have greater floor-to-floor heights than is current practice and, if you work on a floor-to-floor height of about 2.6m (8ft 6in) you may find that you can get an extra floor in as compared to the neighbours. If you are unsure how to calculate the height of adjoining buildings, a good way is to count bricks (each brick course is roughly 75mm (3in) in height) or any other repetitive element on the buildings façade. In addition you can 'hide' an extra storey in the roof space as a way of keeping the height of your proposed building down.

Parking

It is common for areas to have their only parking out on the street, if the locality was developed before the use of cars became commonplace. These days you will want (and probably be required by the planners) to have off-street parking. Each parking space needs to be about 4.8m by 2.4m (16ft by 8ft) so ensure you have space in front of the building for at least one space and possible a garage.

Ease of Construction

If the new property is intended to be a terrace you will, of course, be building right up to the boundary and using the flank walls of adjoining property as a party wall, but you may also want to build right up to the boundary if the new property is detached or semi-detached. This is, of course, perfectly possible, and is done on a regular basis. This practice does, however, lead to some difficulties in construction of the building. The way that a domestic property is usually constructed is by the erection of a scaffolding platform around the outside of the building from which the bricklayers and the roofers can work. If a building extends all the way to the boundary then the building can only be constructed by obtaining the neighbour's agreement to work off their land or by using a process known as 'working overhand', by which the bricklayer works from the inside of the building leaning out over the wall and pointing the brickwork as he goes. This does tend to lend a somewhat unsatisfactory look to the finished wall and it is this that can often be used to persuade a neighbour to let you use their land to build a scaffold. Having built a wall right on the boundary there is, of course, the issue of maintaining it in the future.

If space permits, therefore, it is better to allow a space round the building on all sides to allow construction of the external walls. This will also have the effect of maintaining the 'detached' status of your building even if the neighbour builds right up to their boundary. This space should be a minimum of 900mm (3ft) and can also be used as a mechanism to shape the footprint of your building.

Ground Conditions

A sturdy building demands sturdy foundations and it is of primary importance to ensure that a new building is well founded. In actual fact, you will not be allowed to build anything which doesn't have foundations that are up to the job; the Local Authority's Building Inspector will ensure that this is the case (Building Control is dealt with in chapter 4). The type of foundation depends largely on what the ground conditions are and, in turn, the type of foundation can have an effect on the cost of the project.

At its best the ground will consist of 300–600mm of vegetative topsoil overlaying a firm, stable, substrata. In this case the foundations need only go down deep enough to sit on this substrata and to avoid the top layers of soil that are affected by contraction and expansion caused by frost – this is typically 1m (just over 3ft). There are other situations, however, whereby the level of stable soil might be much deeper or even not present at all. If such is the case you will have to budget for deeper foundations or even piles that are like columns screwed or driven into the ground.

To find out if a prospective site has poor ground conditions one can carry out a soil survey, whereby a specialist firm is brought in to dig sample holes and take 'cores' with a drilling rig. This is an expensive process and is probably not something you would really want to undertake when you are just considering buying a site. Another way is to ring up the Local Authority and ask to speak to the Building Inspector dealing with the area. Building Inspectors have the responsibility for checking all new foundations in the area and the chances are that they will be able to tell you what the ground conditions are like and what sort of foundations they would expect to see.

Another thing you should watch out for is trees, since they tend to suck large quantities of water out of the soil resulting in expansion and contraction of the ground during wet or dry spells, a process known as 'heave'. When building near a tree or large bush you may find that you have to go down a lot further with your foundations, and perhaps treat them in a special way with a slip membrane or a compressible layer round them.

If it does appear from your preliminary enquiries that you may need something special in terms of foundations it might be worth talking to a structural engineer. You can probably get preliminary advice free of charge on the basis that you will use the firm if the job goes ahead and if, instead of calling them out, you turn up at their office with your sketch footprint (with any trees marked on) and photographs. The structural engineer will probably be able to advise you as to the rough cost of the additional foundation work sufficient to assess whether your project will be viable on this site.

Services

Any new building will need to be serviced; the primary services are gas, water, electricity, drainage, and telecommunications. Before opting for a site it is worth checking what, if any, of these services are readily available. In most cases it will be readily apparent from adjoining properties that all the services are available, but in remoter areas it is prudent to check.

The best way to check is to contact the local service providers and ask them for the telephone number of their new connections or planning office, then ring them up and get a contact's name who, on request, will send you an ordnance survey map with local services marked up in the area. There is sometimes a small charge for this and it may take two or three weeks.

If it is clear when the plans are returned that you might not be able to get one of the services on site, this is not necessarily a deadly blow to the site; remote areas have been developed for many years and there is always a solution. You can get a quotation from the service providers to run services to the proposed site and then factor it into your cost plan. If you can't get gas then you can use fuel oil or electrical heating. If you can't get electricity you can consider a generator; water can almost always be run to site; if there is no drainage you can use a septic tank or bio-digester; if there is no telecommunications you can use a mobile telephone. If you have to use a more esoteric form of servicing it is worth getting a quote so that you can factor it into your cost plan.

It is important with any property, even in a built-up zone, that you obtain information on drainage, since the UK is interlaced with culverted streams and public sewers. If one crosses where you want to build, you will need permission to build over or divert it and, again, extra cost will be involved. In addition, if you need to make a connection to a public sewer outside the site then you will need to budget for it.

Access

Getting proper access onto a site is obviously of prime importance. If you need to cross someone else's land to gain access, your solicitor will advise you as to whether or not you have the right to do so. Developers have a nasty habit of leaving narrow strips of land between sites they have developed and the public road, so that anyone who wishes to further develop the land must negotiate with them in order to do so.

In addition, if a site has to have a new road constructed to get to it or even a new crossover over a public footpath, then this will have financial implications and needs to be budgeted for. The Local Authority's Highways Division will, again, probably give you an off-the-record budget cost for any such work.

Listed Structures, Trees and Archaeology

You should be aware that any existing buildings on the site, however redundant they may be, might not be yours to demolish. If the existing buildings are listed you will need permission to alter or demolish them and, be warned, it is extremely difficult to get permission to demolish listed structures. In addition, if the property is in a Conservation Area as defined by the Local Authority you will need conservation area consent to demolish any buildings on site; such consent is generally fairly easy to get providing the existing structures are not of townscape or landscape merit. If there are existing structures on the site and you wish to clear them then it is always worth a telephone call to the Local Authority's planning department to establish if the structures are (a) listed and (b) within a conservation area.

If there are any reasonably substantial trees on the site, especially if they are in a position where you

An existing tree close to a building plot does not mean you cannot build on it.

might want to fell or lop them, you should again establish with the Local Authority whether they are the subject of a tree preservation order (effectively listing for trees) or again within a conservation area, since you will need permission to do anything other than light pruning if this is the case. If the trees are listed or within a conservation area this is not necessarily an insurmountable problem; work or even felling can be carried out on such trees. The best thing to do is to arrange to meet the Local Authority's Tree Officer on site – they will be able to give you a good idea what you can or cannot do.

It is also possible that the site you are interested in is in an area of archaeological interest, that is to say in a location where there have been previous human settlements dating back to Roman times or beyond. If this is the case the Local Authority may impose a condition on the planning that an archaeological survey is carried out. This is usually a desktop study undertaken by an archaeologist. If this exposes anything of interest then you may be required by the Local Authority to carry out trial pits on the land to establish what, if anything, there is of interest. In most cases these are troublesome and can cost a few

hundred pounds, but do not threaten the viability of the scheme. There are cases, however, when the remains of a Roman villa are found and no development is allowed on the site. This is a bit like being struck by lightning – it is very rare, but does happen – and sensible precautions should minimize the chances of it happening. Again, a telephone call to the planners will establish whether or not the site is within an area of archaeological importance and also will quite probably tell you whether any interesting finds have been made in the immediate locality. If this proves to be the case then you can have your own desktop study for the cost of a few hundred pounds to establish if any further work will be necessary. The Local Authority's Listed Buildings Officer or Conservation Officer will generally give you the name of an archaeologist who will give you a quote for carrying out the work.

Site Clearance/Site Contamination

If the site has existing structures on it, which you wish to get rid of, you will obviously need to budget for the cost of this. Local demolition contractors will be happy to give you a price for this. You will need to ensure that they cost for all demolition work, including the grubbing up of foundations and the removal of asbestos if there is any, so write them a letter inviting them to quote for the work making clear all these items.

In addition, there might be site contamination of some sort – this is quite common as pressure for land forces new housing onto sites that had previous industrial use. Common pollutants are diesel, where there have been previous garages or rail sidings, and chemical pollutants, where there have been previous manufacturing processes. Get your solicitor to ask if there has been any decontamination carried out and if the vendor is aware of any pollutants. If you get a noncommittal reply or it appears from previous usage that there may be pollution, then it may be worth getting a soil survey done for a few hundred pounds. The soil survey will recommend what needs to be done and you can then decide whether to go ahead or to budget for decontamination.

There are also hazards such as methane or radon gas present in the soil that can affect whole areas and which cannot be removed. These hazards are generally overcome by construction methods, such as ensuring floor voids are ventilated and that membranes are laid across the site to prior to building to prevent gas seepage. Again, it is worth putting in a telephone call to the Local Building Inspector to establish if there is any ground hazard present and what construction method is advised to get over it.

It may have been a somewhat sobering experience reading this chapter with its litany of what to watch out for, but it would have been irresponsible of the writer not to point out potential problems. There are undoubtedly other possible problems, since each site is unique. The likelihood is, however, that the site you find will have few if any of these problems and that I will have worried you unnecessarily. If such is the case I apologise, but it is always better to get the bad news (if there is bad news) out into the open so that you can take a rational decision based on fact. The approach should always be one of taking a long, clear and dispassionate look at any site. If at the end of this process you are still happy, and your budget still works, congratulations! you have found your site.

CHAPTER 3

Programming and Processes

Not so much a programme, more a way of life!
(Title of a BBC television series 1964)

Once a site has been secured, there is then a procession of things that you will need to do to progress the building. It may seem to be complicated at first, but in essence all these stages are fairly straightforward and can be dealt with in a relatively simple, linear way. This chapter is intended to cover all the processes involved and to assign a time period to each of them. If you intend to assemble a full design team who will provide you with a full service then these processes will largely be carried out on your behalf and this is also the case if you have opted for a developer-led or community self-build operation; nevertheless, this chapter will still be useful as a checklist to make sure all the stages are covered.

The first chapter touched on programming, but the intention of this chapter is also to expand on that diagram, so that you will be able to develop a linear checklist against which you can monitor progress, and which will prompt you (or prompt you to prompt others) into taking the appropriate actions in plenty of time. Although time periods are allocated for the various tasks, it should be realized that, despite the best-laid plans, you will find that times will vary and it is therefore important to regard the programme as a guide document, but one which should be constantly updated to reflect what is actually happening on the ground. What this chapter will attempt to do is to demonstrate ways in which you can minimize delay.

The first thing to do is to develop a list of processes involved; the following is such a list, together with a short explanation of what each process involves. You might find that in your particular case some of these stages are unnecessary, or have already been carried out. You might also find that, as a result of the special circumstances of your project, there are additional processes to be carried out. Whichever is the case, you should find that this chapter will provide a useful framework to carry out your project planning.

Feasibility

Chapters 1 and 2 were designed to provide a checklist for choosing the way to achieve your objectives, and a checklist for site selection. It might be that, for whatever reason, you already have a site and that you have jumped straight to this chapter. It is suggested, however, that you should still go through the feasibility process just to ensure that you do not embark on something that might be ill-advised.

Survey

We have already dealt with the use of ordnance survey maps as a useful basis for feasibility. These can also be useful for providing a base for design and planning applications (see page 45). A measured survey will eventually be required and a decision must be taken as to which stage this survey is carried out. You should be prepared to spend £300–£800 on a measured survey (depending on the size of the site and how difficult it is to carry out a survey) and you obviously will not want to lay out this sort of money until you actually need to.

If you are unsure what your chances are of a successful planning approval then you might want to hold on commissioning a survey until you have got planning approval and, instead, base the initial design on an ordnance survey plan and a few check dimensions. There are certain circumstances, however, when it is prudent to carry out the site survey at the earliest opportunity. These are when:

- The site is very small and/or restricted.
- The site is on a steep slope.
- You are intending to convert or extend an existing structure.
- Adjoining structures must be shown in detail as part of the planning application.

When commissioning a survey it is important that you properly brief the surveyor, since their price will be based on a single visit to site and, if they have to return to take further measurements, they will probably charge you for the privilege. In addition, you will need to consider the medium for the survey. If you plan to commission an architect to carry out the design, the likelihood is that these days they will be using a computer-aided design process and you will need to have the survey in electronic format so that the proposed design can be laid onto it on the computer – it is probably safest to request a copy of the survey as a hard copy on stable film and also in electronic format on a disc.

You should consider the following points when commissioning a survey:

Levels
You will need to know what the levels are and this should be related back to the nearest ordnance benchmark (these will be marked on your ordnance survey plan). If the site is fairly flat then it is generally enough to take levels on a 5m (15ft) grid; if the site slopes noticeably you may have to take levels at more frequent centres.

Services
Make sure that the surveyor picks up the position of any services on site and that, in addition, they measure the cover level of any drainage manholes and also the invert level – this is the depth of the bottom of the drain from datum level and will be needed when a new drainage system is being designed. Also, it is likely that you will want to connect into services out in the road, so it is worth getting the survey to cover any services that are running in any road on which your site fronts.

Trees
Make sure that the survey picks up the position, height, spread of canopy and species of any trees within 15m (50ft) of the proposed building or any hard standings.

Existing Structures
The survey should pick up the outline of any structures that are on site, even if you are intending to demolish them (the planners will often ask them to be dotted on the site plan). In addition, detailed surveys constituting full floor plans and elevations will be needed for any structures you are planning to convert or extend.

Boundaries
A survey should list the type, position and height of any boundary.

Adjoining Structures
If there are buildings hard up against the boundary or even close to the boundary it is prudent to have them surveyed, since the planners will always be interested in how the new building relates to its neighbours, particularly in their height and elevational treatment. If it is not possible to gain access to adjoining sites to carry out such surveys then ask for indicative drawings from your surveyor.

Access
It is quite likely that you will be building a new access onto your site from the adjoining road, or at least remodelling an existing access. If this is the case, it is a good idea to have the road surveyed where it fronts onto your property.

Your requirements for the survey should be carefully set out in a letter that invites a tender from the surveyor.

How long the survey will take is rather dependent on how busy the surveyor is, so you should always invite prices from several surveyors and ask them to specify in their reply how long they will take to complete the survey. For the purposes of initial programming you should allow about three weeks for this process.

Design and Production of Information

What is involved in the various stages of design is covered in Chapter 5, but you should allocate a time for each process for programming purposes. Some suggested times are set out in the sample programme at the end of this chapter.

Planning Approval

Any new buildings (with a few exceptions that do not really need to concern us here) require approval from the relevant Local Authority prior to their construction. As has been mentioned previously, the UK has some of the most stringent planning controls in the world.

A planning application can be one of two types, either an outline or a detailed application. An outline application is when an approval is sought in principle without giving any details such as plans and elevations; it is only really used by someone who wants to realize the potential of the site without spending a lot of time and effort getting a proper design done. Since a detailed application is still necessary before the building can be constructed, the best format for the self-builder will generally be the detailed application.

For a detailed application, plans at all levels, elevations of all external facades and a site plan are all needed at a minimum scale of 1:100, together with a location plan at a minimum of 1:2500. These, together with the application forms which are supplied by the Local Authority and filled out by the applicant, form the bulk of the application.

There is a central government directive which states that all planning applications should be dealt with within eight weeks of registration by the Local Authority of the application. In practice, however, it is practically unknown for this to happen, since the Local Authority will generally come back with queries, design changes and requests for further information. It has to be said that such manoeuvres are quite often a delaying tactic, since Local Authorities are generally overworked and under resourced, and usually struggle to conform to the timescale set out.

It is a fact that when someone is overworked they will often be motivated towards directing their efforts to where they are under most pressure. To ensure that your application is dealt with as quickly as possible, therefore, it is better to keep in touch with the planners regularly to find out what progress is being made, rather than sitting back waiting for things to happen. In doing so it is best to be polite and sympathetic towards the planning officer's problems rather than being pushy and aggressive, since this may have the effect of upsetting the officer and only motivating them to put your application at the back of the queue. It is important that, if unnecessary delay is being caused by lack of effort on the planners part, you let the officer in charge of your case know that you are experiencing inconvenience and frustration; hopefully their conscience will make them act more promptly. The whole planning process is dealt with in more detail in chapter 5.

Building Regulations

As well as applying for planning permission there is also a requirement to apply for Building Regulations Approval. These two processes are often confused with each other, especially since they are administered by the same authority, but they are entirely different. In essence, the Planning Law is all about appearance, siting and zoning of the built environment, whereas the Building Regulations are all about safety, use and environmental impact.

Like planning legislation, the Building Regulations grew out of local byelaws; for instance, a London byelaw prohibited the use of thatch after the part it played in spreading conflagration in disasters like the Great Fire of London. As the rate of building accelerated and there was increasing urbanization during the industrial revolution, it was recognized that safety was of increasing concern and the byelaws became more common and more stringent.

As the years have gone by, the Building Regulations have, as regulations will, expanded and become more far ranging. They now cover not just safety in the form of structural and fire regulations but also moisture penetration, drainage, ventilation, personal safety, conservation of energy and disabled access. Many of the provisions of the Building Regulations only apply to public or commercial buildings, but there is a formidable array of provisions that apply to domestic buildings.

A Building Regulations Application consists of forms that are supplied by the Local Authority and filled out by you, together with detailed drawings. The drawings are generally at a minimum scale of 1:50 and consist of plans, elevations and sections. Rather than dwelling on the appearance of the building, these drawings should concentrate on structure, construction, staircases, ventilation, drainage and heat-producing appliances.

After submission of the application, the Building Inspector will come back with a list of queries and requests for clarification that then have to be addressed. If these are successfully dealt with then Building Regulations approval will be granted. As building proceeds, the Building Inspector will make regular visits to ensure that the building is being constructed in accordance with the approval and to react to unforeseen situations.

It is common practice to start on site before Building Regulations Approval has been given, and the Building Inspector will still visit site and give informal advice as to what is acceptable, which will almost certainly be sound. It is advisable, however, to hold fire until the application has been made and the initial queries have been sent out.

Obtaining Tenders

The whole business of contract is dealt with in Chapter 6 and how much time will be necessary rather depends on how you want to set up the building contract(s). It is important that you do not rush this process, however, since if you do not allow enough time for a contractor or supplier to properly price the job then you might find that they will submit a higher price to cover themselves.

Mobilization

When starting on site, it is not simply a case of suddenly deciding that you want to build and the next moment beginning the building. There is little point in starting work on site only to find that you come to a grinding halt a few days later due to lack of materials. All materials will tend to have an ordering period; this will vary from a day or two for materials that are held in stock and only need to be delivered to

site, to several weeks in the case of more exotic materials that must be specially constructed or delivered from abroad. The trick to mobilizing is to ensure that all the materials you will need immediately are on site before you start, or will be delivered shortly thereafter. You will find that if you are employing a general contractor they will refuse to start until they know that they will have the necessary materials.

In addition, it is important that you ensure that the correct notices and permissions are obtained to let you start before you actually do start. Will your initial works, for instance, involve a road closure or the obstruction of a public highway? If so you will need to obtain the necessary approval.

Also you will need to obtain the things that are necessary to make the site workable, such as toilet facilities, making the site safe with hoarding and arranging for temporary services – water and electricity principally, sometimes a telephone.

Construction and Design Management Regulations

As a business sector, construction has a very poor safety record and is responsible every year for more deaths and injuries than any other industry in the UK. Historically this effect has been exaggerated by the fact that there are a great deal of 'cowboy' builders around – companies or individuals who are not members of any regulatory bodies and who flaunt proper health and safety procedures.

In an effort to cut down on injuries, in 1994 the Government introduced a piece of legislation designed to put the responsibility for safety on site more onto the building owner and the design team, on the basis that it was likely that they would inject more responsibility into the process. This piece of legislation is known as the CDM regulations.

The CDM regulations come into play when construction work lasts for more than thirty days, involves more than 500 person-days of work or has more than five persons on site at any one time. The CDM regulations also come into play if there is any demolition involved, however many people there are on site or however long building work takes. The exception to this rule is if the work is carried out on the residence of a domestic householder, in which case only the design part of the CDM regulations

Notification of project

Note

1. This form can be used to notify any project covered by the Construction (Design and Management) Regulations 1994 which will last longer than 30 days or 500 person days. It can also be used to provide additional details that were not available at the time of initial notification of such projects. (Any day on which construction work is carried out (including holidays and weekends) should be counted, even if the work on that day is of short duration. A person day is one individual, including supervisors and specialists, carrying out construction work for one normal working shift).

2. The form should be completed and sent to the HSE area office covering the site where construction work is to take place. You should send it as soon as possible after the planning supervisor

3. The form can be used by contractors working for domestic clients. In this case only parts 4-8 and 11 need to be filled in.

HSE – For official use only

Client	V	PV	NV	Planning supervisor	V	PV	NV
Focus serial number				Principal Contractor	V	PV	NV

---

1. Is this the initial notification of this project or are you providing additional information that was not previously available

   Initial notification [/]   Additional notification [ ]

2. **Client:** name, full address, postcode and telephone number *(if more than one client, please attach details on separate sheet)*

   Name: *MR J BLOGGS*   Telephone: *0001 001 0001*

   Address: *33 ACACIA AVENUE*
   PASTURES NEW
   WESSEX

   Postcode: *WES 001*

3. **Planning Supervisor:** name, full address, postcode and telephone number

   Name: *CAMP AND FLATTERY ARCHITECTS*   Telephone: *0002 002 0002*

   Address: *NO 1 PAPER CHASE*
   SCALE RULE
   WESSEX

   Postcode: *WES 002*

4. **Principal Contractor**

   Name: *BODGIT & SCARPER LTD*   Telephone: *0003 003 0003*

   Address: *LAST CHANCE SALOON*
   DODGE CITY
   USA

   Postcode: *ZIP 001*

5. **Address of site:** Where construction work is to be carried out.

   Address: *AS ABOVE (ITEM 2)*

   Postcode

6. **Local Authority:** name of the local government district council or island council within whose district the operations are to be carried out.

> *WESSEX DISTRICT COUNCIL*

7. **Please give your estimates on the following:** Please indicate if these estimates are

original [/]   revised [ ]   *(tick relevant box)*

a. The planned date for the commencement of the construction work — *1ST APRIL 2004*

b. How long the construction work is expected to take *(in weeks)* — *32*

c. The maximum number of people carrying out construction work on site at any one time — *7*

d. The number of contractors expected to work on site — *1*

8. **Construction work:** give brief details of the type of construction work that will be carried out

> *DEMOLITION OF AN EXISTING GARAGE AND THE CONSTRUCTION OF A SINGLE FAMILY HOUSE*

9. **Contractors:** name, full address and postcode of those who have been chosen to work on the project *(if required continue on a separate sheet). (Note this information is only required when it is known at the time notification is first made to HSE. An update is not required)*

> *NOT YET KNOWN*
>
> *PRINCIPAL CONTRACTOR AS ABOVE*

Declaration of planning supervisor

10. I hereby declare that ...*CAMP & FLATTERY*......................(name of organisation) has been appointed as Planning supervisor for the project

Signed by or on behalf of the organisation...... *I. M Camp* ......(print name) *I. M. CAMP*....

Date ......*20th AUGUST 1999*...

Declaration of principal Contractor

11. I hereby declare that ......*BODGIT & SCARPER LTD*...(name of principal contractor) has been appointed
As principal contractor for the project. *(or contractor undertaking project for domestic client)*

Signed by or on behalf of the organisation...*BILLY KID*...(print name)..*B. T. KIDD*.......................

Date ...*30.02.04*...

An F10 form, obtainable from your local Health and Safety Executive.

01.04.2004		33 ACACIA AVENUE, PASTURES NEW
		HEALTH AND SAFETY PLAN
		INFORMATION TO BE PROVIDED BY THE DESIGNER
	1	Proposed Designer
	2	Provide written evidence of training in the CDM regulations
	3	Has the company / firm carried out this type of work before in relation to Health & Safety and can references be made available?
	4	Significant hazards or construction sequences that the Contractor should be aware of
	5	Hazardous substances that may be used or present during the construction phase
	6	Significant hazards or work sequences that the Contractor should be aware of when stripping out existing building materials
	7	Provide any known building material that may require to be manually lifted
	8	Fragile materials that will be used during construction work
	9	Provide details of dedicated fire routes to be maintained during construction work
	10	Provide details of any restrictions the Contractor should be aware of when erecting scaffolding/hoists
	11	Provide details of any restrictions the Contractor should be aware of when setting out his work station
	12	Provide details of any poisons being used in the premises
	13	Provide details of any welding or torchwork required
	14	Describe any known unavoidable hazards that the Contractor should be aware of
	15	Describe any other unavoidable hazards the Employer should be aware of for future maintenance/operation of the building

A simple questionnaire can establish the competence of potential designers.

49

apply. So the self builder will not generally qualify, although you are still obliged to inform the Health and Safety Executive via a form F10, which you can pick up from your local HSE office. The CDM regulations do, however, contain some sound provisions to help ensure a safe site, and subsequently a safe building, and you are well advised to take some heed of them.

The responsibility for safety in the CDM regulations focuses on two areas – design and construction. As the building developer you should try to ensure that the design and designers take account of Health and Safety during construction and subsequently, and that contractors take account of Health and Safety during construction. For larger projects there are now special professionals who carry out audits of the design and construction to ensure knowledge of and compliance with Health and Safety procedure. If you are employing an architect they will take on this role for a nominal additional fee. If you are taking part in developer-led, system-built or design-and-build type programme, you are still obliged by law to ensure that the person who is building on your behalf has taken proper account of the CDM regulations.

When others are acting as the developer you should check that they have, in sufficient time for the preparation of a health and safety plan (see below), submitted a form F10 to the local Health and Safety office.

You should ensure that the design team is aware of the provisions of the CDM regulations and that they alert you and the building contractor to any danger in their design or the materials of construction. This is best done by sending out questionnaires to the design team and asking them to prepare a design statement.

The design statement should cover such items as the position and type of any possibly hazardous materials, any possible dangers during the construction process (essentially an invitation to the contractor to ensure that they consider and mitigate the danger in these processes) and any dangers associated with future maintenance of the building (processes such as cleaning windows or roof lights).

During the construction process you (or your agent under the terms of the CDM regulations) will need to ensure that any building contractor working on site is aware of the provisions of the CDM regulations, is competent to work safely and has planned their construction in such a way as to minimize needless risks. To check a contractor's awareness a simple questionnaire can be sent out.

To check a contractor's competence ask to see their health and safety policy. This should typically cover such matters as protective clothing, procedure in case of injury and safe working methods.

For each work process the contractor should produce a method statement setting out how he will deal with any situation that is likely to arise in the special circumstance of your building. For instance, a roofing contractor should be setting out how he will protect himself and his operatives from injury by falling and also how he will minimize the chance of injury to those below caused by materials or tools being dropped.

It should be noted that many small contractors regard the CDM regulations as unnecessary red tape and will resist producing the paper work, often on the basis that they have been doing this for years and can work safely without having to spend valuable time away from the job preparing statements. This is very often true, but you should be aware of the consequences if they don't go through the proper procedure and something happens. These are:

- The occurrence of an injury or death that could have been avoided if the work had been properly thought about and the feelings of guilt related to that.
- The possibility of prosecution of the contractor or even yourself by the Health and Safety Executive.
- The delay and disruption that will be caused to the project by the fact that, inevitably, the Health and Safety Executive will then go over the project with a fine tooth comb to ensure compliance with the provisions of the CDM regulations.

At the end of the project the aim is to produce a Health and Safety File that will set out the nature and position of any dangerous materials used on the scheme, the position and nature of any services such as gas, electricity and water, operating manuals and safety notes for any equipment that has been installed

01.04.2004

	33 ACACIA AVENUE, PASTURES NEW
	HEALTH AND SAFETY PLAN
	INFORMATION TO BE PROVIDED BY THE PRINCIPAL CONTRACTOR
1	Proposed Principal Contractor
2	Confirm that the Company has a Health & Safety Policy
3	Confirm that the Company's Health & Safety Policy conforms with the current CDM regulations.
4	Provide written evidence of training in Health & Safety for Supervisors, general workforce and plant operators.
5	Does the company employ their own professional safety adviser/advisers?
6	Will the safety adviser be making regular site visits?
7	How do you manage hazard identification, risk management and communication of such?
8	Provide method statements for the Works and risk assessments.
9	Will the company provide all personal protective equipment (PPE) and other control measures?
10	Has the company carried out this type of work before in relation to Health & Safety and can references be made available?
11	If any part of the proposed works are to be sub-contracted outside your organisation, please give details (what & by whom)
12	How do you assess the competence (in terms of Health & Safety) of the proposed contractors?
13	Extent of Public Liability Insurance
14	How do you ensure that any plant or equipment used on site is regularly inspected, used only when in a safe condition and found when defective?
15	What documentation is in place for the reporting of accidents & injury?

A typical contractor's questionnaire.

on site, and notes on maintenance and any danger associated with it. This will be very useful to you (and also to any future purchasers) as a house-maintenance manual and will also be of great help when and if you have any future work done on the property. It is well worth including in the Health and Safety File a copy of the as-built drawings.

It is important not to feel intimidated by this whole process – it is simply a way of trying to ensure that you do your bit to protect the builders, yourself and any future users of the building.

Building Guarantee

The majority of new-build houses erected in the British Isles are done so with the benefit of a building guarantee. This is, in essence, an insurance policy, which means that if any building defects occur in the first ten years after completion the insurance policy will cover the cost of rectification. The main provider of building guarantees in the UK is the National House Builders Council (NHBC), although there are other options such as the Zurich.

So common are these forms of guarantee that they are now expected, so that if you decide to sell your house within ten years of completion, a prospective purchaser may either be warned against the property by their solicitor or refused finance by their mortgager if there is no building guarantee in place. If nothing else, an NHBC warrantee is looked on as proof that the building was constructed with a reasonable amount of care and any self-builder would be prudent to consider taking out NHBC or similar cover.

For conventional situations, the way that the NHBC works is that both the developer and the contractor are NHBC registered, and they pay an amount to the NHBC who then provides cover on the building. The essence of this arrangement is that, in the event of a defect appearing, the NHBC will go to both the contractor and the builder to obtain rectification, and only if they default will the NHBC arrange for the work to be carried out.

The difficulty for self-builders is that they are not registered NHBC developers and will often not use registered NHBC contractors. Previously this meant that if a self-builder wanted NHBC cover they had to get the shell of their building constructed by a registered developer. For this reason the NHBC has developed a product that is aimed specifically at self-builders, which is called the 'Solo for Self Build' scheme. The essence of this scheme is that, in return for a premium of £800–£1,100 (at the time of writing) based on size, the NHBC will inspect the plans, do on-site inspections and will provide cover subsequently. There is an excess to be paid on any claim that is made (£500 at the time of writing).

The building guarantee may seem to be another irksome piece of red tape, but in practice it can be a useful check to ensure that the building is being constructed to the high standards you would aspire to.

Demolition

If any demolition is involved it is important that adequate time and consideration is given to this process. It is usually most cost-effective to use a specialist contractor, since a conventional contractor is likely to subcontract these works anyway and a specialist contractor will generally be more competent.

You can, of course, choose to do demolition work yourself since, on the face of it, it appears to be mostly unskilled work, but be aware that demolition is one of the most dangerous tasks on site and you have to be very careful to take down existing structures in a safe way.

If an existing structure is fairly elderly it is advisable to have a hazards check carried out. There are various specialist contractors who do this sort of work, and many of them will visit the building and do a preliminary survey for a minimal cost or free on the basis that they are awarded the contract.

Typical hazards are asbestos and, in derelict buildings, bio hazards such as pigeons and rats.

If asbestos is found, then there is a requirement to notify the Health and Safety Executive prior to commencement of work. Typically, this is a period of a month and will need to be factored into the programme.

Construction

Construction will be dealt with in greater detail in Chapter 6, but for the purpose of programming the following factors need to be taken into account:

Time of Commencement

What time of the year the project is started will have quite a fundamental effect on the programme. The period when the building is 'in the ground' (the construction of basements and foundations in builders' parlance) is of particular significance. Below-ground operations are particular prone to disruption by inclement weather; torrential rain will flood excavations, cave in the sides of trenches and necessitate postponement or pumping, while wet processes such as pouring of concrete and brick laying should not be carried out in freezing conditions, since the structural integrity of the cement may be compromised. While it is impossible to plan for the British weather, there are obviously some times of the year that are more prone to disruption than others. Starting a building late in the year (after September say) will mean that you are carrying out excavation and construction of the external envelope of the building during a period when you are much more likely to be disrupted than during summer.

In addition, holiday periods can play a part. The building industry tends to shut down for three or four weeks over the Christmas and New Year period and starting a building project just before that time can be counter-productive in that, effectively, the site has to be set up twice over.

Having said all this, you should not be too daunted by the exact timing of the start-on-site date; no date is completely ideal and the majority of the British Isles experiences the sort of weather that will be an inconvenience rather than something that will prevent work altogether. It is simply a matter of being aware.

Complication of Construction

How long a building takes to build will depend to a large extent on how complicated it is. If, for instance, the building is in a single-storey timber-framed format then it will be considerably quicker to construct than a four-storey brick-built building (although the ordering period for materials may be longer). If the site is steeply sloping or has restricted access then this will make the construction process more complicated and hence more protracted.

Type of Contract

A building contract is very much a process of management. There are typically a number of subcontractors who provide the various 'trades' and who will do various stages in the project such as ground works, brickwork, carpentry and so on. A conventional contract will have a general contractor who provides the management over the various trades and who ensures that they turn up on site in the right order and as close to one another as possible. It is in the interest of the general contractor to ensure that works are carried out as quickly and efficiently as possible, since these two factors have a fundamental effect on the profitability of the scheme.

Many self-builders will fulfil the role of general contractor themselves, so that they can save money on this element of work and since, for a small project such as a single house, the management process is not over-complicated. You should be aware, however, that you are not likely to carry out this process as efficiently as someone who is a professional at it, and you may also have other commitments and be unable to devote all your attention to the job. It is likely, therefore, that if you opt for a self-managed type of contract you will take longer than you would with a conventional type of contract.

Drafting the Programme

It is important to have a document that you can use to control and monitor the programme. This can be an evolution of the programme you developed for the feasibility stage. The programme will not be a static item, but will move and adapt to the changing circumstances as the project develops. It is worthwhile, if you have access to a computer, to create this document as a spread-sheet.

A useful way to construct the programme is by dividing the sheet into a grid, with each square across the grid equalling one week. At the top of the diagram you can then indicate the day that each week starts, at the left-hand side you can have a column that indicates the various project stages and the amount of time each process lasts can be entered as a solid bar within the grid.

During the early stages you can guess at the time it takes to complete various processes or base them on

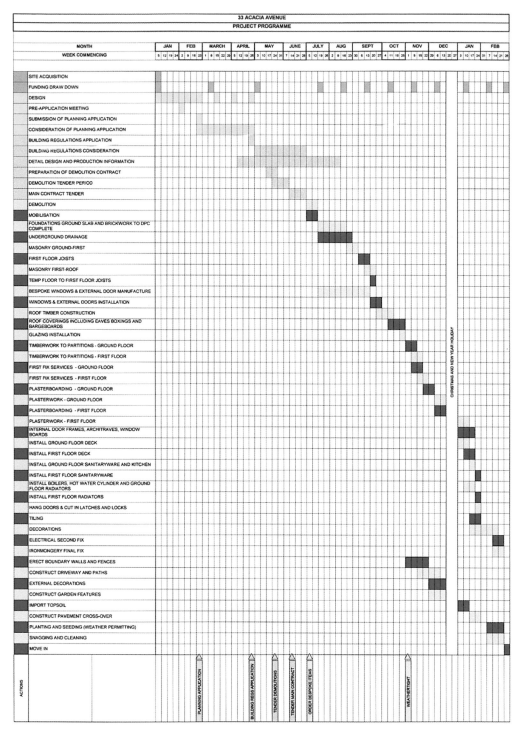

A typical programme.

the diagram above, but try and think about the specific site and construction conditions as dealt with earlier in this chapter. As you progress and start to get feedback from consultants, local authorities and contractors you can then get more specific. Once you are on site you can use the programme to monitor progress and to arrange for a planned draw-down of funds if you are financing the project.

It is also very useful to incorporate an action column in the programme as a reminder to yourself or to other people that a certain process should be instigated on a certain day and by a certain person. Many building processes have a long 'lead-in' time (the time between ordering something and it being instigated) and you can get stranded if you do not plan properly.

Hopefully you will now be at the stage when you have thoroughly planned the project, you will have a good idea whether it is feasible and how long it will take, and you will hopefully have control of a site. So far the majority of the expense has been in your time, but now is the time to fully commit to the project and to start getting some concrete results. The next few chapters will now take you through the actual business of completing the design and getting the building built.

CHAPTER 4

Assembling and Briefing the Design and Construction Team

Work is of two kinds: first, altering the position of matter at or near the earth's surface relatively to other such matter; second telling other people to do so. The first kind is unpleasant and ill paid; the second is pleasant and highly paid.

(Bertrand Russell *In Praise of Idleness and Other Essays*)

Whichever way you achieve your finished house you will need to work with other people; these will be vendors, bankers, fellow self-builders, professionals, local authorities and contractors. It is clearly of great importance to the success of your project that you are able to work well with the other members of the 'team' both from a personal point of view and from the point of view of having common targets, and this chapter is designed to assist you in ensuring that, as much as is possible, this is brought about.

GENERAL SELECTION

To some extent the selection of the design and construction team will depend on the process that you have selected to achieve your aims. In a conventional contract you will have far more control over the various members than in a group self-build, design-and-build or system-build scenario.

Choice of a specific organization or individual for election onto the design and construction team tends to be specific, and this is dealt with under each separate type of service, but whichever process you opt for there are certain ways of establishing the credentials and abilities of any organization that you are dealing with; some of these will be specific to the type of organization you are dealing with and some are general. The specific items will be dealt with under the generic groups below, but to avoid repetition I have listed the important general headings first.

References

It is of primary importance to get references for any company or individual you plan to work with on your project, since it is by these that you can gauge how successful their previous efforts have been.

The best references tend to be direct recommendations by someone who is, or has been working with a person or organization who would be useful to you. These could simply be contacts supplied by friends, neighbours or work colleagues, or it could be that members of the design team will supply recommendations (although you should try to ensure that there is no direct business link when references come through in this manner). Also, self-help groups for self-builders can be a good source of references. Local Authorities will also sometimes endorse particular builders or professionals.

It is common for individuals to have a portfolio of gushing letters of praise from previous clients. I am always a little suspicious of these documents since you do not know for sure at what stage in the project these references were given and whether there was any form of duress or coercion applied to get them. If these are the only references supplied, then I would suggest that you write to the individuals who supplied the letters and find out firstly if they exist, then what work they had done and then what they genuinely think of the company they referenced.

The individual or organization you are intending to use, if legitimate, should have no difficulty with

QUESTIONNAIRE FOR NEWLY REFERRED BUILDING CONTRACTOR

THE RECIPIENT OF THIS QUESTIONNAIRE IS KINDLY REQUESTED TO COMPLETE THIS QUESTIONNAIRE THAT IS DESIGNED TO ESTABLISH THE OVERALL COMPETENCE AND PERFORMANCE OF THE NAMED CONTRACTOR. MANY THANKS FOR YOUR HELP

NAME AND ADDRESS OF CONTRACTOR

(i) How long have you worked with this Contractor

1 year or less ☐   2-5 years ☐   5-10 years ☐   Longer ☐

(ii) What type of work has this Contractor carried out on you behalf

Commercial ☐   Residential ☐   Institutional ☐   Other ☐

(iii) What was the category of the work they carried out:

Refurb ☐   New - Build ☐   Civil ☐   Other ☐

(iv) What is the value of the *largest* job this Contractor has carried out for you

£100k or less ☐   £100-£1million ☐   £1million-£5million ☐   More ☐

(v) What is the value of the *smallest* job this Contractor has carried out for you

£100k or less ☐   £100-£1million ☐   £1million-£5million ☐   More ☐

(vi) How would you rate this Contractor's performance on *programme*

Very Good ☐   Good ☐   Average ☐   Poor ☐

(vii) How would you rate this Contractor's performance on *quality control*

Very Good ☐   Good ☐   Average ☐   Poor ☐

(viii) How would you rate this Contractor's performance on *health and safety*

Very Good ☐   Good ☐   Average ☐   Poor ☐

(ix) How would you rate this Contractor's performance on *after care / snagging*

Very Good ☐   Good ☐   Average ☐   Poor ☐

(x) How would you rate this Contractor's performance on *claims*

Very Good ☐   Good ☐   Average ☐   Poor ☐

(xi) How would you rate this Contractor's *overall performance*

Very Good ☐   Good ☐   Average ☐   Poor ☐

(xii) Please enter any other comments below (or on another sheet of paper)

A user-friendly questionnaire is more likely to get a response than a non-specific enquiry.

supplying the contact details of several people with whom they have dealt in the past. Make sure that the contacts given are people who are similar to yourself rather than potential business partners of the referenced company.

It is suggested that all the references are taken up and that you ask certain specific questions; it is often a good idea to set these questions out in documentary form as a questionnaire, this can then be altered and adapted to serve as a basis for any organization or individual that you come across throughout the design and build process.

When sending out for references it is important to remember that the referee does not stand to gain from your request, so you are acting on their goodwill. Try to make the questionnaire as user friendly as possible, with boxes to check rather than lines to fill, and supply a self-addressed envelope so that it is easy for the referee to reply.

The main criteria in any situation when taking up references are:

- Accessibility.
- Relevant experience.
- Flexibility.
- Ability to perform.
- Financial Security.
- Quality of work.

Any process of selection should ensure thorough coverage of all these topics and, although taking up references will assist in ensuring that they have been covered, there are also other ways of learning more about them. To assist this we will go into more detail below on each of them.

Accessibility

It can be extremely difficult to deal with any organization if they do not respond to your approaches and requests during the course of the works, so it is important to establish a point of contact and to satisfy yourself that, when you need to, you can get a response.

It is, unfortunately, quite common for an organization to be very open and friendly prior to receipt of your order and then keep you at arms length once they have received it, but you should be able to get a

reasonable idea at an early stage as to whether you think that this will be the case by asking the right questions as follows:

- Size of company – to some extent when dealing with a single housing project 'small is beautiful' can be the case. You need to ensure that your business is important to the company and that you will get proper consideration – you may find that when you are dealing with a larger company you will be put down the pecking order or assigned to a junior although this must be balanced against 'Resources', as dealt with below.
- Chain of command – establish who is in charge and where the buck stops; also who will be dealing with you on a day-to-day basis. Get a commitment that they will deal with you personally and then confirm the arrangements in writing.
- Contact arrangements – if your only access is through a switchboard it is easy to brief the receptionist to avoid your calls, so try to get a direct number for your point of contact even if it is only a voicemail; mobile and e-mail numbers are also very useful.

When an individual or organization is busy or under pressure they will often respond to the person who shouts the loudest, so once you have obtained contact details do not be afraid to use them.

Relevant Experience

However much a company or individual is recommended, such recommendations count for little if they are of no relevance to your particular project, so it is important to establish whether they have experience on similar projects. If they do not, but you like the organization and feel that you would like to do business with them, you can consider the closest project to yours that they have been involved with.

When assessing someone's experience, the first port of call will be the portfolio of similar work; ask to see photographs of projects together with lists of clients and contract values. It is a good idea, if possible, for you to visit other projects they have been involved with and ascertain for yourself the quality of the job. This is also a good opportunity to canvass the opinion of the people who are using the system of building. In this process try to establish that the quality is good, that the users are satisfied, and that the project is neither much bigger or much smaller than yours.

Flexibility

It might be that your self-build project is the first time that you have been involved in the construction of a building, or you might have had limited experience in the field, and therefore you might find drawings and specifications difficult to understand. Chapter 4 deals with the 'reading' of plans but, whichever way, even professionals who study drawings on a daily basis sometimes like to change things as they get deeper into a project, so it is important to give yourself the ability to change things during the course of the design-and-build process, without incurring excessive penalties.

Some individuals and organizations will charge significantly if you change your mind during the course of a project. This is perfectly understandable if it means that a lot of extra or abortive work is involved, but you should ensure that there is a mechanism in place with any contract that allows you to vary the works and also allows you to be charged a reasonable rather than exorbitant amount for any variations that take place.

It is important that you build-in checking stages in any contract; points at which you are allowed to review the work and make any changes that are needed. If changes are made, it is also important that there is a mechanism for valuing it, so that you know how much money you are in for and can make an informed decision as to whether you want it done. For professionals an hourly rate should be incorporated for abortive or extra work, and if you instruct changes it is always better if you can get your consultant to quote a maximum sum for the change. Similarly, for contractors, you should ensure that there is a clause in the contract ensuring that any changes or extra work be charged on a pro rata basis with similar work already priced.

Whatever happens you will want changes and extra work, be they minor or major, so try to avoid signing any contract that does not allow you to change.

Ability to Perform

However well recommended an individual or organization comes, it does not mean that they can perform at the same level now as when they worked with their referee. Typically with this sort of work there tend to be considerable fluctuations in workload and it is important to establish what an organization or individual's existing commitments are before signing contracts. This is easy to say but harder to do; if the work is valuable to the person you are negotiating with then they may be tempted to tell you that they can perform while at the same time having secret doubts. You can ask them what their previous year's turnover was and what their current year's turnover is likely to be, and get this in writing. If there is a big variation beware; it may be that they are either over-extending or in danger of going out of business. This is also part of the 'Financial Security' section below.

When you are dealing with a specific item such as, perhaps, a kitchen, it is important to establish what the *lead-in time* is – this is the amount of time between when you place the order and the work is done. If the work arrives out of sequence then the whole programme can suffer and you may be involved in extra expense for delay to others. With contractors it is quite common to have a penalty clause, whereby if the contractor fails to perform he is charged a fixed rate per week overrun, such rate being based on any financial loss (such as additional interest on a loan) that you might suffer.

When you are obtaining competitive tenders for work it is a good idea to carefully compare the various prices. If one price is significantly below the others then look carefully at it – the cheapest is not always the best. It may be that there is a mathematical mistake in the cost or that the price is unrealistic. Either way, if the contractor has messed up the cost you might find them dragging their feet or even refusing to work when the mistake becomes apparent.

Financial Security

Establishing financial security has been touched upon above in the context of ability to perform. The importance of the financial security of an individual or company involved in your project cannot be overstated. The building process is a delicate fabric of co-operation, based on a series of actions that rely on other actions being carried out in the correct order and within a certain time. If a hole opens up in the knitted fabric, it can lead to disruption and tearing of the surrounding strands and, to stretch a metaphor, the whole affair being knotted and tangled and having to be, to some extent, unpicked with consequent loss of time and money.

The building industry is a fairly volatile one and you can never be totally sure that anyone involved with it will be absolutely secure, but there are ways to check that they are reasonably secure at the point at which you sign up with them, as follows:

Bank and Trade References

Any legitimate business should be happy to supply bank references. They are, however, of limited use since they are generally restricted to confirmation that they bank with them, their company status and the length of time they have been with the bank. The things to look out for are that the company or individual has been banking continuously for a reasonable amount of time and that the reference appertains to the individual or company involved; if an organization trades under a different name from their bank account it can imply a certain amount of 'slipperiness'

Trade references are of limited use, since an individual or company is bound to put forward as referees companies or individuals whom it knows will give them good press. When taking up trade references it is important to establish how long trading has been going on and what the credit limit (if any) is. If trade has been going on for a long time it implies that you are dealing with a secure situation and a large credit limit obviously implies trust on the behalf of the referee.

With a contractor it is better to get as a reference a sub-contractor or a supplier of materials or plant, since these organizations tend to suffer most in the case of insolvency and tend to be the most cautious.

Company Searches

When you are dealing with an individual or a partnership, then the individual's estate is up for grabs if they fail to honour a debt. It is, therefore, a more difficult option for them to simply disappear if they

run into trouble compared with a limited company, although it is still difficult to extract money from an individual or to compel them to perform. A limited company in financial difficulty is much more difficult to 'get at', since it can go into liquidation, any remaining assets will be divided by the liquidator and you will rarely get what you are owed.

Companies based in the UK have to post accounts and these are a matter of public record. A number of organizations have been set up that will do a company search and will inform you of the company structure, date of creation of the company, trading address, directors and credit rating. There is a relatively modest cost associated with carrying out a company search such that it is probably not worth considering if the work they are doing for you is minor, but well worth doing if the work value runs into thousands of pounds or if it is pivotal to the project.

VAT Registration

The small domestic sector of the property market has become synonymous with the 'black' economy, and rightly so. A lot of transactions take place between individuals and a cash transaction will often carry a discount for the purchaser, and a chance to avoid income tax and VAT for the supplier.

You should, however, be wary of individuals or organizations offering discounts for cash. This may be a genuine offer based on the avoidance of delay and charges in processing cheques, but is more likely to be a 'black' economy offer. Such an offer implies a certain amount of financial 'slipperiness' and thus insecurity.

The other thing to look out for is VAT registration, which should be shown on a company's invoices and letterheads. Unless you are dealing with a single individual or tradesman it is likely that most organizations you are dealing with will have a turnover large enough to justify being VAT registered. If they do not have a VAT registration number then they are either not making very much money or are, again, 'slippery'. Customs and Excise are very strict with people who try to defraud them and will clamp down on individuals and organizations that try this, so lack of VAT registration does tend to imply, in itself, a lack of financial security.

Quality of Work

Once the excitement of the whole self-build process is over and you are left with your finished house, things like cost, delays, arguments and so on will gradually fade from your memory, but what will linger on will be the quality of the scheme. This will be reflected in the quality of the design, the quality of its execution and the quality of the legal and statutory arrangements you have been left with. In some ways, therefore, quality is the most important of the factors to be used when selecting a member of the design team, although never to the exclusion of the other criteria.

There are a number of ways of establishing a team member's credentials on the quality front; some of these are specific to the type of service provided and will be dealt with under the individual headings, but, again, some of them are universal. There are the reference sources already touched upon above and also the visits to similar projects that have also been touched upon. With visits to other projects, what you are looking for should be tailored to the service being provided and will be dealt with under each design team member's heading below.

Another source for finding out about someone's ability to deliver quality is by looking at what trade organizations they belong to. This again varies according to the type of service offered and will be dealt with in greater detail later but, basically, membership of certain trade organizations implies a certain level of expertise and professionalism.

Any recognition in terms of awards is obviously a good indicator of the quality of someone's work, although some of them carry less prestige than others.

SPECIFIC SELECTION

There are some members of the team whose selection you will have no say in and whose actions you will have no control over; typically these will be members of Local Authorities and insurance groups such as the NHBC. In the case of these individuals it is still necessary to establish a working relationship, so it is well worth getting to know the individuals involved. Where you do have some control as to selection you should exercise it. Set out below are some of the ways you can do it in relation to the various disciplines.

Group Self Build

If you have opted for the community-led form of self-build then you are severely restricted as to the choice of design team since, to some extent, the other members of the team are selecting you rather than vice-versa. It is therefore up to you to find a way of working with the other members.

The important aspect of team working in group self-build is co-operation; there may be things you believe could be done better or someone else's input could be improved upon, and it is important to be forthright about such matters rather than letting them fester. Ultimately, however, it is the group that decides the way forward.

Design-and-Build and System Build

With a design-and-build or system contractor you will find, again, that your control is not as strong as with a conventional set-up and that once you have 'signed on the dotted line' your ability to influence matters will be limited; if you try to change things it is likely to be expensive.

It is important with this sort of arrangement, therefore, to try and make sure that the organization you are contracting with is the right one, and that you are satisfied that you have set the ground rules to your satisfaction before you embark on the process.

Before committing yourself to a specific design-and-build or system-build contractor you will need to go through the six key points as set out above in the 'General' section, but in this situation of equal importance is the actual design or system that you will be using as the platform for your house.

If the arrangement is a turnkey type of operation with the design already complete, then you will need to ensure that the design meets your needs and this will require careful perusal of the plans and drawings. This process is covered in chapter 5. It is another disadvantage of the design-and-build arrangement that this needs to take place somewhat out of sequence and you will have less influence on the final design than in a conventional situation. The design-and-build contractor will also try to minimize the

Awards may be a good indicator of quality of work.

AWARD

FOR OUTSTANDING
CONSERVATION

in recognition of the contribution
that the restoration of

Richmond House
The Epsom Beaumont

has made to the architectural
heritage of the Borough

1996

Awards Panel
.... Chairman of Planning Committee
.... Vice-Chairman of Planning Committee
.... Borough Planning & Engineering Officer
...17...OCTOBER.....1996.......... Date

amount of work they do before you sign up and the pressure will be on you to base your order on a generic model rather than on something tailored specifically to your needs. This pressure may well be accompanied by assurances that you will be able to alter things at will at a later date, but it is not unusual for companies to be a lot less cooperative once you are 'in the bag'.

When dealing with system builders you need to satisfy yourself that the system suits your tastes. Building systems vary quite considerably, from Scandinavian 'modern' through to vernacular pastiche, and you need to be comfortable with the one you have chosen. Studying photographs of similar completed projects is of prime importance, as is visiting other projects. You should pay particular attention to detail, since some of the systems are design to slot together with the minimum of fuss and, as a result of this, the detailing can be a bit crude.

Solicitor

It is probable that you have a solicitor who has worked with you on previous property dealings, such as buying and selling houses, and you may wish to keep this relationship going. This is fair enough and in many ways desirable, but property transactions involving development have slightly different criteria and specialists in the development field will generally employ specialist solicitors.

You need to ensure that the solicitor you employ will be giving you the correct advice for a self-builder. To some extent this is a matter of briefing, which is dealt with later in this chapter, but there are also some more specialist items that may need to be addressed and if your solicitor is not comfortable with these issues then you should consider employing someone who is more familiar with them. Much of this is covered in Chapter 2, but you need to ensure that your solicitor will be able to guide you on restrictive covenants, easements, planning restrictions and, if necessary, contract law. The best way of doing this is to ask and also request examples of similar work.

If you do decide that you need to source a solicitor, for whatever reason, and have not heard of a suitable one on the grapevine then there are a couple of other ports of call you can try.

There are, of course, the *Yellow Pages*, which will at least narrow your search since the majority of solici tors will have in their advertisement a guide as to what they specialize in. The key words here are conveyancing and housing; if a solicitor advertises as a specialist in either of these fields then you are halfway there. In the case of conveyancing it is an advantage if a solicitor advertises as specializing in commercial and residential conveyancing, since the commercial side will give them an additional edge in the planning status and contract law side. The difficulty is, however, that this method of sourcing a solicitor is a bit general and it may be that it will take a while before you find someone who has the particular expertise you are looking for.

Another option is to contact the Client's Advisory Service at the Law Society. They will provide a list of suitable local solicitors, but you should be very specific about what you are looking for when you contact them. Make sure that you emphasize that you want a small-developer's solicitor rather than an ordinary conveyancing solicitor.

Perhaps the best option, however, is to target advertisements by solicitors in the self-build publications and on the net, since solicitors who advertise in this way will be specialists. In addition, planning offices may carry advertisements on their folders by solicitors who are involved with small developments.

Whichever way you source a solicitor, do make sure that they *are* a proper solicitor. It is possible to carry out conveyancing without being a solicitor – this is fine for simple cases of house purchase, but you will need someone with a bit more expertise. Solicitors will generally carry various logos on their advertisements and letterheads, and these can be a good indication that they have professional recognition, but the important thing to look out for is registration with the Law Society, which means that they have to carry out their business in a professional and ethical manner or face being disbarred.

Accountant

It may be that your project and the financial arrangements necessary to realize it are not complicated enough to warrant the involvement of an accountant. You do need, however, to be careful about VAT and about capital gains tax as mentioned in Chapter 2, and a relatively modest amount spent on an accountant may save you money in the long run.

If you do decide to get advice from an Accountant there are again a number of ports of call.

Again, the *Yellow Pages* can give you leads to local accountants, but here the categories of specialization can be even more vague than for solicitors and hence your search may be longer.

You can once more take the option of searching the advertisements, but since most self-builders do not engage an accountant it is unlikely that you will find many useful leads.

This leaves us with a recommendation from the professional body, which is the Institute of Chartered Accountants (RICS). Again, you need to be very specific about the project you have in mind and the issues that need to be addressed, and make sure that you fully brief the advisor at the Institute.

Once more, there are various people who offer accountancy advice who are not chartered or qualified accountants and these are best avoided, so if you do use an accountant's services check that they are RICS members.

Architect

If you do not have a system-building or design-and-build type of arrangement the architect is the key to the design team and is its most important member. If you select the right architect you should end up with an aesthetically pleasing house that is efficient to run and soundly constructed; if you select the wrong architect his inefficiency or lack of commitment can spread throughout the design team. It is therefore of paramount importance to ensure your architect is up to scratch.

All the other members of the design team provide a service that someone of similar experience within their profession can equally well provide. An architect, however, will have a unique vision, different from other architects. Therefore, it is obviously very important that the architect of choice has a vision that most closely matches your own. The way to ensure that this happens is to collect images of the sort of building you want, preferably by the architect you want. If you are looking for a solidly conventional building you do not want a 'way out' architect but, equally, if you have a vision of something quite radical you do not really want a run-of-the-mill architect.

Useful sources of material are the various self-build housing and lifestyle magazines, and you can even subscribe to the architectural publications if you are so inclined.

Another way to select an architect is to go to the Clients Advisory Service of the Royal Institute of British Architects (RIBA) and ask for recommendations. They will give you a list of two or three local architects who specialize in the type of project that you have in mind.

Another organization that can be useful is the Association of Self-Build Architects (ASBA), which is a group of architects who have set up a cooperative organization aimed at self-builders. There is no strin-

gent membership requirement, but at least you know they are interested in your business.

Another possible organization is the British Institute of Architectural Technologists (BIAT), which issues a qualification of a more mundane type – members are often perfectly competent to design a house and may even be more practically minded than some architects. An architectural technologist, however, is unlikely to have as much flair or imagination as a good architect.

Anyone who claims to be an architect may not be a member of any of the organizations above, but should always be a member of the Architects Registration Board (ARB), which means that they have to carry out their business in a professional and ethical manner or face being disbarred.

You can look in the Yellow Pages for local practices and then ring them to establish whether they are interested in your project – again this can be very time consuming.

The option of looking in self-build magazines is again an option – and a good one, in that the people who advertise in this sort of way will have self build as a specialization.

Again the key is to ensure that you are dealing with someone who is capable of doing the job to your satisfaction. There are a lot of people advertising architectural services, such as drawing up plans and obtaining planning approvals, at reasonable prices. But architecture is a field where you get what you pay for and the cheapest is not likely to be the best. It cannot be overstated how important it is that your house is well designed and saving a few hundred pounds on your architect's fees is generally a false economy.

Do make sure that any architect that you deal with is a member of RIBA or registered as an architect with the Architect's Registration Board, but do not rely solely on professional qualifications; it is vital to ensure that the architect is the sort of person you can get on with and whose work you like.

When you have assembled a short list of architects the next thing to do is to meet with them. Most architects will not charge for an initial meeting, although it may have to be at their offices rather than at your house. Ask them to have a portfolio of their work and a list of similar projects to yours ready.

What you need to establish when you meet the architects is, firstly, do you think that their approach concurs with the way you see things, secondly, can you work with them on a personal basis and, thirdly, are they practical?

There are a number of ways that you can establish the first of these criteria – whether or not you see things in a similar way. The first of these is to scrutinize their previous projects carefully. Ask yourself do you like the look of the building, does it give you what you want to see in terms of feeling, quality, comfort (or lack of it) spaciousness light and colour? In doing this there is no question that the best way is to visit one of the projects in the flesh; it may not always be possible to see the building internally, but you should at least be able to get a good idea from the outside. If there are no buildings that the architect feels confident enough about or is on good enough terms with the client to allow you to view internally, then this should tell you something about them in itself (unless you have decided to take a risk and go for a young inexperienced architect). Ask the architect to talk you through the philosophy behind the building; what is good and bad about it and how they reacted to the brief. Also, get the architect to do a 'walk through' of the plans of a scheme describing to you how the plan works and how this project is special. The very act of doing this will give you a good idea of how they will be able to transfer their ideas across to you when the time comes.

Another way to select an architect might be to get them to put their initial ideas down on paper so that you can know roughly the direction you are headed in. You can, of course, try to get this work done free of charge on the basis that they will get the job if you are happy with their approach. You are likely to have limited success with this approach, since the initial ideas stage can take quite a lot of time and your scheme is unlikely to be big enough for them to be able to finance free work of this magnitude. You can also negotiate a cost for initial work, with such cost being knocked off their final fee if they get the job. This is a good approach, but can prove expensive if you are talking to several architects or cannot find one you like straight away.

Whilst establishing whether or not you like the quality of an architect's work, it is also important to find out whether you think they are organized enough and whether you can work with them on a personal basis. Architecture is not just about pretty designs and design ability; the architect must also be technically proficient, organized and able to administer contract law. Ask the prospective architect whether they have had any claims made against them recently and whether the projects they are managing generally come in on time and on budget. Personality is very important – you will be seeing a lot of this person and you might also be relying on them to lead the project to a successful conclusion. The qualities you are looking for are not just whether you like them, but whether they seem to have good attention to detail, are forthright about their views, knowledgeable and also whether you feel they have a strong enough personality to 'bang the table' in meetings with recalcitrant contractors and suppliers.

It is also important when selecting an architect to make a judgement on their information technology and computer skills. The world of architecture is becoming inextricable enmeshed into the world of computer-aided design (CAD) and although these skills are not essential – after all buildings have been being constructed for millennia without them – a lack of ability can betray an old-fashioned approach or an inability to keep abreast of the latest innovations. And you yourself may want to take advantage of such things as 3D simulation and e-mail.

If you have some special requirement for your project that is a little beyond the ordinary, now is also the time to check and make sure that the prospective architect has the expertise or can acquire the expertise to action your preferences. Such preferences might include environmentally friendly building, low-energy building or, perhaps, feng shui.

Most architects will base their fee on a percentage of the likely construction cost, so the more expensive a building, the more their fee will be. You may like to pin them down to a lump sum to remove the temptation to not hold the purse strings tightly if they are involved with the project on site. Remember that the cheapest fee is not necessarily the best and try to ensure that, if you do employ a competitive-fee tendering approach between a number of architects, they are all quoting for the same thing and that there

The ability to produce computer drawings shows technical prowess and can be a useful tool to help you envisage your building.

is no room for claims for additional services later (see the 'Briefing' section later on in this chapter). Expect to pay between 5 and 11 per cent of the contract sum, depending on the degree of complication of the project and whether the site is in a conservation area or has physical difficulties like being on a big slope.

Another factor in choosing an architect is their professional indemnity insurance. This is a policy that they will carry to cover them for any expense that you might suffer as a result of negligence on their part, so that in the event of some blunder (they do happen!) you will not be out of pocket. It is suggested that you should ensure that they carry at least the cost of the contract sum and ask for a copy of the cover note from their insurers.

Structural Engineer

The other consultant you may need is a structural engineer, who will design and size the structural members in the building, such as foundations, floor and roof structure.

If you have an architect, choosing a structural engineer is easy – ask them. It is important to have a professional team who are confident of each other's abilities and who are used to working with each other. It is very unlikely that your architect will recommend an engineer who is not up to the job. An architect may also include the necessary structural work within their fee, referring to a structural engineer if one is needed.

If you have not, for whatever reason, engaged the services of an architect but still need a structural engineer, then there are other ways of sourcing one.

There is, again, the *Yellow Pages* option and, once more, you should be very precise about what service you expect and should be prepared to spend some time ringing around. Alternatively you may like to get in touch with the Institute of Civil Engineers (ICE) who will refer you to practices in the area that they believe will be able to offer you the kind of service you require.

Once you have found a likely structural engineer you will, once again, need to take up references and ensure that they are used to the kind of work you have in mind. Structure is not something that you can easily check out on site, since it is almost always buried out of sight, so references are of more importance than for the other parties. A list of similar projects completed in the last five years is a good guide.

A check on the professional qualifications of a prospective engineer is advisable; they should be a member of the Institute of Civil Engineers (ICE). It is also advisable to check on their professional indemnity insurance, which should be on a similar basis to that of the architect.

Financier/Banker

Financing the scheme properly is fundamental to its success. There is a plethora of options available and making the selection that is correct for you is not always easy.

It is easy to assume that the best deal is going to be the one that costs you the least but, although cost is very important, it is not necessarily true. You need to ensure that a prospective financier conforms to the general criteria at the head of this chapter. In addition, it is worth considering using a better known company rather than an obscure one, since the last thing you want to do is be in the middle of a project and suddenly find that finance, for whatever reason, has been withdrawn.

Choosing a method of finance is not easy; there are so many options available and the situation is constantly changing. In general you will probably find it more cost-effective to go for one of the available self-build mortgages rather than a straight loan. The problem with self-build mortgages is that the mortgager tends to look at how heavily mortgaged you currently are and your ability to pay. This can be difficult if you are already a home owner and you want to stay in that home while you are building your new one. You can obviously sell your old house to finance the new one, but this can be disadvantageous.

The alternative to a mortgage is a bank loan, whereby the whole process is looked at as a commercial deal, with the lender making available a sum of money and then including the likely interest in the loan, so you don't have to make any payments until you have finished your house and can sell your old one, mortgage the new one and pay off the bank loan. The problem with this method is that it tends to be more expensive, with commercial lending rates and arrangement fees applying.

It can be quite a lengthy process investigating which is the best deal for you and quite confusing establishing what the terms of the deal actually are. For this reason, many people will go through an agent, who will arrange the loan for you and will take a commission from the lender to cover their fee – such commission cost not generally being passed on to the borrower except in the most general sense. The disadvantage with this method is that you may find yourself steered towards the lender who offers the best commission to the agent or to whom the agent is affiliated – you should check that any agent is independent.

Before signing up with a lender you need to check the small print and it can be worth showing the contract to your solicitor. Terms to be careful of are: hidden costs, such as arrangement fees including back-end fees when you pay the loan off; valuers' and surveyors' fees; repayment terms, which sometimes include 'on demand' terms whereby you are agreeing to pay back the loan any time the lender asks you for it; and security offered if you default on the loan through no fault of your own due to accident illness or unemployment – if the lender doesn't arrange for insurance you should consider taking out your own.

Contractors

After the architect, contractors are the most important pieces of the design and construction team, since you are relying on them to ensure the building is built in a cost-effective, safe and quality-controlled way. The importance of the choice of contractor can vary from the fundamental if you are relying on one contractor to build the whole house, to fairly minor if you are arranging the contract as a series of subcontracts. For this reason this section is split into two subsections – 'Main Contractor' and 'Subcontractor'. You may still want to source subcontractors even if you are using a main contractor, since it might be that there is someone who you believe to be especially good or you may want specialist work done. In this case you can bring the subcontractor in on a 'nominated' basis, by which you tell the main contractor to employ the subcontractor in question.

Main Contractor

A main contractor is a single person or organization with whom you contract to carry out the general building works. This does not have to mean that he is contracted from beginning to end, from foundations through to fitting the number on the front door. You can employ a main contractor to, for instance, do the walls and roof and leave the building weatherproof so that you can do the fitting out, or even to plaster and do the electrical and plumbing fitting out leaving you to do the decorations. The advantage of employing a single main contractor is that you are only dealing with one body, rather than a number of different people, and if there is a problem then, legally, it is generally the main contractor's obligation to sort it out or to take responsibility. It is also easier to impose penalties for lateness or poor workmanship if you are dealing with just one party. The disadvantage, of course, is that essentially it is quite likely that all a main contractor is doing is providing management and maybe a labourer or two, while the rest of the work is done by a series of subcontractors. If you opt to manage the contract yourself you can save the main contractor's costs, but beware of false economies; unless you have some expertise you can find the project taking all your time and taking twice as long. You need to quantify how much your time is worth and also the additional money it might cost you in interest if the project takes much longer than expected.

It is common practice to assemble a list of main contractors and then get them to price competitively against one another. This is a valid approach, but can lead to a contractor under-pricing the job and then trying to make up costs later. The alternative is to negotiate with a single contractor, but that can be more expensive. If you do decide to assemble a list of contractors then you will have to be reasonably satisfied that they are all capable of doing the job, but you do not need to go into fine detail on taking up references and so on until tenders have come in and you can whittle it down to one or two.

You will find that, if you have applied for planning permission, there will be some contractors who write to you offering their services. This is generally because they have perused the list of planning applications in their area (they are a matter of public record), or subscribed to one of the business journals that publish lists of planning applications. Contractors who write to you can be a useful source of potential inclusions onto the tender list, since they are generally local, think the job is the right size for them and are also hungry for the work.

Another way of sourcing contractors is to ask the professional team - the architect and structural engineer. It is likely that they will have worked with a number of building firms over the years and will know who are the good ones and who are not.

It is also possible to ask the Local Authority Building Regulations Department on an informal basis. They will know which contractors have produced a good product locally and which have been lax or sloppy; they will not, however, know whether the contractor was cheap or expensive.

You can, of course, also try the *Yellow Pages*, but this is a little risky since a lot of builders who have the biggest banners in the directories are looking to attract people who are not experienced in the building trade and they can be not as good as you would like. If you do go for this method of procurement then it is suggested that you restrict your search to those who are in the Federation of Master Builders.

The Federation itself will also supply a list of its members who are local to you and who it believes would be interested in the kind of job you have on offer, but they will stop short of actually recommending someone.

Building contractors have, over the years, had very poor press and have become a byword for 'cowboy' activity. This is to a certain extent true; there are certainly a lot of firms who will provide a sloppy and unreliable service and then try to charge you through the nose for it. Even well-established and so-called professional firms can set their stall out to make as many claims as possible during the job in order to inflate the contract sum. It is, therefore, of paramount importance that you go through the checking procedure as thoroughly as possible

The building industry has recognized the problem that it has with public perception, and has been fighting for many years to improve its image and to raise the standard of professionalism generally. There has been a lot of activity on the trade standards front and there are quite a lot of trade associations whose logo you will see on the builder's notepaper and advertisements. The ones to look out for are the Federation of Master Builders and the NHBC. The Federation is quite strict about its membership and will actually exclude people when they have allegations of misbehaviour or negligence proved against them. The NHBC also demands a reasonable standard of workmanship from its membership and, since they have to arrange for the work to be carried out if the contractor defaults, membership implies a commitment to the job, even when it is finished, and a certain amount of longevity.

Final selection of a contractor means going through the processes outlined at the beginning of this chapter with particular care. Of special importance are visits to buildings previously completed by the contractor. It is worth reiterating the point that, when the excitement of the building process has died down, it is the quality of the building that will stay with you and it is of primary importance that the quality is good. Try opening windows and doors, make sure they fit properly, and look at the smoothness of plasterwork and the evenness of brickwork. It is also common for contractors to lose interest a bit when the job is nearly complete, so make sure everything is finished. It is a good idea to look particularly in out-of-the-way places, such as cupboards and

behind doors; if the quality is good where it might not be seen or detected then it shows an attention to detail throughout. A site visit is also a good opportunity to ask the building users whether they have any major problems with the building or the contractor (there will always be minor grievances) and what the aftercare service was like.

The financial stability of the main contractor is of more importance than that of any other member of the design and construction team, since a contractor going out of business in the middle of a job causes a great deal of delay and, usually, additional expense, so it is a good idea to be particularly stringent in your checking process when taking up business references.

It is not unusual for contractors to go for more jobs than they can actually handle, on the basis that usually some of them will fall through prior to signature of contract and, anyway, feast is better than famine. But if a contractor has too much work then this can crucially effect your building programme, so again you need to ask detailed questions about how much other work he has got on. When checking a potential contractor's ability to perform it is important to get them to draw up a works programme, check that it is sensible (your professional team will be of help here) and then make it one of the contract documents.

Look for quality in detailing and workmanship in out-of-the-way places.

The final thing to look at when selecting a contractor is to make sure that they are adequately insured. You need to check that they have both public and employer's liability insurance since, if persons on your property are injured and he is not covered, you may find a claim being made against you. Contractor's all-risk insurance should be in place for damage to your or a neighbour's property during the course of the works.

Subcontractors

You may find yourself involved in the selection of sub-contractors in three situations. These are: when you are managing the works yourself; when you particularly want to use an individual person or firm because of their specialist knowledge or because they are so good; or because the main contractor wants to subcontract part of the works and has asked you whether this is acceptable.

In every case the three key items are quality, ability to perform efficiently and safely, and insurance. You should bring to bear some of the stringency of your investigations into the main contractor into the examination of a potential subcontractor.

If you are using a main contractor, but would also like to use a particular subcontractor then you can nominate; a process by which, in essence, you instruct the contractor to use a particular sub-contractor. Hopefully, the contractor will agree to employ the subcontractor as domestic (basically as their own employee). If you can't get them to do this then you may find, depending on the form of contract, that if the nominee causes delay or extra expense the contractor will try and pass any costs on to you.

Suppliers

Le Corbusier, the famous French architect, coined the phrase 'a machine for living' in relation to a house and the analogy is a good one; a building is essentially a complex machine providing shelter, comfort, retreat and entertainment, and like any machine it relies for its success on the integrity of its component parts. It is in your power to influence the quality of those component parts and, therefore, the successful function of the machine. Components can vary from the obvious (kitchens, bathroom suites, light fittings)

through to the concealed (pipe work, cabling, insulation). Since the contractor is running a business, if he is given the choice he is likely to go for the cheapest option, so if you want something different from the base level you need to specify it,

A typical, but only partial, list of items you might like to choose would be:

*   External Finishes – bricks, roof tiles, windows, doors and the like.
*   Internal Finishes – paint type and colour, wallpaper, tiling, floor finishes.
*   Internal Fixtures – doors, staircases, architraves, skirting, fireplaces.
*   Internal Fittings – kitchens, bathrooms, light and electrical fittings, ironmongery.
*   Systems – heating, ventilation pipe work, wiring, energy efficient and 'green' issues, central vacuuming.
*   Components – conservatories, porches, pools, cupolas.

The best way to choose these items is by looking at them, handling them and seeing them installed – and in a comparative way. As you can see from the list above, there are a lot of things to choose and the sooner you start the easier it will be, so as soon as you have decided to start building your own home you should start collecting photographs and samples of the materials you would like to use. There are many ways you can source these components as follows:

*   **Publications.** Just looking through lifestyle, home and trade publications will reveal a great number of suggestions as to particular components and details of the manufacturers who make them. It is a simple matter to ring the people who are mentioned or who advertise and get them to send their literature and/or samples.
*   **The Professional Team.** If you have employed an architect or designer it is, to some extent, their job to assist in the selection of components. Ask for samples and catalogues of recommended materials to be brought to meetings. You will, of course, get examples of what the architect or designer likes and this might not accord with what you want, so

if you are not happy then be forthright about it, after all it is you that will have to live with it.

- **Exhibitions.** There is an increasing number of trade exhibitions across the country where products and systems are displayed to the public, with sales staff on hand to explain their characteristics. These are an extremely important source of inspiration when it comes to selection of materials and components; there is a unique opportunity to compare and contrast materials, and to get the low-down on them from people who are in the know. To find out about where and when these exhibitions are occurring you will need to keep your eye on the various publications and also get the programmes from the various exhibition centres. Most of the exhibitions will charge an entry fee, but it is common for the companies you have telephoned for literature to offer free or concessionary tickets to shows where they are exhibiting.
- **Retail Outlets.** Shops are an obvious source of inspiration, especially the specialist ones like lighting and bathroom suppliers. Again, the advantage here is that you can compare and contrast the products in the flesh, and the people who run such outlets are generally quite knowledgeable about what they are selling. The disadvantage about sourcing materials through retail outlets is that they tend to be quite expensive, since they add a percentage onto the goods to finance their operation. It is generally cheaper if you can manage it to go straight to the manufacturer or to a supplier who deals directly with the building trade.

When you are dealing with bespoke items like conservatories or kitchens you will not be able to view a product that is exactly the same as the one you want, so it is important to treat the item as you would a main contractor's work. If it is a large item you need to go and see an example of the system as-built and concentrate on the quality of the materials and their assembly. Again, if you can see the item on site it will give you an opportunity to pick the brains of the person who is living with it on a day-to-day basis.

When specifying products and components, you have to bear in mind that if you insist that the contractor uses something you want rather than something he wants, then if, for whatever reason, the item fails to turn up on time or is faulty you will find that your position is weakened contractually and contractors may seek to pass any costs they incur on to you. For this reason it is a good idea, if possible, to specify the material, product or system before you sign the contract with the main contractor so that there cannot be the excuse that the programme was prepared without knowledge of when the item would be ready. When you have not been able to specify pre-contract it is important to check when the contractor will need the item on site and then check with and obtain written confirmation from the supplier that they are comfortable with this timetable. Similarly, if something you have specified fails it is more difficult to blame the contractor, so it is a good idea to seek guarantees, warrantees and quality assurance items, such as BS numbers and membership of trade associations. You also need to let the supplier know what the conditions of the main contract are, so that they are aware of the implications of default on their part.

GENERAL BRIEFING

When you have gone through the selection process and appointed a new individual or organization to the design and construction team, you need to tell them what it is you want. This is the briefing process. A good brief will be one that leaves the member of the team with no doubt about what your objectives are and what precisely you expect them to do. To some extent you will find that a brief tends to be a movable feast, the further you get into the process the more you will refine your ideas, and in some cases you may change your mind completely. This is a completely normal and healthy thing, so you also need to make sure that the brief is kept up to date and that any parties that need to know are aware of changes that come along from time to time.

Mission Statement

It is a thoroughly worthwhile activity to produce as early as possible a statement of exactly what it is that you want – a *mission statement*. This is worthwhile for two reasons: firstly it will let those on the design and

Go and see examples of the workmanship of bespoke items either at showrooms or, preferably, on site.

construction team know what the primary objectives are; secondly it will concentrate your mind and force you to make some decisions about what it is you want.

There is no set format for a mission statement; it can be in written, pictorial or even aural form. It is not the format, it is getting your ideas across that is important. This section of the book should not be looked at as a hard-and-fast framework, but merely as some suggestions for how you could go about things.

Images

In Chapter 1 it was suggested that you start collecting images of things that attract you and it is now that these items will come into play. You can assemble a series of images in digital or analogue format that sum up what it is that you want your house to look and feel like. This can range from the straightforward

to the esoteric. You can have photographs of a particular bath or kitchen, montages of photographs of buildings (internally and externally) to show what it is you would like your building to look like, colour and fabric swatches to show what your preferences are and maybe even a favourite painting, sculpture or photograph to illustrate what it is you would like your house to feel like both inside and out.

Primary Objectives

A mission statement should set out what are the must-haves in your project. What you believe to be essential can vary, but a few of the primary objectives you might have are set out below:

- Budget – it might that you cannot, in any circumstances, exceed a certain cost, if this is the case it should be stated clearly and simply right from the beginning.

Collect images of what it is you are after.

- Accommodation – it is always a good idea to decide on the absolute minimum you will accept in terms of accommodation and your mission statement should include a list of rooms you must have, to include ancillary accommodation such as garages, sheds, utility areas and so on.
- Size – this is somewhat linked to budget, but a statement of maximum and minimum sizes is very useful.
- Timescale – it might be that you have to be out of your existing house by a certain date, or something similar; if so, this should be stated, but it is very hard to be absolutely sure that this objective can be achieved.
- Special requirements – if there is anything unique to this project it should be stated; you may need the house to be disabled- or unsighted-friendly, or be capable of future extension, or even to have the right conditions to store your wine collection.

When setting out the primary objectives you should try and be as realistic as possible, since you can find people refusing to get involved if they think you are trying to achieve the impossible or are going to be too demanding. For this reason it is worth canvassing the opinions of the design and construction team as to the validity of your primary objectives; if you are dreaming the impossible dream you need to know sooner rather than later, before you commit too much time and money.

Secondary Objectives

Having established what are items which are essential to the project's success, you can turn to things which you would like see but are not necessarily deal breakers. This is likely to be a bit more esoteric than the primary objectives, but here are a few suggestions:

- Additional rooms for activities and so on.
- Aspect of particular rooms.
- Quality and type of fittings and fixtures.
- Spiritual matters such as feng shui.
- Environmental issues such as sustainability, energy efficiency and recycling.

Again your design and construction team will be able to help you decide which of your secondary objectives are practical. You will need to be flexible – the whole point of this list is to commit to paper what you would like to see but are prepared to let go if it proves impossible.

Enablement

Any member of the design and construction team has a vested interest in the financing of the project; after all, if it fails due to collapse of funding it is likely that they will lose money at the same time. A simple statement outlining how you are achieving your funding is therefore a good idea; you don't have to be too elaborate about the exact amounts or even the parties involved, something along the lines of 'I have raised the finance for this project partly by the sale of my previous property and partly by a self-build mortgage' will suffice.

Form of Contract

All of the design and construction team will want to know what form of contract you are intending to use, since it will shape the way that they carry out their duties and how they structure their costs. This item will change and become more elaborate as things progress and as you get advice from various people along the way. Contracts are dealt with in detail in Chapter 6, but your general brief will probably start off by saying things like 'I intend to enter into a conventional contract with a main contractor' and end up saying 'the contract will be a JCT Intermediate with specification and drawings'.

Programme

The design and construction team will need to know your intentions as to time scale and when briefing each new member it is important to let them know when their input will be required. I have covered programme in the last chapter and it may be that you give members of the design and construction team a copy of your preliminary programme or, later on, a copy of the contractor's programme. In some cases it is enough to state the date and time when a certain thing will be required on site.

SPECIFIC BRIEFING

Each member of the design and construction team, in addition to knowing the general project details, will need to know specifically what their duties will

be and, in many cases, exactly what those duties are will form the contract between you. In addition, it is the case with almost every member of the team that you will have duties towards them, such as payment, and this should also be spelt out in the briefing document. Often you will work with the prospective member of the design or construction team to formulate their brief and in some cases they will simply tell you what they intend to do, when they intend doing it and how much it will cost you. It is difficult, therefore, to have a brief ready-prepared for each member of the team, but I will work through the special requirements using the same categories as for the selection stages above.

Briefing Your Solicitor

An exchange of letters is the normal way of briefing your solicitor; you will write to the prospective firm and they will write back confirming their ability to carry out this work and what their costs will be. Solicitors will generally try to charge by the hour unless the tasks are very specific but, if pushed, they will generally give you a lump-sum quotation for work. What you want them to do will vary according to the nature of your particular project but the headings might be as follows:

- Acting for you on the conveyancing of a site or property.
- Acting for you on negotiating rights of way or easements.
- Acting for you on removal of, imposition of or insurance against implementation of restrictive covenants.
- Advising you on contractual matters with developers and others.

If you do pin your solicitor down to lump sums, you should also negotiate an hourly rate for anything else that might come up.

Briefing Your Accountant

As for your solicitor, the brief and contract with your accountant will consist of an exchange of letters, where you will set out what is expected and they will confirm their costs for carrying out the same. Again, an accountant generally charges by the hour since it is uncertain exactly what they will have to do, but in your case it may be that you only need some quite specific advice on VAT or tax and an accountant will generally give you a lump-sum quotation. Services that you may require an accountant to perform could include:

- Advice on whether the work will be zero or standard rated for VAT and how to verify this.
- Advice on tax matters such as how to prevent your project being the subject of capital gains tax.
- Advice on how to raise finance for the project.
- Advice on bookkeeping and control of finance during the project.

Again and as with your solicitor, if you do get lump-sum quotations it is worth getting an hourly rate confirmed for any additional duties.

Briefing your Architect

The architect's role and duties can be the most complicated of the briefing process and a brief outlining those duties is generally more complex than a simple exchange of letters. The Royal Institute of British Architects produces various useful publications dealing with the commissioning and briefing of an architect, and it is worth ringing them to obtain the latest booklets.

Basically, an architect's involvement breaks down into various stages and you need to decide for which of these you would like to commission the services of an architect.

The Royal Institute of British Architects has broken the various work stages down and assigned letters for them from A through to L. You do not have to commission your architect to do all of these stages – you may be intending to do all the detailed design and site management yourself and only want them to get planning permission for you, for instance. For ease of selection of exactly what your architect should do, the various categories as taken from the Royal Institute of British Architects' 'Appointment of an Architect' booklet are shown in boxes.

Of the services outlined you may have done some of these and may just want a general discussion about the scheme that can be the subject of an initial

---

Work Stage A: Inception

1.1 Discuss the client's requirements, including timescale and any financial limits; assess these and give general advice on how to proceed; agree the architect's services.
1.2 Obtain from the client information on ownership and any lessors or lessees of the site, boundary fences and other enclosures, and any known easements, encroachments, underground services, rights of way, rights of support and other relative matters.
1.3 Visit the site and carry out an initial appraisal.
1.4 Advise on the need for other consultants' services and on the scope of these services.
1.5 Advise on the need for specialist contractors, sub-contractors and suppliers to design and execute part of the works to comply with the architect's requirements.
1.6 Advise on the need for site staff.
1.7 Prepare where required an outline timetable and fee basis for further services for the client's approval.

---

meeting. Many architects will carry out the initial inception meeting free of charge. There are a couple of items in Stage A that will be premature in the type of project you are carrying out; these are 1.5 and 1.6.

Work Stage B: Feasibility

1.8 Carry out such studies as may be necessary to determine the feasibility of the clients requirements; review with the client alternative design and construction approaches; advise on the need to obtain planning permissions, approvals under building acts or regulations, and other similar statutory requirements.

The standard terminology of Work Stage B concentrates on the architectural feasibility, whereas your own feasibility study may well have been more far-ranging. It may be, therefore, that this stage is rolled into Stage A as part of the initial meeting.

With a project of the kind you are undertaking it is unlikely that you will want (or need) to engage other consultants' services at Work Stage C, so the architect tends to be by himself. The approximation of the contract cost will be a useful tool and, depending on the experience of the architect, can be quite accurate. It should be noted, however, that costs at this stage are based on a sketch and this could change considerably as the project evolves and develops. Costing buildings is not the architect's speciality; they can only give you a rough idea based on their previous experience. It is also at this stage that you can expect the meter to start ticking in the matter of fees.

Work Stage C: Outline Proposals

1.9 With other consultants where appointed analyse the client's requirements; prepare outline proposals and an approximation of the construction cost for the client's preliminary approval.

Work Stage D: Scheme Design

1.10 With other consultants where appointed, develop a scheme design from the outline proposals taking into account amendments requested by the client; prepare a cost estimate; where applicable give an indication of possible start and completion dates for the building contract. The scheme design will illustrate the size and character of the project in sufficient detail to enable the client to agree the spatial arrangements, materials and appearance.

1.11 With other consultants where appointed, advise the client of the implications of any subsequent changes on the cost of the project and on the overall programme.

1.12 Make where required application for planning permission. The permission itself is beyond the architect's control, and no guarantee that it will be granted can be given.

Work Stage E: Detail Design

1.13 With other consultants where appointed, develop the scheme design; obtain the client's approval of the type of construction, quality of materials and standard of workmanship; co-ordinate any design work done by consultants, specialist contractors, sub-contractors and suppliers; obtain quotations and other information in connection with specialist work.

1.14 With other consultants where appointed, carry out cost checks as necessary; advise the client of the consequences of any subsequent changes on the cost and programme.

1.15 Make and negotiate where required applications for approvals under building acts, regulations or other statutory requirements.

It is not until Stage E that a clear picture of the actual cost of the project will begin to emerge, since it is only now that you will actually get to the nitty-gritty of the specification. It is also at this stage where you can revert to a design-and-build type of contract if you wish, by which the contractor takes over the design of the project based on the planning drawings and an outline specification. This is dealt with in more detail below in 'Briefing Your Contractor'. It is also at this stage that you will probably need to engage the services of a structural engineer.

Work Stages F and G: Production Information and Bills of Quantities

1.16 With other consultants where appointed, prepare production information including drawings, schedules and specifications of materials and workmanship; provide information for bills of quantities, if any, to be prepared: all information complete in sufficient detail to enable a contractor to prepare a tender.

For Stage F and G, depending on the size of your project, you may not require a bill of quantities (see 'Briefing Your Contractor' below).

Work Stage H: Tender Action

1.17 Arrange, where relevant, for other contracts to be let prior to the contractor commencing work.
1.18 Advise on and obtain the client's approval to a list of tenderers.
1.19 Invite tenders from approved contractors; appraise and advise on tenders submitted. Alternatively, arrange for a price to be negotiated with a contractor.

Work Stage J: Project Planning

1.20 Advise the client on the appointment of the contractor and on the responsibilities of the client, contractor and architect under the terms of the building contract and arrange for it to be signed by the client and the contractor; provide production information as required by the building contract.

Work Stage K: Operations on Site

1.21 Administer the terms of the building contract during operations on site.
1.22 Visit the site as appropriate to inspect generally the progress and quality of the work.
1.23 With other consultants where appointed, make where required periodic financial reports to the client including the effect of any variations on the construction cost.

It is important to note that the standard wording of Stage K allows for inspection only, there is no management element, so if you want your architect to take a more proactive role in a management of the works sense, you should make this clear.

Work Stage L: Completion

1.24 Administer the terms of the building contract relating to the completion of the works.
1.25 Give general guidance on maintenance.
1.26 Provide the client with a set of drawings showing the building and the main lines of drainage; arrange for drawings of the services installations to be provided.

The standard Architects Appointment sets out the bare bones of an architectural service, but there are many other services that you may want. If this is not stated clearly at the outset then you might find that your architect will resist carrying out any additional services or will charge more for doing them, typical additional services are:

- Project Management – managing the rest of the team and coordinating and advising on finance.
- Planning Supervisor – managing and advising on the terms of the Construction and Design Management Regulations (Health and Safety).

- Interior Design – selection and specification of internal finishes, furniture and soft furnishings.
- Landscape Design – design of external landscaping including planting, hard and soft landscape.
- Visualization – preparation of computer and scale models, computer and hand perspectives allowing visualization of the building prior to commencement.
- Party Wall Surveys and Awards – necessary when you are building closer than 1m to any adjoining structures belonging to someone else, or when there is any question of undermining a neighbour's foundations.
- Research and Advice – on specialist items such as environmental issues, feng shui and disabled access.

The Royal Institute of British Architects advises that payment of fees should be broken down as follows:

Work Stage	Proportion of Fee (%)	Cumulative Total (%)
C	15	15
D	20	35
E	20	55
FG	20	75
HJKL	25	100

It is my opinion that this breakdown of fees is somewhat front-loaded, this is natural since most architects work in arrears, carrying out the work prior to invoicing. You will find, however, that if you call off the project at the end of, say, Stage G you may have paid an unfair proportion of the fee. You may like to put forward the proposition that in return for prompt payment of accounts or even a 50 per cent up-front payment on each work stage you adjust the payment of fees to the following:

Work Stage	Proportion of Fee (%)	Cumulative Total (%)
C	10	10
D	20	30
E	15	45
FG	20	65
HJKL	35	100

All the above might seem very dry; it is obviously needed but does not get to the heart of things, which is what the building will look like and feel like, and it is for these reasons that your visualizations and images are of such importance. In addition, it is important to the job that you find out from the architects as quickly as possible where they are going with the design. It is suggested, therefore, that you make it clear to your architect that you require visualizations at the earliest possible stage and give yourself an escape clause, whereby you can end the architect's involvement if you are really not seeing things eye-to-eye and only pay for the work actually completed.

It is suggested that, given the complicated nature of the architect's service, you base the brief on the Royal Institute of British Architects' 'Standard Form of Agreement', which is available from the RIBA bookshop or from the architects themselves. This document is in the form of a contract between the parties (you and the architect) setting out exactly what is required in terms of duties on both parts, to be signed by both parties – this will make things much easier if there is any discussion during the course of the works as to exactly what you wanted done.

Briefing Your Structural Engineer

The structure of a domestic house will tend to be fairly simple, and a structural engineer will usually quote a lump sum and base his service and brief on the basis of a simple exchange of letters.

You do need to set out exactly what you require the Structural Engineer to do and these can include:

- Substructure design, including foundations and retaining walls (walls to hold back earth in the case of basement construction or when the building is on a sloping site).
- Wall design, including density of brick or block work, steel or concrete columns and lintels over windows.
- Intermediate floor design, including any beams required.
- Roof design, including any beams or columns required.
- Site inspections and approval of sub-contractors' drawings.
- Road and/or drainage design.

It is worth also thinking about whether you will require any special services. For instance, do you want double or triple height-space in your house? Would you like solid-concrete intermediate floors rather than lightweight timber ones for acoustic reasons? Or would you like your engineer to design pieces of external structure like pergolas?

It is suggested that you, at least, refer back to the Institute of Civil Engineers' Standard Form of Agreement, a copy of which you can obtain from the ICE or from the engineers themselves.

It is quite likely that the engineer will not be required until you have planning permission (although it is worth consulting an engineer on acquisition of site if you are thinking of converting an existing building, taking away support of an adjoining structure by demolition or the ground conditions are unusual). Sending copies of the planning drawings together with a letter outlining their duties can brief the engineer.

Briefing Your Designers

If you have decided to employ designers in addition to architects, for instance landscape or interior designers, a letter of appointment should be sufficient as a brief. Again, you need to address exactly what it is you want from them. Typical items are as follows:

For Interior Designers
* Wall floor and ceiling finishes.
* Interior layouts including furniture.
* Soft furnishings.
* Light fitting and ironmongery.
* Bespoke furniture.
* Kitchens and sanitary ware.
* Direct acquisition of items (rather than through a contractor).

For Landscape Designers
* Hard and soft landscape design.
* Specification of plants.
* External furniture design and/or specification.
* Design of bespoke external items (pergolas, summerhouses and the like).
* Boundary treatment.
* Direct acquisition of items (rather than through a contractor).

Briefing Your Contractor

Apart from the mission statement and general briefing there are three main ways of briefing your contractor, these are:

* The Health and Safety plan.
* The Contract.
* Drawings and Specifications.

The Health and Safety plan has been dealt with in the last Chapter so I will concentrate here on the contract, and the drawings and specifications.

The Contract

The form of the contract will, to some extent, dictate the drawings and specifications, so the first thing to do is to decide what contract you would like to use.

First, ensure that you do have a contract; you are strongly advised not to do things on a handshake or by a verbal agreement. However well you know someone, things can go wrong in the building business and a properly written contract should cover all eventualities. A contract in letter form is better than nothing, but it is far better to use a properly written contract.

Construction contracts form a large and complicated body of work. There have been a considerable number of unsatisfactory contracts over the years: contracts written by the employer (you), which are unfair to the contractor; and contracts written by the contractor, which are unfair to the employer. Whoever writes the contract tends to write terms that favour themselves. Therefore it is best to avoid a contract that is prepared by one of the parties to it. The particular slant given to a contract by who writes it has been recognized over the years and, to get over this, a body called the Joint Contracts Tribunal (JCT) was set up in 1931. This body has representatives from client, contractor and professional bodies sitting on it, and their job is to make sure all the parties to a contract are fairly represented by its terms. It is suggested, therefore, that the first decision you take is to use a JCT form of contract, since this way the contractor will know he is adequately protected and will price the job competitively and you will know that your rights are also protected.

It is sometimes impossible to avoid using a contract that has been prepared by the contractor – for instance most of the system builders will want to use their own contract. It is suggested that, if you come across a party who has their own contract, you persevere with suggesting that you use a standard form, since a contractor will often give in rather than lose the order. If you do have to sign a non-standard form of contract it is suggested that, before you do so, you get your solicitor to look over it and suggest changes to clauses that are disadvantageous to you. Particular things to *avoid* are requirements for payment up-front and payment for extras; particular things to ensure are *included* are requirements to make regular progress with the work and the mechanism for you to walk away if such regular progress is not being made.

There are numerous different forms of contract and the first decision you need to make is whether you want a conventional or a design-and-build contract.

A conventional contract requires the contractor to price and work to detailed drawings and specifications provided by you. The advantage of this form of contract is that you have much more control of what is produced and the quality of it; you get to control and work closely with the designers and it is also much easier to make changes during the building works. The disadvantage of this form is that it is more complicated for you to arrange – you have to employ the professionals yourself and it is difficult to claim back the VAT on their fees.

A design-and-build contract requires the contractor to price outline drawings and specification either provided by you or, alternatively in the case of the system-builders, drawings provided by the contractor, and then to produce their own detail drawings and specifications that they will then work to. The advantage of this form of contract is that it is generally faster on to site than a conventional one, since you do not have to wait for the detail drawings to be prepared, and you will be able to save the VAT on any professional fees, as they are all wrapped up in the contract sum. The disadvantage of this form is that you get far less control of the job and the quality of it, and you can find yourself being charged through the nose for any changes made during the process of work on site.

For both forms of contract the Joint Contracts Tribunal has produced a variety of different types depending on size of job and what form the accompanying drawings, specifications and schedules take. If you have employed a professional team they will advise which is the most appropriate form, or you can ring the JCT who will tell you (and sell you) the correct contract. It is likely that you will use either a minor works or intermediate form for a conventional contract, or a standard form with contractors' design for a design-and-build contract.

Much of a contract is about eventualities that will probably not come into play at all with your particular project, but have to be there 'in case'. There are also clauses that deal with the normal day-to-day running of the contract, such as valuing for making payments, how to make changes and how the work is to be insured. The contract will also deal with start and completion date and what valid reasons there are for an overrun.

The Drawings and Schedules
The contract drawings and schedules are, in essence, your brief to the contractor on how you want the building to look and function, and so it is of primary importance to get them right. The only way to do this is to go through them with a fine-tooth comb, in the fashion described in Chapter 5, and not to be reticent about getting them changed if they are not to your satisfaction.

In a design-and-build contract the drawings will depend on whether you are going for a system-built arrangement or whether you are going to a contractor to design-and-build to drawings that you have already had prepared by an architect or designer.

In the case of a system-built house, the contractor will have a fairly standard set of scheme drawings, which will be altered and adapted to reflect the nature of your own particular project. The thing to look out for here is the level of detail – what will your windows look like, how does the kitchen look, what is the ironmongery and sanitary ware and so forth. Obviously, the latter items are difficult to reflect in drawing form and this is where the schedules come in, since they are lists of items specifying make and type.

Scheduled items will include the following:

- Ironmongery.
- Sanitary ware.
- Doors.
- Windows.
- Wall and floor finishes.

Each schedule should have a means to refer back to the plans, such as door and window number, a description of the type of object, its size (where appropriate), the manufacturer and reference, and the colour when possible.

There should be no grey areas in the documentation – you need to know what you are buying right down to the colour of the paintwork and the type of taps in the bathroom.

When you are employing a design-and-build contractor to work on a scheme that you have already designed or had designed, it is common to work from a set of planning drawings and a document that is known as the 'Employers Requirements'. The Employers Requirements is a list of what is important to you in your particular project, and can vary from schedules and specifications through to detail drawings of areas that are important to you, such as fireplaces, staircases and fixed furniture. The more detail

Schedules should show the item in question, its manufacturer and its location.

LOCATION	WC	WC SEAT	CISTERN	TOILET ROLL HOLDER	WASHBASIN	TAPS & WASTE	TOWEL RAIL	GRAB RAIL	SHOWER	BATH	SPECIAL EQUIPMENT	COMMENTS
ALL FITTINGS TO BE AS SUPPLIED BY TWYFORD CARADON LTD UNLESS OTHERWISE SPECIFIED												
FIRST FLOOR FAMILY BATHROOM	GALERIE ELITE GE 1148 WH	GALLERIE ELITE GE 7810 WH	GALLERIE ELITE GE2671 WH	ECLIPSE EL 6801 WH	ARIA WB 3050 WH WASHBASIN WITH RUGBY JOINERY NICE V96RD VANITY UNIT AND GREY GRANITE WORK TOP	CLASSIQUE CQ 5126 CP MONOBLOC MIXER WITH POP-UP WASTE	C.P.HART CT4 HEATED TOWEL RAIL WITH WALL STAYS AND DECORATIVE VALVE HAND WHEELS	AV 5802 WH GRAB RAIL ABOVE BATH	NONE	CONSTELLATION AL 9502 WH 1700x700 BATH WITH PP 1321 WH FRONT PANEL AND CLASSIQUE CQ 5215 CP TAPS	ECLIPSE EL 6873 WH TOOTHBRUSH HOLDER, EL 6850 WH SOAP DISH, EL6856 TOILET BRUSH HOLDER, 600mm DIAMETER ROUND SILVER MIRROR	FIX EQUIPMENT IN POSITION INDICATED ON DRAWINGS ENSURE GRAB RAILS HAVE NOGGINS TO ENSURE SECURE FIXING
FIRST FLOOR MASTER BEDROOM ENSUITE	GALERIE ELITE GE 1148 WH	GALLERIE ELITE GE 7810 WH	GALLERIE ELITE GE2671 WH	ECLIPSE EL 6801 WH	ARIA WB 3050 WH WASHBASIN WITH RUGBY JOINERY NICE V96RD VANITY UNIT AND GREY GRANITE WORK TOP	CLASSIQUE CQ 5126 CP MONOBLOC MIXER WITH POP-UP WASTE	C.P.HART CT4 HEATED TOWEL RAIL WITH WALL STAYS AND DECORATIVE VALVE HAND WHEELS	NONE	760x760x180 RISER TRAY YGWH WITH YO 0004CP WASTE, XV1050WC PIVOT DOOR, AV 7900WH FOLD-DOWN SHOWER SEAT AND THERMOSTATIC SHOWER SF 7063 CP WITH FIXED HEIGHT SHOWER ARM	NONE	ECLIPSE EL 6873 WH TOOTHBRUSH HOLDER, EL 6850 WH SOAP DISH, EL6856 TOILET BRUSH HOLDER, 600mm DIAMETER ROUND SILVER MIRROR	FIX EQUIPMENT IN POSITION INDICATED ON DRAWINGS ENSURE GRAB RAILS AND SHOWER SEATS HAVE NOGGINS TO ENSURE SECURE FIXING
FIRST FLOOR BEDROOM 2 ENSUITE	GALERIE ELITE GE 1148 WH	GALLERIE ELITE GE 7810 WH	GALLERIE ELITE GE2671 WH	ECLIPSE EL 6801 WH	ARIA WB 3050 WH WASHBASIN WITH RUGBY JOINERY NICE V96RD VANITY UNIT AND GREY GRANITE WORK TOP	CLASSIQUE CQ 5126 CP MONOBLOC MIXER WITH POP-UP WASTE	C.P.HART CT4 HEATED TOWEL RAIL WITH WALL STAYS AND DECORATIVE VALVE HAND WHEELS	NONE	760x760x180 RISER TRAY YGWH WITH YO 0004CP WASTE, XV1050WC PIVOT DOOR AND THERMOSTATIC SHOWER SF 7063 CP WITH FIXED HEIGHT SHOWER ARM	NONE	ECLIPSE EL 6873 WH TOOTHBRUSH HOLDER, EL 6850 WH SOAP DISH, EL6856 TOILET BRUSH HOLDER, 600mm DIAMETER ROUND SILVER MIRROR	FIX EQUIPMENT IN POSITION INDICATED ON DRAWINGS ENSURE GRAB RAILS AND SHOWER SEATS HAVE NOGGINS TO ENSURE SECURE FIXING
GROUND FLOOR ENTRANCE HALL WC	RHAPSODY RH 1148 WH	RHAPSODY 7810 WH	RHAPSODY RH0614 WH	ECLIPSE EL 6801 WH	RHAPSODY 355 WASHBASIN RH4812 WITH SR 5367 XX WALL HANGERS AND WF 8463 CP BOTTLE TRAP	CLASSIQUE CQ 5205 CP TAPS AND CQ 5823 CP CHAIN WASTE	ECLIPSE EL 6865 TOWEL RING	NONE	NONE	NONE	ECLIPSE EL 6850 WH SOAP DISH, EL6856 TOILET BRUSH HOLDER, 600mm DIAMETER ROUND SILVER MIRROR	FIX EQUIPMENT IN POSITION INDICATED ON DRAWINGS ENSURE GRAB RAILS ARE PLACED FOR SINK FIXING
GROUND FLOOR NANNY ROOM ENSUITE	GALERIE ELITE GE 1148 WH	GALLERIE ELITE GE 7810 WH	GALLERIE ELITE GE2671 WH	ECLIPSE EL 6801 WH	MINA 455 WASHBASIN WB 1120WH WITH SR 5307 XX WALL HANGERS AND WF 8463 CP BOTTLE TRAP	CLASSIQUE CQ 5205 CP 5823 CP CHAIN WASTE	ECLIPSE EL 6865 TOWEL RING	NONE	700x700x142 EUROLUX SHOWER TRAY YS WH WITH YO 0004CP WASTE AND THERMOSTATIC SHOWER SF 7063 CP WITH FIXED HEIGHT SHOWER ARM	NONE	ECLIPSE EL 6873 WH TOOTHBRUSH HOLDER, EL 6850 WH SOAP DISH, EL6856 TOILET BRUSH HOLDER, 600mm DIAMETER ROUND SILVER MIRROR	FIX EQUIPMENT IN POSITION INDICATED ON DRAWINGS ENSURE GRAB RAILS ARE BOLTED TO SECURE FIXING
GROUND FLOOR GRANNY ROOM ENSUITE	RHAPSODY RH 1148 WH	RHAPSODY 7810 WH	RHAPSODY RH0614 WH	ECLIPSE EL 6801 WH	RHAPSODY 580 WASHBASIN RH 4212 WH AND RH 4910 WH PEDESTAL	CHROME PLATED CHAIN WASTE 1.25" WF 4330 CP AND PAIR OF CHROME PLATED LEVER TAPS 1/2" SF 5245 CP	AVALON AV 5801 WH 450MM GRAB RAIL	NONE	800 QUADRANT EUROLUX SHOWER TRAY YG WH WITH YO 0004CP WASTE AND THERMOSTATIC SHOWER SF 7063 CP WITH FIXED HEIGHT SHOWER ARM	NONE	ECLIPSE EL 6873 WH TOOTHBRUSH HOLDER, EL 6850 WH SOAP DISH, EL6856 TOILET BRUSH HOLDER, 600mm DIAMETER ROUND SILVER MIRROR	FIX EQUIPMENT IN POSITION INDICATED ON DRAWINGS ENSURE GRAB RAILS ARE BOLTED TO SECURE FIXING
BASEMENT SAUNA						NORDIC SAUNA REF 11A						
BASEMENT EXERCISE ROOM	NONE	NONE	NONE	NONE	NONE	NONE	NONE	NONE	NONE	JACUZZI OPALIA TWO PERSON SPA BATH IN WHITE WITH CHROME FITTINGS	NONE	NONE
BASEMENT SHOWER ROOM	NONE	NONE	NONE	NONE	NONE	NONE	NONE	NONE	760x760x180 RISER TRAY YGWH WITH YO 0004CP WASTE, XV1050WC PIVOT DOOR, AV 7900WH FOLD-DOWN SHOWER SEAT AND THERMOSTATIC SHOWER SF 7063 CP WITH FIXED HEIGHT SHOWER ARM	NONE	NONE	FIX EQUIPMENT IN POSITION INDICATED ON DRAWINGS ENSURE SHOWER SEAT HAS NOGGINS TO ENSURE SECURE FIXING
BASEMENT WC	GALERIE ELITE GE 1148 WH	GALLERIE ELITE GE 7810 WH	GALLERIE ELITE GE2671 WH	ECLIPSE EL 6801 WH	ARIA WB 3050 WH WASHBASIN WITH RUGBY JOINERY NICE V96RD VANITY UNIT AND GREY GRANITE WORK TOP	CLASSIQUE CQ 5126 CP MONOBLOC MIXER WITH POP-UP WASTE	ECLIPSE EL 6865 TOWEL RING	NONE	NONE	NONE	ECLIPSE EL 6850 WH SOAP DISH, EL6856 TOILET BRUSH HOLDER, 600mm DIAMETER ROUND SILVER MIRROR	FIX EQUIPMENT IN POSITION INDICATED ON DRAWINGS

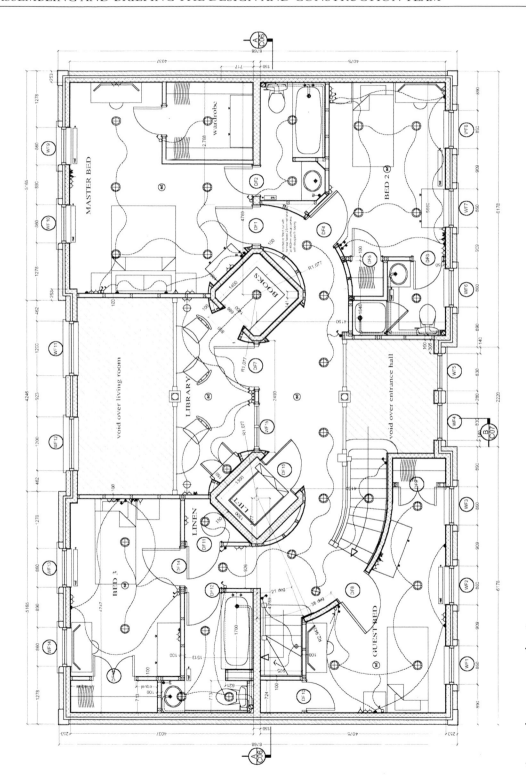

A general arrangement drawing.

the Employers Requirements document goes into, the better you will know what you are getting. Your architect will prepare the Employers Requirements document on your behalf.

With a conventional form of contract the idea is to give the contract a detailed set of drawings which describe the building in its entirety; there will inevitably be more drawings produced as the project progresses, which will be requested by the contractor to explain in more detail what the architect is after, but this should be limited.

Drawings should consist of, at a minimum, the following:

- Plans of every floor level at a minimum scale of 1:50 showing construction of walls and partitions, the position and size of columns and beams, dimensions to allow the setting out of every wall and door and window opening, electrical layout, drainage runs, window and door references and, preferably, a furniture layout.
- Sections and elevations at a minimum scale of

1:50 showing wall and roof construction, floor to floor heights and the height of window and door sills and heads.
- A site plan at a minimum scale of 1:100 showing external drainage, areas of hard and soft landscaping and external levels.
- Typical details of window heads, jambs and sills, thresholds, eaves, ridges, valleys and any other typical situation at a minimum scale of 1:5, showing nature of construction and with notes as to precise materials.
- Drawings at a minimum scale of 1:10 showing any bespoke items such as conservatories, porches, dormer windows, pergolas, fixed furniture or other features.
- Structural drawings at a minimum scale of 1:50 showing foundation width, depth and type, any steels and their position, the size and spacing of any floor joists and rafters.
- Structural drawings at a minimum scale of 1:10 showing any specialist connections, such as between steel members or steel/floor judgements.

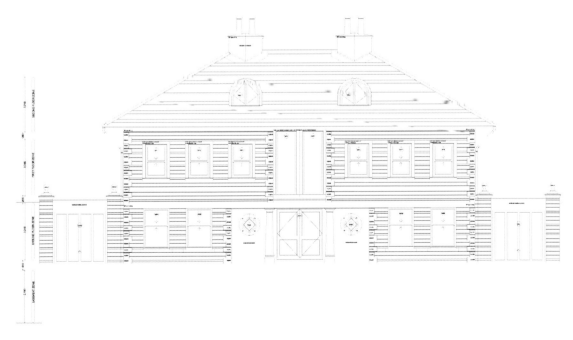

A typical elevation.

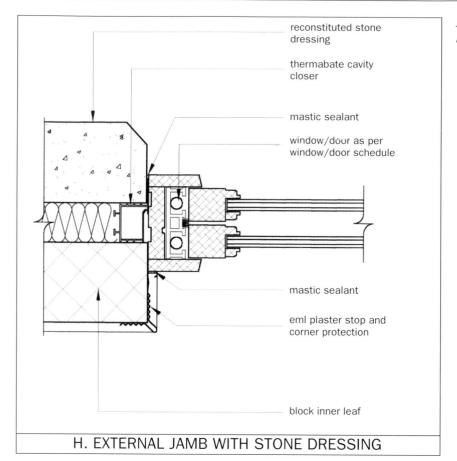

reconstituted stone dressing

thermabate cavity closer

mastic sealant

window/door as per window/door schedule

mastic sealant

eml plaster stop and corner protection

block inner leaf

H. EXTERNAL JAMB WITH STONE DRESSING

A typical detail drawing.

The Specification

In addition to drawings and schedules your brief to the contractor should include a specification.

The specification is a document designed to fill in any gaps in the information on the drawings and schedules; it is essentially a technical document listing special contract conditions, working methods and codes of practice. It is generally broken down into three subsections as follows:

The Preliminaries

This section will refer back to the contract itself and will say which contract conditions apply and which do not, and will also list start and completion dates, damages for non-completion and insurance amounts. The aim of this item is to précis the contract so that the contractor will be able to pick out the relevant points without having to wade through it all.

There will also be items on site access, working hours and any other special site provisions.

The Preambles

This section will refer to working methods and materials; the aim being to ensure that all work is carried out to a good standard, using quality materials and to the latest working standards. A preambles section will, for instance, refer to: storage of a material; where it comes from; how it should be used; and any applicable standards and codes of practice (see box for an example).

The Works

This section will contain a list of the various works, generally broken down into the trades that will carry them out, and is designed so that the contractor will price each separate item. This can be used in the

> ### Curing and Protection
>
> All concrete shall be protected within one hour of completion and cured in accordance with Clause 6.6 of B.S. 8110 except that the use of damp absorbent materials, damp sand or watering shall not be permitted on reinforced concrete.
>
> No load shall be placed on concrete beams and slabs until they have reached their twenty-eight-day strength.

future for valuing how much of the work has been done at interim valuations.

Typical work sections are as follows:

- Demolitions.
- Ground works.
- Concrete work.
- Brickwork and blockwork.
- Carpentry and joinery.
- Roofing.
- Plaster work.
- Mechanical services and sanitary ware.
- Electrical services.
- Decorations.
- External works.

The Collection

This is a list of the various sections in the specification, including all the works section, and will ask for a cost against each item so that this can be condensed into a single contract sum.

A variation on the specification and works schedule is the *Bill of Quantities*. This is a document that is generally produced by a quantity surveyor and will not just list all the works, but will also measure them so that you will know how much skirting board, for instance, you are using down to the nearest linear metre. The advantage of this document is that it makes the valuation of any variations much easier. You can, for instance, add an additional door and the Bill of Quantities will tell you not just the value of the door, but also how much blockwork and plaster will be saved, the cost of additional architrave and

paint and so on. The disadvantage of a Bill of Quantities is that it is more expensive to prepare than the normal specification and, depending on the type and size of contractor you are using, can be so daunting that they may increase their price as a result.

Briefing Your Subcontractor

A subcontractor is like a smaller and more specialized version of a main contractor who will need to be briefed in a similar fashion with a contract, drawings and specifications. However, since their work is likely to be less fundamental, the nature of all these documents can be much simpler.

Quite how you brief your subcontractor rather depends on how you are running the contract. If you are using a main contractor, but have certain subcontractors you want to use, then you will have to nominate them. The key to nomination is to tell the contractor that you intend to nominate certain sections of work at the tender stage; that way there can be no discussion or argument when the time comes. If you are actually managing the works yourself then you may be letting sections to individual subcontractors.

In the case of using a main contractor, then you will need to inform the subcontractor what the contract arrangements are (as previously dealt with). This is best done by sending a copy of the preliminaries with your invitation to tender – this should be accompanied with the relevant section of the preambles and the works section. If you are nominating the subcontractor on to the main contractor, then the contract will be between those two parties.

If you are managing the contract yourself then you will need the same general documents, but the contract will be between you and the subcontractor.

This chapter has dealt with selecting and briefing the design and construction team as if they are all being commissioned at the same time, whereas, in reality, they will be sourced at various stages throughout the whole process. The next two chapters deal with the design and construction process and will deal with when, in this process, it is appropriate to source any of the design and construction team.

CHAPTER 5

Designing the Building and Getting What You Want

Architecture is the art of how to waste space.
(Philip Johnson *New York Times* 27 December 1964)

To some extent the last four chapters have been all about getting into a position where you have 'all your ducks in a row', are comfortable that you have limited your risk and have the right components to go forward. Some of this has involved a lot of legwork and you may have found some of the tasks were chores. This, however, is where the fun really starts; you are now in a position to let your imagination loose, realize your dream and get on with the business of design.

There are a number of ways of arriving at the design of your own home: you can buy a site which already has planning permission; you can design it yourself; you can commission someone else to design it on your behalf; you can inherit a design through a group self-build or design-and-build operation; or you can pick a standard design from a pattern book. Whichever way you do choose to go about things, however, there are a few fundamentals that can be applied in establishing what it is that you want and ensuring that you then get it.

This chapter is intended to give you a step-by-step guide as to how to envizage the building, make a positive input to its design and ensure that you actually get what you want.

GETTING STARTED

In previous times building was a fairly ad hoc affair. Building types and methods were mostly fairly traditional and tended to evolve quite slowly; people generally just started on a house along the same lines as they always had done and any adaptations, specialities or design features were done in a seat-of-the-pants kind of way on site. Architecture was kept for wealthy individuals, public buildings and places of worship. Things have changed considerably in the last hundred or so years, with the increasing regulation of the building process, so that now even the humblest dwelling must be properly designed and thought about prior to start on site. This has had a negative effect in some ways, in that it has led to estates of 'pattern book' buildings that all look the same, as opposed to the organic villages of yesteryear, but also a positive effect in that it has led to a situation where no two buildings need to be the same. There has also been an explosion of new technology and new ideas.

The problem with the new way is that to design and build a building economically you have to have it pretty much completely designed before you even dig a hole for the foundations. You can alter things as you go along but, be warned, this is expensive both in terms of delay and disruption to the natural progress of the works and you may need to get new permission from the Local Authority. Alteration during the process is, therefore, best avoided and for this reason visualization of the building prior to start on site is of primary importance. There are several ways of doing this, from the more technical such as architectural plans and elevations, through to three-dimensional sketches, renderings to scale and computer models.

If you have no experience in the building trade and are not au fait with these methods, it is important that you learn enough about them to allow you to understand the information that is being imparted and also to give yourself the ability to impart your own ideas to other people.

You will need a number of simple purchases to get you started, these are:

- An architectural scale – obtainable from most specialist stationers this will allow you to measure architectural plans.
- A supply of tracing paper – obtainable as above, this will allow you to trace over drawings and indicate any changes you would like.
- A roll of masking tape – this will allow you to tape-down drawings and keep them stationary when you are tracing over them.
- A flat surface to work on – this can be, at its simplest, a dining-room table or, at its more complicated, a drawing board. The drawing board will come equipped with a T-square or parallel motion, which will allow you to draw precise lines at right angles to each other, while the dining-room table approach relies on you having a good eye or working over a sheet of graph paper.
- A plentiful supply of pencils, pens, erasers and crayons.

There are also an increasing amount of architectural visualization packages for computers available for the technically minded, although these are generally for drawing the building once it is designed and you will probably still need all the above.

Having equipped yourself to do battle, here is a guide to the various forms of visualization.

Architectural Plans and Elevations

It may be that you already work in an occupation that involves reading architectural drawings, or you have experience through some previous project, if so you may like to skip this section.

Architectural drawings will generally be to scale and it is here where your architectural scale will come in. An architectural scale is essentially a ruler that measures, instead of actual size, the scaled size of things. If you look at the ruler you will see that it is marked on each of its sides with a figure which represents the scale of what you are measuring, such as

1:100, 1:50 and so on. It is obviously not practical to have a drawing that is life sized when you are representing a whole house. A 1:100 drawing, therefore, is a drawing of whatever you are looking at reduced to one hundredth of its actual scale, such that one centimetre actually represents a metre. The architectural scale allows a ready conversion of this without any arithmetic involved; thus on the 1:100 side of the scale a centimetre will actually read as a metre. To find out what scale the drawing you are looking at is, look for a title block or something similar, which should tell you.

Architectural drawings are essentially a two-dimensional way of representing a three-dimensional object and, as such, are always going to be limited in their scope. That said, however, these drawings are absolutely fundamental to the building trade and are tremendously useful tools. At their simplest, architectural drawings break down into three main groups: plans; elevations/sections; and detail drawings.

Plans

A plan is basically a diagram of a particular element of the building drawn as if you were hovering directly over the top of it, as if perspective didn't exist and all layers of the building that are in the way have been removed. The plan of a top floor of a building, therefore, will be as if the roof and the upper section of the wall have been removed leaving approximately the first meter (or yard) of any element above floor level – walls, doors, widows, furniture, kitchen and bathroom fittings.

If you look at the example diagram you will note that the closer the object you are looking at is to the hypothetical cut through the building the darker it is, so that the things which have actually been 'cut' (the walls, doors, and door and window frames) are darker, while the things that are further away (the window sills and sanitary ware) are lighter. You can also see that the doors are drawn in an open position and there is a light arc drawn between the leading edge of the door and the door frame; this describes the area that the door covers between opening and closing.

It is a very useful exercise, if you are not familiar with reading plans, to try to get hold of a set of plans of an existing building. Start by looking at the plans

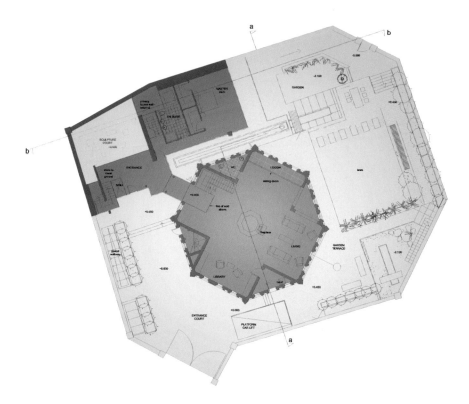

Floor plans – a horizontal section through the building.

and try to envisage how the building will look; then actually visit the building with the plans and walk through it, comparing what you see with what there is physically on the ground.

Another form of plan is the site plan, where the whole building plot is drawn as if the observer is hovering over the roof.

Sections and Elevations

In the same way that plans illustrate what a building would look like if it was sliced horizontally, a section illustrates the same process, but with a vertical slice.

The same rules apply as with the plans, the closer something is to the 'cut', the darker it is.

The idea of a section is to illustrate the heights of things like floor to ceilings, floor to window sill and so on, and also to illustrate how internal features like staircases or double-height spaces might work.

Elevations illustrate the way a building would look if you were hovering halfway up the building and at ninety degrees to the wall. Again no perspective is employed.

The darkness of the lines still shows things that are closest to the viewpoint as being the darkest, but also shows things that are more important or prominent in a darker line, hence window openings are darker than brickwork hatching.

The weakness of elevational drawings is that, because of their lack of perspective, unless the building in question is very flat sided they do not show any layering in the façade and can make the building seem a little flat.

Detail Drawings

Detail drawings tend to be more technical in their nature and represent how a particular element is constructed. Because of their technical nature they

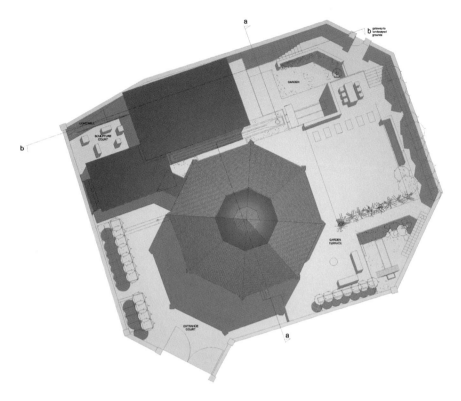

Site plans – a bird's eye view of the whole building plot.

tend to be even more diagrammatic and thus even harder to read, since they will emphasize things that are particularly important constructionally. They tend to be still based around the same plan/section format (although you will encounter the occasional three-dimensional sketch) but in more detail. An example of a detail drawing was shown in the last chapter.

Although architectural drawings attempt to show how a building looks they will never be more than diagrams, and they rely on the viewer to interpret them in the correct way. If you want to see how the building will actually look, you need to enter the realm of three-dimensional representation.

Perspective Drawings/Renderings

We are all familiar with photographic images and are bombarded on a daily basis with two-dimensional representations of three-dimensional things. It is easy to forget, however, that reading perspectives is an acquired skill and the field of anthropology is dotted with cases of isolated peoples, unused to photographic or pictorial representations, struggling to make the connection between the image and the reality of an object.

A perspective drawing can be giving out several pieces of information, and how well it does this is a function of the artists skill and their ability to visualize. Remember, this is not a situation where an artist can set up his easel in front of a building and paint it from life – he or she is actually visualizing the building and then committing that vision to paper. The various pieces of information can conflict or complement and would break down broadly into 'accuracy', 'feeling' and 'colour'.

Accuracy
A perspective drawing represents an image of the object as if you were standing looking at it from a

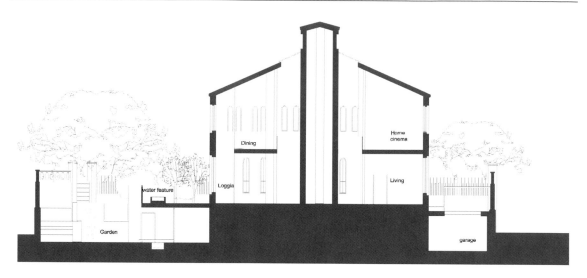

Sections – a vertical slice through the building.

certain viewpoint. There are various techniques used in creating a proper perspective, which have been honed since Renaissance times, and it is now possible to use these techniques to set up a completely accurate image of a building. In practice, however, these techniques are somewhat tedious and artists are more likely to use their skills to improvise an image rather than to create a completely accurate one. In addition an artist will always want to flatter a building by showing it in its best possible light, as a portrait painter will try to show their subject to advantage, so that you will be pleased with the result. Oliver Cromwell in the pomp of his Puritanism famously instructed a portrait artist who was trying to flatter him to alter the canvas and paint him 'warts and all'. If there are any warts on a potential design you need to find out about them, so if you do employ an architectural illustrator you should instruct them to paint

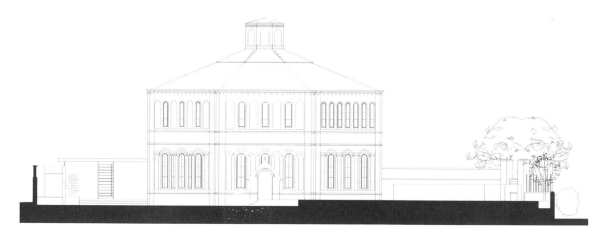

Elevations – a flattened-out 3-dimensional image.

90

A perspective drawing.

And the finished product.

your building 'warts and all'. This is a working diagram, as much as it is something to hang on your wall, and should be treated as such.

Feeling

I am hesitant to enter into a discussion of this item since it is such a nebulous (and controversial) subject, the basis hypothesis being that a painting or drawing with 'feeling' can be more descriptive than a strictly accurate representation. This is quite correct in many ways; who can argue that Monet's *Water Lilies* does not convey the feeling of a beautiful pond on a sunny day better than an accurate diagram of it including brackish water and floating debris.

The problem here, however, is that you are in the presence of greatness – will your perspective artist be capable of the same? A good artist should have the ability to get across some of the feeling of the building and should be allowed to sacrifice some of the accuracy to do so, but you should remember that you may well be seeing the building as it might be on a sunny day. Remember – 'warts and all'.

Colour

A lot of architectural representations tend to err towards the monochrome; it is easier and quicker to do a line sketch than a full rendering and you may not have made up your mind about what the final finishing materials will be. It is important, however, to think about colour as soon as possible – after all, brickwork will be almost the first thing that will appear on site. It is better to have an attempt early and at least open the debate.

It may appear from the above that I am rather down on perspectives, but this is not the case, I believe them to be an extremely useful tool, and I also believe that any perspective is better than no perspective at all.

There are, however, other ways to consider how a building will look and you need to consider these as well.

Scale Models

Scale models have always been a useful tool for both designing and envisaging the building, giving as they do a three-dimensional view of the whole. The model comes into its own in three primary ways: as a working model; as a massing diagram; and as a full presentation model. Whichever the main thrust of the model, there are certain things that need to be borne in mind when looking at it.

You will probably be looking at the model from above and this will give you a very unusual view, unless you plan to do a lot of hot-air ballooning over your property. A model always appears very 'roofy' and this is a view you will very seldom get. It is important, therefore, to try and look at the model in the same way that you will see the building. Try crouching down (or holding the model up) so that your eye level is about at the same level as the front door and you will get a reasonable facsimile of what you would actually see. An alternative is an endoscope, which the model maker might have. This is a tiny flexible camera which can be arranged in such a way that you will be able to set up typical views in and around the building.

Another thing with models is to try and arrange the lighting as it will actually be. Light and the way it changes plays an important part in the way a building works. For a model whose primary purpose is to illustrate how the building will look from the outside, you need to look at it from the way the sun interacts with it. The sun rises in the east, sets in the west and in between describes an arc to the south, which varies in its angle from the horizontal depending on the time of year. A crude but effective way of recreating this process is with an angle-poise lamp. Start off by putting the lamp at a low level on the eastern side and look at the effect; the shadows cast and the areas illuminated will be the way the building will be at breakfast time. Then shift the lamp round so that its rays are shining down at an angle of about 45 degrees from the south and again take note of where the shadows are cast and what areas are illuminated; this is what it will be like at lunchtime. Finally, shift the lamp round to the west at a low level, which will recreate sunset. This exercise will help you to lay out gardens – where are the sunny spots? Internal rooms – it is nice to get morning sun into breakfast rooms, evening into dining rooms and may even move you to revise the design.

The purpose of the three types of model is various and overlapping, but I will attempt to separate them.

The Working Model

A working model is essentially a crudely constructed diagram of the building that helps one to think about the way it (or elements of it) look in three dimensions. Some designers find it easier to envisage the building they are working on in three dimensions by building a model as they are designing it. If you are employing an architect it may be that they are doing this – it is well worth asking them – and if they are ask to see it, however crudely executed it is, since it might also help you to understand the building better. If they are not building one you might like to do it yourself. As the sketches arrive you can construct a crude model with card, a scalpel and some glue that will help you to both visualize the building and get to know it better. If you are designing the building yourself it could be a valuable tool; just cut the walls out of card, cut where you intend to have windows and then construct the roof out of inclined planes of card – this is especially useful for working out the geometry of a pitched roof.

It is also common to use working models to visualize internal spaces, either by having a lift-off roof or by leaving the roof off entirely; this way you can see tricky spaces like double height areas, staircases and the like in three dimensions.

The Massing Diagram

Another common use for a model is to illustrate how the building sits next to its neighbours. It will answer some key questions as to scale and neighbourliness; does the building have an overbearing effect on adjoining properties? is it higher? does it cast a shadow on their gardens? and so on. A massing diagram can be relatively crude, doesn't have to show any windows and can be in monochrome, but it is important to show as much of the surrounding buildings as possible. If you are building the model yourself, you cannot really go and measure all the surrounding buildings so the best way is to 'guesstimate' them. A common trick of the trade is to count brick courses. The majority of buildings have brick on them somewhere or somewhere close by and each brick course measures approximately 75mm (3in), so if there are, say, eight courses from ground level to the sill of a window you will know that this equates

to eight times 75mm or 600mm (2ft). Once you have established the height of one element you can stand back and compare it to another that maybe doesn't have any brickwork; is the height from top of window to eaves four or five times the height from the ground to the sill?

Planning officers will be particularly keen on massing diagrams since it makes one of their jobs (thinking about how the new house relates to surrounding buildings and to the general environment) so much easier, but take care! A massing diagram can also expose areas that the planning officer might believe is a problem but which you might not. If this is the case don't show them. Let them find out for themselves (if they can).

If you do build (or have built) a massing diagram, it is worth making the section for your building lift out, so that as the building alters or adapts you can alter or adapt it in the massing diagram without having to rebuild the whole model each time.

The Presentation Model

The object of a presentation model is to sell the model to some body (or bodies). These might be you, your financiers or the planning committee. Whatever the purpose, a presentation model will be as realistic as possible, with, in all probability, lifelike details and materials. It is, therefore, more expensive to produce than the other two types of model and is not really worth doing until you are pretty sure that you have got the design right.

If you are building the model yourself, a trip to a model-making shop will be useful. You can buy clear acetate for the windows, sheets of realistic materials, such as brick, to stick on your card sub-base and even add-ons like cars, trees and people to give the model a spark of life.

Computer Models

In the last twenty years there have been enormous strides in the field of computer-aided design (CAD). Once the exclusive province of specialists who used huge mainframe computers to turn out crude drawings, CAD is now the territory of most designers who can use personal computers to turn out photo-realistic renderings of buildings.

Computer visualizations can be external …

A computer model of a building or part thereof is, basically, a life-size model on which you can experiment using different lighting, surface materials and colours. Creating a computer model is rather an exact business and quite difficult to alter once it is done, so they tend to appear at the end of the initial design process and are not extremely useful during it. A computer model, however, can be a very useful tool for the detailed design process; it is easy to change a material on the surface or move a light and a variable camera position allows you to look at out-of-the-way corners, giving you exactly the view of the building that you want (particularly useful for the 'warts and all' approach).

… or internal.

Computer visualizations can be taken from a distance.

If your architect or designer is reluctant to spend the time on preparing a computer model or does not have the necessary skills, it is also possible to do your own computer model. There are various packages available that, for those with reasonable technical skills, will allow you to create a computer model of your building by working off scaled plans and elevations. Although these are not as good as the professional programmes they are good enough to create perfectly presentable computer images of your building and, again, this process will allow you to get to know your new house really well.

INITIAL DESIGN

If you are designing the building yourself this section will give you some guidance as to how to go about it, if you are not it will give you an insight into the process that will hopefully allow you to work in a meaningful way with your designer or even produce some rough sketches to serve as a brief for your designer.

The initial design process is all about formulating your ideas and creating a platform from which you will be able to create a fully designed house. Your site is, at this precise moment in time, a blank canvas and

you need to create the initial brush strokes, which can be filled out into a complete painting.

Desire Lines

A good way to start is to decide which part of the site your building is going to inhabit and a useful tool for doing this is to start drawing desire lines on a site plan. As a base for this activity you will need a site plan showing adjoining buildings (if there are any), roads adjacent to the site, all major trees on the site and any trees outside the site that are immediately adjacent to the boundary, levels or contours, and any natural features such as rock outcrops, streams etc. The idea will be to create on this plan a building zone, using lines or hatching to show where you would like to site the building and where it is unlikely that you can. There are a number of factors that will come into play here and they are as listed below.

Building Lines

This item is generally of more importance in built-up areas and villages, and not so relevant in the country (although it can still play a significant part). If you look at most townscapes you will notice that the buildings therein have some conformity in their relationship to each other, front and back. A street of houses will quite often share the same relationship to the road, at the front, and a similar relationship to each other at the back, This means that you do not get any properties 'sticking out' and they tend to be fairly neighbourly to each other, in the sense of not overshadowing each other's front and back gardens. However, this is not always the case and some older neighbourhoods tend to go backwards and forwards so that only the immediate neighbours are the ones that create the context in terms of the front and back walls.

The line that is created by the surrounding properties' front and back is called the 'building line' and is generally quite an important criteria in creating the building zone. It is by no means impossible to project forwards or backwards beyond the building line, but you may find that you will get more resistance from neighbours and the planning authorities if you do so. It is less controversial if you project small elements such as porches, bay widows or feature towers beyond this line.

Having made a study of the adjoining buildings you will now be able to draw a line front and back that you believe will be the rough zone for the maximum front and back extent of your new house.

Boundaries with Adjoining Properties

Having established front and back building lines, you now need to have a look at adjoining properties and what relationship they bear to your boundary. In a similar way to the building line, there is likely to be a convention in the area as to what relationship buildings have with their neighbours. This will vary according to the density and nature of the existing building fabric.

In a street where the buildings are 'terraced', that is to say built right up against each other, it is acceptable and often desirable for any new building to be built right up against the boundary and to extend to the full width of the site. In an area of detached or semi-detached properties within a townscape environment you may find that houses are spaced back from the boundary by a metre or two, allowing access to the rear garden via a side alley. In this kind of area you may find it advisable to space your building back from the boundary by a similar extent. This does not

always apply; you can build right up to the boundary, but you should be aware of the problems, which are:

- The planners may frown upon building right up to the boundary and you may not get planning permission.
- Building right up to the boundary may bring objections from neighbours, who may agitate against you building with the planners, or you might 'start off on the wrong foot' with them in terms of friendly relations.
- Building right up to the boundary will make the building difficult to construct unless you have permission from your neighbours to erect scaffolding on their property.
- Building right up to the boundary may restrict access to the rear of the property and mean that you have to take things like garden waste through the house.

In rural areas you may find that the criteria are completely different and that the relationship with the boundary may be restricted by overlooking; that is, you will want to site the building where it can't be seen from adjoining properties.

Having gone through the above exercise, you will hopefully be able to draw other lines at the sides and back to set out other boundaries to the building.

Parking

If you want to have off-street parking with your new house (and most Local Authorities will insist upon it) you need to consider where that will be. A parking space needs to be, at a minimum, 4.8m (16ft) long by 2.4m (8ft) wide. If your house has the usual straightforward relationship to a road (facing straight out on to it), you will need to have an area where there is at least 4.8m (16ft) from the back of the pavement to the front of the building. You may find, in areas which are older and do not have much off-street parking, that this is behind the general building line; in this case you do not have to set the whole building back, but just the area for parking.

Sight Lines

A related topic to parking is that of sight lines. These are basically lines of vision – both pedestrian and vehicular – that allow you to see what is coming in either direction before you pull out onto the street. An accepted way of doing this is to take a line 2.4m (8ft) back from the back of pavement, which is approximately where you will be sitting if you are in your car, and draw a line from there to the back of the pavement 11m (36ft) in either direction. This zone should then be clear of any obstruction higher than 1m (3ft) to give you a view of whatever is coming. You may find that this impinges on other properties and is thus impossible, but it is still desirable.

Trees

Your prospective site may have existing trees on it that you want to keep or which the planners think are important and have imposed a tree preservation on. If this is the case you will need to ensure that your new building is not too close. If you are too close you may find that the new foundations will destroy much of a tree's roots and it will die, or that the tree will cause damage or overshadowing to your house.

What tends to govern the relationship of a building to an existing tree is its canopy, which is the area covered by the branches, twigs and leaves of the tree when it is in a mature state and which will usually describe a rough circle round the tree's trunk. It is not impossible to build viably under a tree's canopy up to about a third of its area, but this rather depends on the species of tree and its age. If you do build under a tree's canopy you are risking damage from falling branches and the chance of clogging up the gutters with leaves.

On your desire-lines diagram you should inscribe circles around any trees that describe any areas you believe should not be built upon.

Natural Features and Services

The next thing to consider is the position and type of any other impediment on site. This can vary from the obvious, such as streams or rocky outcrops, to the not so obvious, such as buried services. It is not impossible to build over, near or on natural features and services, but you should be aware that they can cause problems.

If you have any water on or near your property you should do some research on the flood area – the National Rivers Authority carry records of most flood areas in the country. It is advisable to avoid areas that flood, not just from a practical point of view but because you may also find it hard to sell, finance or insure a property sited on a flood area.

Most sites will have services running to, from and sometimes through them; after all, a house cannot function as a house without them. You need to consider the route and type of these services when planning the position of your house. If the services are only serving your property you do not have to concern yourself, since you will probably be repositioning them as part of the construction process anyway. It is services that actually pass through the property that you need to be aware of. The public utilities (gas, water, electricity and drainage) will often have services running through private property. If they do, you will usually find that they have rights to enter your property for the purpose of maintenance and repair, and you will also often find that there is a provision whereby you are not allowed to build over, or within a certain distance of these services. You generally have a right to move these services if such a move is possible, but doing so generally means that you have to pay the cost (which can be considerable) and it is better to avoid them if you can. In addition, you may find (and this is a common occurrence) that there is a sewer running through your property that is not in the public domain but is serving your neighbour (or neighbours). If this proves to be the case and there is nothing specific on your title deeds about it, then all your neighbour has is an easement (see Chapter 1) and you can move the drain without their consent, providing that you maintain the service.

There are also other features that you may want to avoid; these are generally geological in nature. If your soil survey (see Chapter 1) has turned up pockets of soft soil that require the use of expensive piled foundations you may wish to avoid these. Similarly, if you have areas of rocky outcrop then you may want to avoid them since it is quite expensive to level areas of rock so as to make them proper bearing for a new building.

Desirability

So far the positioning of your desire lines has been dictated in reactive way – you have reacted to restrictions on the site. You may also like to react in a proactive way – that is to establish which area of the site is most desirable. There are a number of criteria you may wish to consider when establishing desirability, such as:

- View – do certain areas of the site enjoy a better view than the others?
- Aspect and Natural Light – are there certain areas of the site that enjoy a preferable aspect of the compass or more natural light?
- Overlooking – are there certain areas of the site that you would like to avoid because they overlook or are overlooked by adjoining properties or public thoroughfares?
- Natural Features – are there certain areas of the site that are by natural features that you would like to be close to, such as ponds, trees, or perhaps a bluebell bank or natural hollow?

By now your site plan should be crisscrossed with lines and hatched areas.

Hopefully this will be of sufficient size to allow you to site your building within the 'desire zone'; if it isn't don't panic – just re-examine your desire-line criteria. Can you extend beyond the building line at the front or back at a single storey so that you will not offend the neighbours? Can you prevent overlooking by planting trees rather than avoiding an area completely? And so on. If your design area is still too small then you may need to look at other ways of expanding it. Can you (and the planners) live with one more storey than you originally intended, or can you site some of the ancillary activities (garage, utility room, guest bedroom or workshop) in a separate annexe or outhouse? If you still do not have enough room you may need to consider abandoning the project on that site or going for something altogether smaller.

Spatial Relationships

Having established where on the site (roughly) the building should go, it is now time to consider how the spaces inside should be organized.

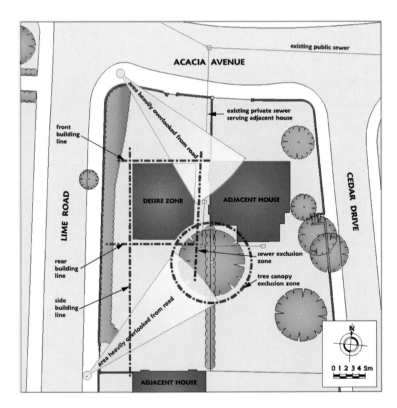

Creating a building zone with the use of 'desire lines'.

The first thing you need to do is to list the accommodation you want within your house. There are two ways of doing this, either by activity or by rooms. Which course of action you take rather depends on your style of living; if you favour a loosely organized, open way of living then the non-compartmentalized option is the one you may favour; if you like a more traditional way of living, with different rooms for different activities, then the compartmentalized option is probably the one for you. Either way the activities are similar, thus:

Compartmentalized	Non-Compartmentalized
Living room	Living
Playroom	Playing
Dining room	Dining
Study	Inside working
Kitchen	Cooking
Utility room	Laundry
Downstairs WC/Cloakroom	Toilet
Storeroom	Storage
Garage	Parking
Workshop/shed	Outside working
Bedrooms 1, 2, 3 …	Sleeping
Ensuite	Individual toilet/washing
Family bathroom	Family toilet/washing
Guest bedroom	Guest accommodation
Hall/Lobby	Horizontal circulation space
Staircase	Vertical circulation space

You will probably want to add to this list yourself to reflect your particular circumstances.

The idea of this exercise is to set up a hierarchy of spaces by which you organize the various areas into a logical pattern according to certain criteria, the principal of which would be: proximity, aspect and importance.

Proximity

It might be simpler for this exercise to split up the activities by floor (assuming that you intend to have more than one floor) since the sheer number of activities can get quite complicated. We are then trying to achieve a form of Venn diagram, by which activities overlap each other if they are related and are separate from each other if they definitely should not be related. For instance, you may want the kitchen to adjoin the dining room and the ensuite to adjoin the main bedroom.

Hence the ground floor and the first floor Venn diagrams might look like those illustrated.

When organizing the spaces there are several important things to bear in mind:

- Convenience – the kitchen may need to be close to the dining area so you do not have to carry hot plates too far; the garage may need to be close to the kitchen for carrying shopping and so on.

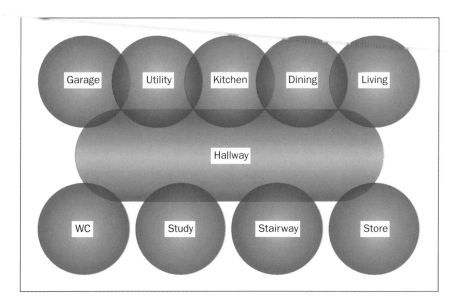

Overlapping circles mean rooms (or spaces) that should be adjacent to each other – this is a ground-floor proximity diagram.

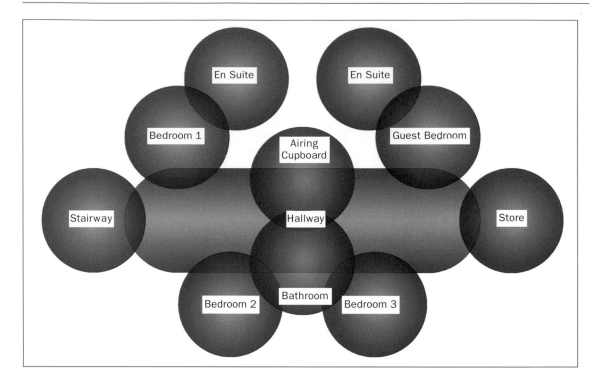

First-floor proximity diagram.

- Visual or Aural Proximity – you may want the kitchen to overlook the playroom so that you can monitor the kids while you are cooking. You may want the living room to be separate from the study so that you can work without being disturbed by the TV. You may want the family bathroom separate from the bedrooms so that you don't get disturbed in the middle of the night by the toilet flushing.
- Smell – you might not want the kitchen close to the living room in case you get cooking smells pervading the lounge.

In doing this exercise you need to be quite analytical about your lifestyle and you need to ask yourself how your present living accommodation works, what works about it and what doesn't, and how you would like to modify your lifestyle from now onwards.

Aspect

It seems a bit obvious to state that, in designing a house, it is important to bear in mind not just how the internal spaces relate to each other, but how the internal space relates to the external. Unfortunately this is something that is often forgotten, especially by those who practice 'pattern book' architecture – that is, using of standard plans rather than designing each house for the site in question.

When considering aspect you need to think of what you are facing, what is pleasant to look at, hear and smell, and equally what is unpleasant for the same reasons. In addition you need to think about light, both from the point of natural sunlight and from the point of shade.

The best way to go about considering aspect is to draw a diagram in a similar fashion to the way that you drew the desire lines – you will need the same basic site plan to work off. It is suggested that you do not use the site plan you have already marked up, since to add to it would be too complicated and you will get to amalgamate the diagrams at a later date, but it is worth drawing an area on your plan where the 'desire zone' is; the reason for this will become apparent later.

Shadows will be cast on your building by external objects.

A demonstration of the effect a 10m (30ft) tree will have at various times of the day.

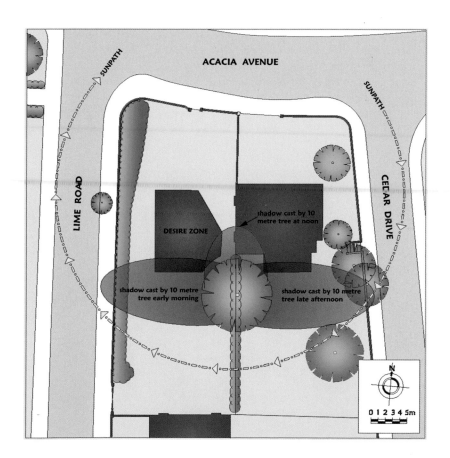

101

Start by describing an arc from east to west in the same way as you did for the desire lines, this being the sun path. At the same time mark on any heavy areas of shade. You can do this by basic trigonometry. Make an estimate of the height of any large physical objects on, or adjacent to, the site – these will be mainly trees and buildings. All these objects will cast a shadow, which will vary according to both time of day and time of year. The shadow cast will obviously rotate around the object casting it as the sun begins its journey from the eastern to the western horizon, with the shadow cast being at its shortest at midday and at its longest as the sun nears the horizon at either end of the day. In addition, the angle of the sun will vary according to the time of year, passing almost directly overhead during the summer and sticking closer to the horizon in mid-winter, so that shadows are longer in the winter than they are in the summer.

There are ways of predicting the patterns of shade – morning, noon and afternoon – on each day of the week throughout the year. However, you can suffer an overload of data in this case and it is not worth doing unless there is a physical object that is very close to a critical portion of the building – a tree which prevents all natural sunlight reaching your living room, for instance. A rule of thumb way of doing this is to assume that the sun will be at 45 degrees to the ground, shining from due north at lunchtime. At 45 degrees the object will cast a shadow to the north, which is exactly the same length as its height and of the same width as its width; this shadow should be marked on your plan in one colour. The next step is to predict the morning and afternoon shadow. For this a rule of thumb method is to assume that in the morning the sun will be 12 degrees from the horizontal due east, and 12 degrees from the horizontal due west in the afternoon. When the sun is at 12 degrees, an object will cast a shadow four times its length, but of the same width, so draw these next two shadows on in different colours.

You should now have a diagram of the shadows cast by various objects on your site. It is important to remember that the shadows will be longer in the winter and shorter in the summer. It is also important to remember that you have not marked up the areas of shade cast by one of the most dominant elements on your site (the house itself) and you will not be able to do so until you have designed the house, but you can still bear in mind the areas of shadow that will be cast.

The idea of considering the sun path is in order that you can organize the accommodation on site so that it takes advantage of the sunlight. If you are a fan of direct sunlight you might like to, for instance, site

A view out is important to any living space, but remember others can also see in.

your breakfast area on the easterly side of the building out of any pools of shade, so that you can take advantage of the morning sun, and your dining room on the west side of the building out of any pools of shade, so that you can take advantage of the evening sun.

In addition you will need to mark on the plan the various stimuli to the senses, so that you can make informed decisions as to what you want to experience from each space.

Take sight as your first factor; mark on views as arrows emanating from the desire zone both positive and negative. In doing this, also bear in mind that you may also like to consider views from the outside into your property, so mark any overlooking from the road or neighbouring properties in the same way, using blue for good and red for bad. Mark on each arrow what it represents, for future reference.

Take sound as the second factor, once again marking positive sounds, perhaps birdsong or the sound of a stream as arrows coming into the desire zone, and mark negative sounds, perhaps traffic noise or the sound of neighbours in the same way. Then once again mark on each arrow what it represents.

The same exercise can then be repeated with smells. Positive smells might be flowers or the sea, negative smells might be the smell of traffic fumes or the neighbouring farmer's silage heap.

With all the above you should be aware that there are a lot of things you can do to change the status quo. A positive view can be created by good landscape design and landscape features can screen a negative one. Similarly, negative sounds can (to some extent) be screened by landscape features or masked by the creation of positive sounds such as wind chimes or a tinkling fountain.

When you have completed this exercise you will have a site plan with various arrows going in and out of the desire zone to act as an aid to siting activities.

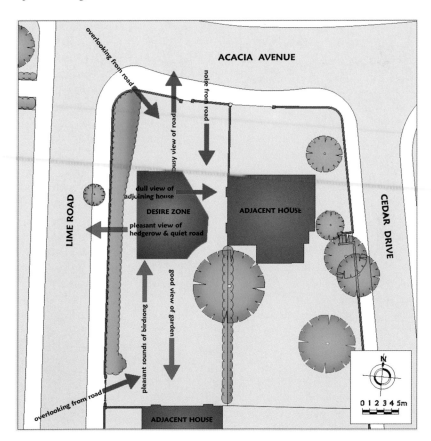

The various aspects will allow you to position the appropriate rooms to take advantage of them.

The idea is now to organize the spaces, as per the proximity diagram, by drawing a Venn diagram over the top of the aspect diagram. What you will need to do is organize the various activities in accordance with what you would like to hear, see and smell from each space and, similarly, what you would like not to hear see or smell. Here are a few examples of what you might think important:

Activity	Important	Not Important
Living room	View of the garden, as much light as possible	Noise
Kitchen	View of the road visitors arising, easterly aspect for morning sun	Noise
Bathrooms	Privacy	Noise, light
Dining room	Westerly aspect for evening sun	Noise
Main bedroom	Easterly aspect preferable for morning sun, quiet, view of the back garden	
Bedroom 2/3	Quiet	View, light
Guest bedroom	Quiet	View, light
Study	Quiet, view of quiet part of garden	Light
Store rooms/utility	Nothing	View, light noise

The above is only an example and you need to put into the table what you think is important for each activity; for instance, you might abhor the morning sunlight coming into your bedroom rather than welcome it.

Having decided which aspect is important for each activity, you need to do another diagram on the aspect plan with each of the activities shown in the area that best suits them. Ignore for the time being the relationship between the rooms that you have already considered.

You should then end up with diagrams like those shown opposite.

Importance
You will now have two diagrams showing how the spaces in and around the building might be organized, one in accordance with proximity and one in accordance with aspect. You now need to try to amalgamate the two into one. For this exercise it is worth cutting squares of the rough size of each room, since they will fit together better than circles. You might find that by experimenting with moving the spaces around you arrive at a diagram that achieves the best of both worlds; if so, great, otherwise you have to decide which are the most important areas and which are secondary, and also which of the 'important' items can be sacrificed or achieved in some other way.

You may consider the main bedroom to be more important than the guest bedroom; thus you may want to keep the main bedroom on the quiet side of the building and site the guest bedroom on the road side of the property but with some sound mitigating measure, like secondary glazing.

After this exercise you should arrive at a compromise diagram such as those shown on pages 106 and 107.

This is an important stage to have reached. You can see how the diagram is beginning to take on the appearance of a building plan, but we now need to move it on to the next stage, which is the actual Scheme Design, or Work Stage D as defined by the Royal Institute of British Architects (see Chapter 4) – the leap which carries the scheme on from a diagram into becoming a recognizable building.

SCHEME DESIGN

As in the initial design, this chapter is being written as if you are designing the building yourself. If you are not it will help you to understand the process and work more closely with your architect/designer; if you are it may not be the exact way you want to go about things and you may prefer to go your own way. Either way, it will hopefully be a useful guide and checklist so that you can take things forward.

The scheme-design stage is of crucial importance, it is at this stage that the whole design philosophy, look and function of a building is crystallized. Also, critically, it is at the end of this stage that planning permission is applied for and you will find that fundamental changes to the house become difficult, time consuming and expensive once this stage is completed.

Ground floor – each room or space is positioned to take advantage of the optimum aspect.

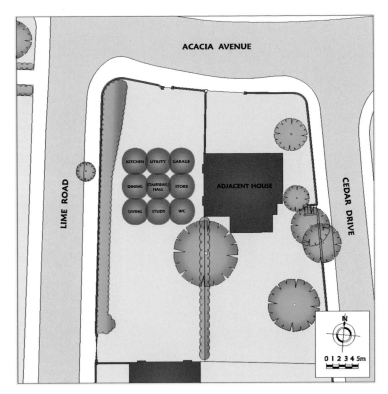

First floor – areas will be as quiet, noisy, private, overlooked, shaded or sunny as you want them to be.

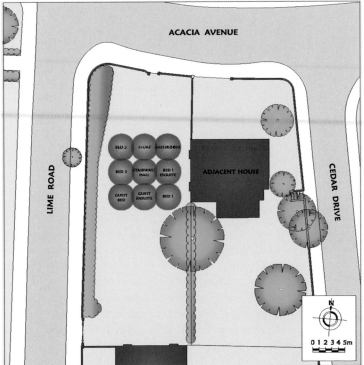

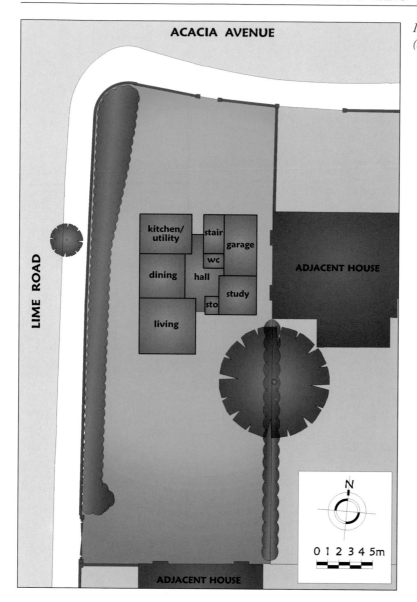

Plans begin to emerge (downstairs).

The aim is, at the end of this stage, to arrive at a design that is complete in terms of the position of external walls and windows, roof design, and general materials of construction. It is also necessary to settle the size, juxtaposition and number of internal rooms. It is a good idea to also settle as much as possible the position and handing of internal doors and staircases, although there is a certain leeway here since their exact positions can be settled after the planning process is complete.

In undertaking the scheme design there are two main categories of endeavour; these break down into what you might term the esoteric and the practical. The esoteric qualities of the building could also be termed the feel of the building and its look, and will revolve around the design philosophy. These qualities will also spill over into the practical, since the feel and look will, to some extent, be generated by the function of the building. The practical side of the building will be its function and will be about how

106

Plans begin to emerge upstairs.

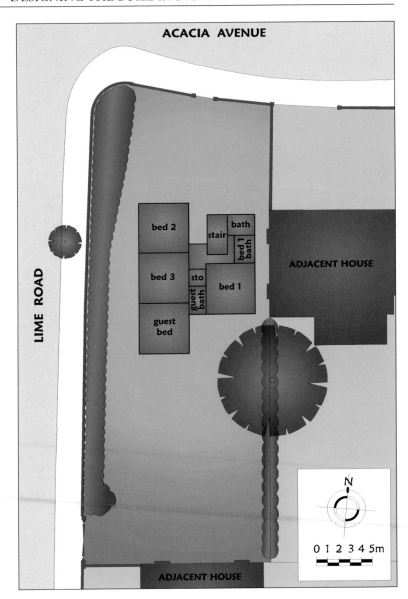

the building will work on a day-to-day basis from the point of view of ease of use, practicality of spaces and ease of maintenance.

Design Philosophy

Design philosophy is a nebulous thing; there are many designers whose only philosophy is that a building should work practically and there is a strong argument that this is a good and valid way of going about things. There are many examples of good buildings that have been produced without any strong design philosophy, such as the UK's fine legacy of vernacular buildings. It can equally be argued, however, that a strong design philosophy has produced all the best buildings in the world. You might therefore find this section of the book a useful and interesting thing, or unintelligible gibberish; either way do not feel that you are missing out, as countless buildings have been produced over the years, both with and without a design philosophy.

Most designers will tell you that if a strong design philosophy has been developed it makes the usual design decisions easier, since the philosophy will guide you into making a choice.

A design philosophy is a difficult thing to describe, since it can mean different things to different people and also covers a huge range of different approaches. A design philosophy could be described as a way of looking at, feeling or using a building ,which generates the form, look or feel of a building – a 'theme' for want of a better word.

If you are going to try to develop a design philosophy to go with your building, now is the time to think about it, before you find that you are tied down by the development of the plan and form of the building.

Design philosophy could perhaps be broken down into four categories; these are *spiritual, ethical, lifestyle* and *style.*

Spiritual

A spiritual design philosophy could be about religion, harmony, feeling or perhaps simple mood altering.

A good example of a spiritual design philosophy is feng shui, which is a philosophy that originated in China over 4,000 years ago and has a long history throughout the East. The idea that the 'spirit' or atmosphere of a place has an effect on your well-being is common in most cultures and philosophies, but in feng shui it has developed into a complex system of theory and practice that embraces almost every aspect of people's lives.

The underlying idea behind feng shui is that everything in your surroundings, down to the smallest details of furnishing and décor, can be advantageous or disadvantageous to your aims or ambitions and to your well-being.

The detail of feng shui is too complicated to enter into at length here, but if you decide that this is the way for you to go there are a number of books that set out the way to design with feng shui in mind. Some of the ideas that are used as a base will stretch the credibility of the more cynical, while others are based on common sense.

Another way to look at the building is the way it might alter your mood and there are certain things you can do which will help you get into the mood you would like to be in. The basics of this are form, lighting, décor and exposure. Décor and artificial lighting is something that is best dealt with during the detail design process, but form and natural lighting are very much something of the scheme design phase. It might be that you want different properties for a space at different times of the day and this can be achieved by careful design. The best way of setting about deciding what mood-altering qualities you would like and at what time of the day you would like them to manifest is to list the space in a chart with the mood you would like to have against them at each time of the day. Below is a guide, but you should fill in the table to your specific requirements.

When you have decided which mood you would like to be in and at which time of day, you can then bear this in mind as you design each room or, if you are having the building designed for you, you can hand this list to the designer and use it to monitor the design as it emerges.

You will have already used exposure to noise, views, sound and smell as part of your initial design

Mood-altering qualities of rooms			
Function	**Morning**	**Noon**	**Night**
Living area	Liveliness	Calm	Cosiness, privacy
Kitchen	Liveliness	Peace	Liveliness, companionability
Bathroom	Liveliness	Privacy	Privacy, serenity
Dining room	Vigour	Peace	Sophistication, conviviality
Bedroom	Liveliness	Peace	Cosiness, sleep
Study	Endeavour	Vigour, privacy	Peace
Hall	Calm	Friendliness	Privacy

Light plays an important part in the feeling of an area.

process and all these will come into play as part of the mood-altering properties of your house. If you are looking to be in a peaceful frame of mind you will need to ensure that all external stimuli conform to that criteria; you will not want irritating stimuli such as traffic noise, passers by peering in or unpleasant smells; you will want either no external stimuli or what external stimuli there are to be peaceful, possibly a fountain, a view of a secluded part of the garden or the scent of flowers. If you are looking to have a lively state of mind you might find that lots of busy external stimuli is the thing you need; perhaps a view of the comings and goings in the street, the sound of children playing or the smell of cooking. If you are looking for a cosy or private state of mind you might want to seal off all external stimuli completely.

Natural light is also a key factor when setting a mood; generally speaking, plenty of natural light will make you feel livelier whereas subdued or indirect light will feel calmer and cosier. In addition, direct sunlight will generally make people feel happier and livelier but less calm. It is possible to use the sun path to create different moods at different times of the day; thus, if you would like somewhere to be more lively in the morning but more peaceful in the after-

noon opt for an easterly aspect, conversely, if you want morning calm and evening liveliness you could opt for a westerly aspect. You may also want somewhere to feel calm and serene but with plenty of natural light; in this case it is best to use a northerly aspect, or baffles and blinds. You may also note that direct sunshine at noon can have a soporific effect when the sun is at its hottest.

Form can also have an effect on state of mind. This has been recognized for many years in the design of places for people who might be disturbed mentally, where you will find that dead ends are avoided since they lead to confusion, tall narrow spaces are avoided since they can give a feeling of isolation and low ceilings in small spaces are avoided because of their claustrophobic qualities.

You can influence your own state of mind in a much more subtle way by the form of a space. An enclosed space where you are not exposed to open areas will make you feel safe and cosy. A busy space with lots going on in terms of angles, elements, fittings and so on will make you feel lively. A minimal space without much going on in formal terms will make you feel calm. It is also argued that the proportions of a space will have an effect, with square or proportionally generous spaces (1:1.5 and less) feeling more harmonic and serene than long narrow spaces. This would seem sensible – a long narrow space is very linear and focussed and makes you feel like hurrying on, while square and circular spaces make you feel like staying for a while.

It is important to bear in mind that the form of a space can be varied according to the activities that take place in it, therefore a living area can have a day area that is lively, light and open and an evening space that is cosy, enclosed and intimate, so try to avoid thinking of each area as being just one open space.

Ethical

An ethical design philosophy would be based on something that you feel strongly about and which you wish your house to reflect. Such philosophy can be proactive – taking an active part in encouraging a certain thing, perhaps energy efficiency – or reactive – not wishing to use certain things in your design, perhaps products of a certain nature, or from a particular country or company.

In recent years, as concern has grown about the future of the planet, the 'green' issue has emerged as the front runner in all the ethical design philosophies. There is now a thriving community of businesses and organizations keen to advise on and supply green products and systems.

Green philosophy can be passive or active as follows:

Passive Options:
- Increased insulation.
- Using materials from renewable sources only.
- Using local materials (to avoid environmental damage caused by haulage).
- Using materials that do not create environmental damage by their manufacture, use or disposal.
- Using recycled materials.
- Using materials which come in bio-degradable packaging.

Active Options:
- Using solar energy for heating or power.
- Using heat exchangers to warm incoming air with heat gleaned from expelled air.
- Using 'grey' water recycled from appliances, or from rainwater harvesting.

- Using wind, water or geothermal sources to provide power.
- Using passive stack ventilation (as opposed to electric fans) for ventilation purposes.

How these components or systems are used could be (and is) the topic of a separate book. Some sources of advice and materials are given in the 'contacts' section of this book.

It needs to be born in mind that being green does not necessarily mean being cheap. Like most industries, the construction business is based largely on supplying things as cheaply as possible and, generally speaking, there is a price to pay for acquiring systems or materials from sources that have different motives. How much extra you pay depends to a large extent on how far you want to go, but there are some items that are very green and very cost effective – the cost of extra insulation, for instance, can quickly pay for itself in cheaper heating bills. Most green suppliers will provide some sort of financial audit if they are supplying something that purports to save energy.

Lifestyle

The lifestyle of the occupants has long been used by designers to generate a design philosophy. There are two ways of going about this; you can either study your own lifestyle and then ensure that the design of your new house reflects it, or you can think about the lifestyle you aspire to and then set about designing a space which encourages that. In order to properly react to matters of lifestyle you need to think about it not just from your point of view, but also from the point of view of everyone using that space. This can be partners, children, parents and visitors.

In some cases people have embraced a radically different lifestyle simply by the space that they live in. For instance, there are those who favour open-plan living, whereby all the activities within the house happen in one huge space or, alternatively, the softer version of this where all the cellular activities (like bedrooms, kitchens and bathrooms) open onto one huge space, which then becomes the core of the house. Such attempts at sculpting lifestyle are exciting social experiments and have, on a number of occasions, changed people's lives fundamentally. However, it should be remembered that our cellular lifestyle, with different rooms for different activities and the ability to get away from the hubbub to places of privacy and tranquillity, has evolved over a number of centuries and there is a reason why things are done this way. So be very sure you want an alternative lifestyle before committing yourself.

It is suggested that you take a good hard look at your lifestyle and the lifestyle of those who will be using the house, and then decide what works well, what you would like to discard and what you would like to institute as a completely new life activity. You will, no doubt, want to fill in your own priorities but here is a theoretical example of what you might produce:

Retained Lifestyle Elements

It is good to be able to be involved with the activity in the living area when cooking; it is nice to be able to move easily between the living and the garden areas so that they can become the same space in the summer; we need to keep an isolated study area because I work at home; and so on.

Rejected Lifestyle Elements

The all purpose dining/living room space doesn't really work since the kids eat at different times to us; it is impossible to have teenage kids in the same living room as us and they need to have their own living area; and so on.

New Lifestyle Elements

We would like to try out a system of living whereby circulation space was absorbed into the living rooms, such that when people want to get from one area of the house to another they have to pass through the living room – this will encourage a feeling of family/community; it would be nice if we could have a bathtub in a room that can be opened up to the garden, so I can have a lazy soak and feel like I am sitting out in the garden.

Style

The final element in the design philosophy is one of style or theme. This crosses over into appearance, which is a practical element – after all, all buildings have to look like something. But it is also possible to look at style in such a way that it pervades all aspects of the design. Have you, for instance, always liked that organic Japanese style with its natural materials, harmonic proportions, sliding rice-paper screens, floor-based living style and Zen garden? If so, now is your chance to recreate it in your own home. You will find that, having taken a decision such as this, all the design decisions will come naturally and you will have a clear framework for each function internally and externally. Such a decision will also cross over into lifestyle, since style of appearance is often a product of the way you live.

Here are a few of the different style options you could adopt, although this list is by no means exhaustive and you might have a particular enthusiasm that you would like to adopt.

Minimalist – simple spaces uncluttered; a few quality objects have more value than many; everything unsightly is hidden in cupboards; materials are natural and colours are muted. This is gradually becoming quite a classic style.

Hi-Modern – features uncompromisingly modern materials in a thoroughly modern way. An off-shoot

Minimalism – the art of simplicity.

Uncompromising modernity – a classic style in its own right.

of this style is Hi-Tech, when the building is designed to seem like a machine, featuring glass, cables stainless steel, rubberized flooring and the like; the architecture can be boat-like in its feeling. Again this style is gradually becoming a classic, but there are only certain locations where it will be accepted by the planners.

30s/40s/50s/60s/70s/80s (probably soon 90s) revival – simply get a book on what was cutting-edge domestic design at that particular moment in time and then recreate it. Beware, these revivals tend to come and go with great frequency and you can end up inhabiting something, which is a bit 'yesterday's news'.

The 'Out of Africa' Look – simple rectangular rooms; light and airy; painted in light colours or even left as natural timber, masonry and plaster. Accessories can include oriental antiques and ethnic art, such as masks and statuary. Again, quite a classic look.

The English Cottage – a vernacular feel; cosy rooms with low ceilings, small windows and features like inglenook fireplaces; materials can be brick, timber boarding, tile hanging, and rough plaster. Also quite a classic look.

The New Naturalism – an increasingly popular look which combines traditional and modern materials in a harmonious way; allows the nature of the material and its natural finish to be expressed without an applied finish.

The Historic Look – pick an historic period and try to recreate that look; for Georgian try high rooms with high rectangular widows, simple rectangular rooms and severe facades; for Tudor take the English Cottage look and add half timbering and stone floors with slightly more generous proportions. Be aware that this type of approach is commonly used by the mass house-builders who will often apply a pseudo-historic façade to a modern house, so you may find that your house blends into the mass, but this is quite a safe look.

The Oriental or Japanese Look – as already discussed above.

And there are many, many more. If you do establish a style you would like to use, then get as much literature as you can on your chosen style and make a collection of images as a source of inspiration that you can refer to from time to time as the project progresses.

Practical Design

Even when you do spend the time and effort to establish a design philosophy, you will still need to go through the process of practical design. The design philosophy will just be something that you apply as you go along.

The new naturalism – the materials of construction shine through.

Many architects use the plan and the elevation to design a building, planning the building first and then elevating it to establish its look, and then going back to the plan to incorporate any changes. This is a rather simplistic way of looking at things, since the design of a building can be generated in a three-dimensional way. The plan/elevation approach is a useful platform, but it is better expressed, perhaps, as *organization* and *appearance*. These two items should really be treated in tandem, so that as you are thinking about the organization you are at the same time considering the appearance.

Getting Started

It is important to have the appearance of your house in mind when you are working on the way it is organized, since the way you want it to look will have a strong influence on the way the various elements will work together. If you have established a style as part of a design philosophy, then you will have already considered the appearance. It may be that you have a unique vision of how you want the building to look in your mind's eye and do not need to consider this any further. You may have also been collecting images for some time, as suggested in Chapter 1, if so then you may also have done enough. If you have not been through any of these processes yet, now is the time.

Have a good look round for buildings that you really like; it will help if these buildings are of the same type and general size as yours – you may love the Eiffel tower, but this doesn't mean that it is suitable for a domestic situation. If you do find a building that you really like do take a lot of photographs of it. You should not just photograph the house but also all the details like windows, doors, chimneys, eaves and so on, since the look of a building depends on the harmonious relationship of all its parts.

When you go on to the organization part of the process, try to arrange the elements of the building to recreate the key features of the house. If you are going for the classical look, for instance, you will probably want to have a very rectangular plan with the entrance in the centre of the façade and a symmetrical arrangement to the windows. If you are going for a more romantic look then you will need to arrange the elements in a more haphazard fashion, with a more random arrangement of windows, types and sizes, and with different levels and roofs.

Organization

The next step is to work on the organization of the building. You already have the Venn diagram that you perfected in the 'outline design' stage of this chapter and this will form the basis of the organization.

At the moment the Venn diagram is a number of circles, but doesn't have any particular size or scale, so the thing to do is to start working on the size of the building. For this you can refer back to the room sizes that you looked at when undertaking the feasibility exercise for the footprint in Chapter 1. It is also possible that the various processes that you have gone through in this chapter will have given you different ideas as to the size of the various spaces.

In establishing the size of a space it is a useful exercise to consider what actually will be going in it. It is suggested that you make a list of the various items of furniture you will be putting in each space and then make a cut-out of each item. To do this you can either measure existing items of furniture and make scale models of them at, say, a scale of 1:100, or alternatively you can trace the diagrams shown opposite for each item of furniture.

Arrange the items of furniture in the way that would seem sensible in a room and including space around each item for circulation. When you have done this, draw a square round the furniture, quite tight to the furniture, and this should establish the size of the space. You will probably find that this is too big and that, during the course of the design process, you will rationalize it to a more sensible size, but it will still be a useful starting point. Measure each side of the area you have drawn with your scale and multiply them together to get the area of the space – for example 5.5m times 4m equals 22sq m.

Work through each space and you will now have a list of sizes. For each space take the square root of the area and cut out a paper square to that size at a scale of 1:100. Thus 22sq m will mean that you have a square of paper that measures 4.7cm by 4.7cm. Write clearly on the paper what space it represents.

The next step is to divide the squares of paper up according to floors – it might be that you don't end up with this subdivision exactly, but again it is a useful starting point.

You can then start organizing the various spaces, starting with the ground floor. The squares should be arranged over the site plan with the desire lines drawn on it, at the same scale. The idea is then to refer back to the diagram you made for the initial design and see if you can arrange the squares of paper that represent the various spaces in an approximation of the diagram.

You might find that the squares will not fit together in the same arrangement as the diagram; if this is the case you can look at changing the proportions of the various squares so that they fit together better. If this still doesn't work then you will have to consider changing their relationship to each other.

You may also find that the squares of paper will not fit the desire zone on the site plan. Again, you can try altering the proportions of the squares to make them fit into a more compact area. If this does not work you then have four options:

- Do you really have to be that far from the boundary? Perhaps you can alter the desire zone by extending beyond the building line at the back, but only on a single storey. This may be the time to challenge some of the assertions you made when setting the desire zone.
- Does all the accommodation you have shown have to be on the ground floor? It is quite common in urban areas to use a 'townhouse' format, by which you have a garage, utility room,

Furniture templates: adjust the size on a photocopier to get templates to experiment with on the plans, or create your own templates by measuring pieces of furniture you would like to reuse.

WORK STATION/DESK	DOUBLE BED	DINING TABLE
SINGLE BED	BATH	RUG AND COFFEE TABLE
WARDROBE	DRESSING TABLE	CHEST OF DRAWERS
TELEVISION	SOFA	CHAIR
WC	SHOWER	SMALL BASIN
SMALL KITCHEN SINK	KITCHEN SINK WITH WASTE DISPOSAL	LARGE BATHROOM BASIN
DISHWASHER/WASHING MACHINE/OVEN	KITCHEN RANGE	HOB

0   1   2 METRES

study or possibly a bedroom on the ground floor, with the main living and kitchen accommodation on the first floor. And bedroom accommodation again on the upper floor(s).

- Are all the rooms necessary? Can you have the study doubling as a dining room or second bedroom? Can the kitchen and utility room be one and the same? And so on. Bear in mind that if you do save rooms the construction cost will fall accordingly.

- Are any of the areas too big? This is the time to get your furniture cut-outs arranged again. It may be that you have left too much space round the furniture – have a look at the furniture in your existing house and the amount of space around it and adjust accordingly. It may also be that you could be more creative about the furniture – could the dining table be pushed against the wall when not in use, or could you use a drop-leaf dining table? It might even be that you are replicating furniture which could be multi-tasked – could the dining table also serve as a study table for instance?

When arranging the ground floor try to keep in mind the style or look of your house; also bear in mind the hallway or circulation space and where you will have your staircase. For houses of only two storeys it is permissible to have a staircase that is situated in living accommodation, but if you have a building of more than two stories the staircase needs to be enclosed in its own hallway at all levels, the logic being that fire is unlikely to break out in the staircase and, if your escape is cut off, a jump from a first floor window is a lot safer than one from a second floor. As a rule of thumb a standard domestic staircase will consist of thirteen risers and twelve treads, the treads being about 230mm in depth. There are a number of standard staircase formats as illustrated on the following pages.

When you have managed to get the ground floor into some kind of order, it is time to move to the upper floors. It can be complicated to fit one plan onto another, so try to be as flexible as possible with room sizes and be prepared to go back to the ground floor to alter things if need be.

It is technically possible to fit one plan on top of another which bears no resemblance to it, providing that the staircase is in the same place on both plans. To make such a plan work, however, you need to employ technological solutions, such that if the first floor is bigger than the ground floor you will need to employ cantilevers and support columns, and if the ground floor is bigger than the first floor you will need to employ steel beams to support the upper walls. Such devices can be expensive and can often lead to strange external appearance, so try to keep the walls lining-through as much as possible and restrict projections to bay windows and the like. When the first floor sets back, try to keep the span of

supporting structure to a minimum and look at where the beams will span from and to.

When positioning the upper floors it is also worth bearing in mind sanitary accommodation. All bathrooms will have to be vertically drained at some point and, although you have some flexibility by running a drainage pipe horizontally before it goes vertically, you need to make sure that a vertical pipe will be against a wall at the ground floor (rather than free standing) and also, preferably, in an area of secondary importance, such as a store, utility room or toilet, since a drain pipe will make some noise when it is in use.

The other thing to look at carefully when arranging the accommodation is to ensure that you can get at all the rooms. It may be fine to access the kitchen by walking through the living area, but it is considerably less desirable to only be able to get to the family bathroom by walking through one of the bedrooms.

When you have finished arranging the pieces of paper, draw round them carefully and write on the function of each space. You should then have a fairly crude diagram of each floor with no windows or doors shown on them.

Appearance

You will have had, hopefully, a picture in your mind of the general aims you were trying to achieve in terms of appearance when you were arranging the accommodation, so you might find that the appearance part of the design process will be fairly straightforward. If you now find that you are not quite where you want to be, you will need to be flexible and prepared to alter the arrangement if necessary.

It is suggested that you start by establishing the coordinating heights of the building. Ceiling heights will typically be between 2.3m (7ft 6in) and 2.6m (8ft 6in). The 2.3m height will give you a comfortable cottage-type of feel; you can go lower but be careful you do not bump your head – an absolute minimum should be 2m (6ft 7in) – or you will create a claustrophobic feeling. The 2.6m height will give you a grander feel. It can also be worth going to double height or storey-and-a-half height in places like living areas or hallways to give that feeling of grandeur; if you do this you should keep in mind the

A section of a typical straight-flight staircase.

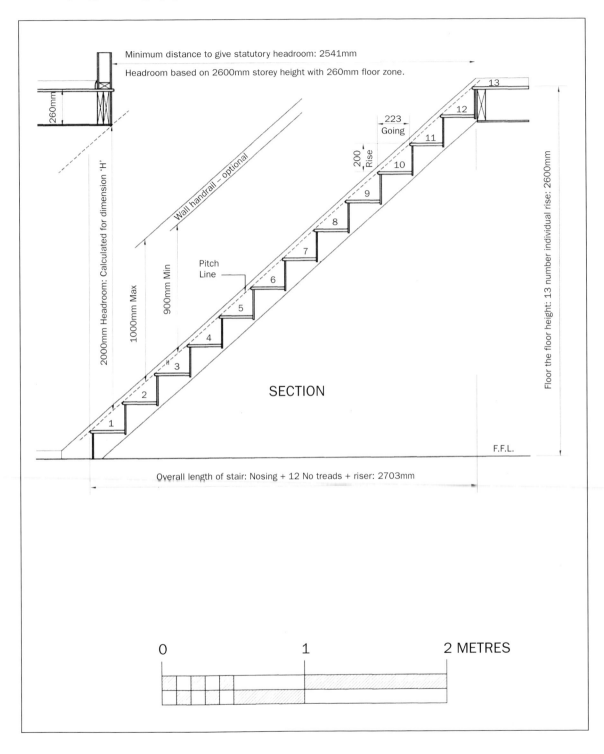

Minimum distance to give statutory headroom: 2541mm

Headroom based on 2600mm storey height with 260mm floor zone.

260mm

2000mm Headroom: Calculated for dimension 'H'

1000mm Max

900mm Min

Wall handrail – optional

Pitch
Line

223
Going

200
Rise

Floor the floor height: 13 number individual rise: 2600mm

SECTION

F.F.L.

Overall length of stair: Nosing + 12 No treads + riser: 2703mm

0   1   2 METRES

The plan of a typical straight flight staircase.

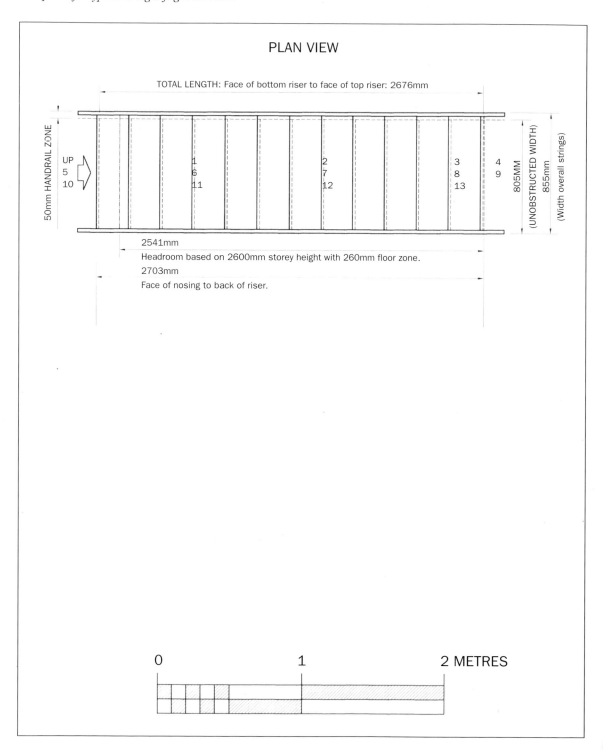

PLAN VIEW

TOTAL LENGTH: Face of bottom riser to face of top riser: 2676mm

50mm HANDRAIL ZONE

UP
5
10

1
6
11

2
7
12

3
8
13

4
9

805MM
(UNOBSTRUCTED WIDTH)

855mm
(Width overall strings)

2541mm

Headroom based on 2600mm storey height with 260mm floor zone.

2703mm

Face of nosing to back of riser.

0   1   2 METRES

A plan of a typical dog-leg staircase.

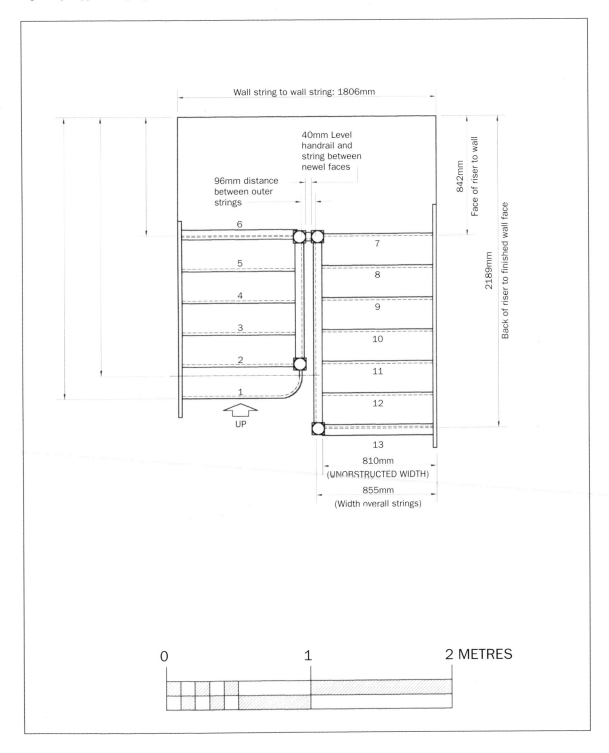

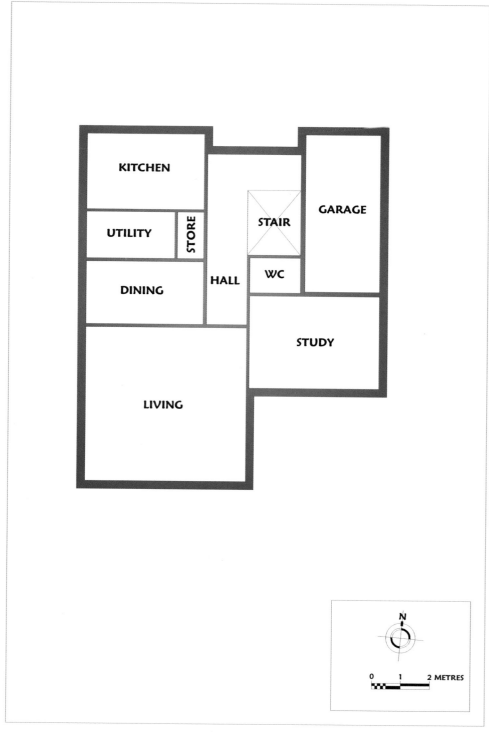

Ground floor block diagram.

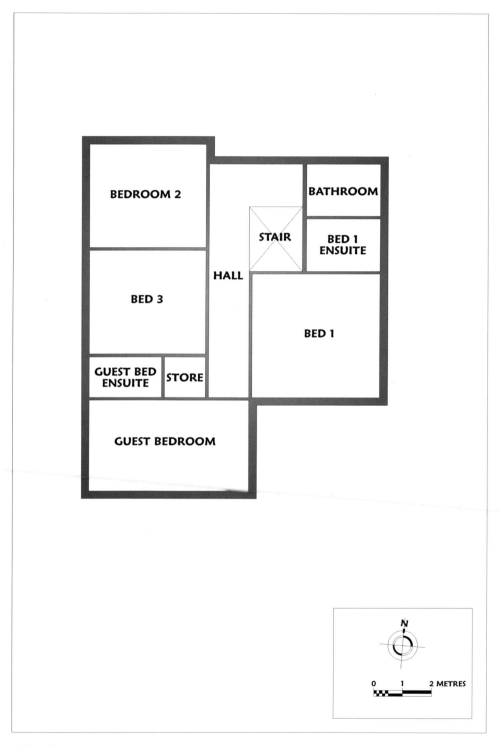

First floor block diagram.

implications for the upper floors. In addition, if your property is close to other existing ones, bear in mind that if you substantially exceed their floor–floor heights your building may look out of scale with them.

At a scale of 1:100, start by drawing the ground-floor level, to which we will give a datum level of 0.00m. Then draw a line parallel to this, at your chosen ceiling height – for the purpose of this exercise let us say 2.4m away. We then have to establish the floor zone; this will vary according to the span of the floor, but at this stage it is safe to assume that 250mm will be sufficient, so draw another parallel line 250mm away from your ceiling. This is the first-floor level and in this case its datum level would be 2.65m. Other floors can then be added in the same manner.

When you get to the roof you need to consider the roof geometry, if you have not already been thinking about it. First of all you need to decide what your roof covering is, because this will dictate the pitch – its angle from the horizontal. It is very rare to find a roof that is truly flat; even roofs which are supposedly flat are actually pitched, but at a very shallow angle, so that water does not stand on the roof but flows away to where the roof outlets are.

If you are using asphalt you can have a roof pitch as low as 1 degree; if you use interlocking concrete-tile you can go as low as 17.5 degrees (depending on the tile); if you are using slate you can go as low as 22.5 degrees; and if you are using plain clay-tiles you can go as low as 35 degrees. The finishing material needs to be selected bearing in mind the look you are trying to get, the material that is indigenous to the area and the height of the building overall.

If you are looking at using a so-called flat roof, working out the roof geometry will be very simple; you can simply cover the top plan area completely, without bothering with things like ridges and valleys.

If you are using a pitched roof then you will have to consider the way the geometry works. There are lots of different ways of doing this, and a lot of it will depend on the way you want the building to work. There are various different types of pitches, as illustrated.

If you do not have a simple rectangular or square shape, then you will have to have roofs joining together to form the whole. This is best done by deciding where the main roofs are going to be and then running secondary roofs into them.

It is preferable, if possible, to avoid various roofs of different pitch since this makes their junction a little difficult to resolve.

When you have decided on the roof form, overlay the roof plan on the top floor plan. If you have used the same roof pitch throughout, you should be able to draw all the hips and valleys at 45 degrees to the walls.

When you have established the angle of the roof, try drawing a typical ridge and eaves height on your coordinating dimensions drawing.

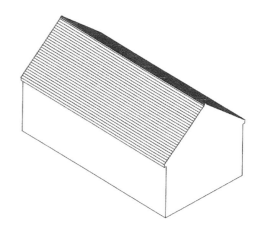

A simple pitch is the basic form.

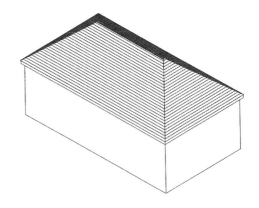

Any kind of pitched roof can also be hipped at the end, rather than gabled …

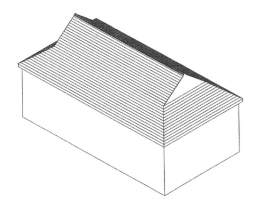

… or you can combine the two to form a hipped gable …

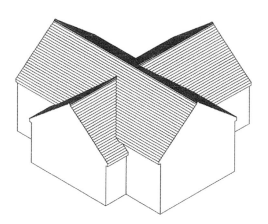

Decide where the main roofs are going to be, and then run secondary roofs into them.

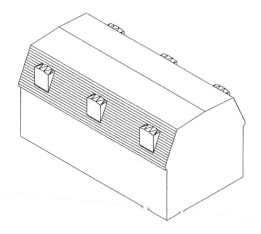

… or even have an area of flat roof and near vertical sides – the mansard roof – that has the advantage of being able to have accommodation in the roof.

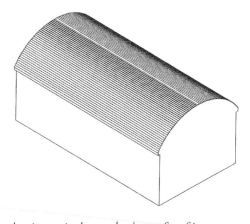

Another increasingly popular form of roof is the barrel vault, although unconventional, this can lead to some interesting roof forms.

When you have sketched in the roof on your section try to set window heights generally. It is best to keep window head-heights at about the same height as internal and external doors, since this means that everything within a room will line through and give a feeling of unity to the space. Door and window head-heights tend to be either 2.1m (6ft 11in) or 2.025m (6ft 7½in) above floor level, allowing for standard doors. Sill heights vary from nothing for French windows and upwards. When setting the sill height bear in mind what furniture or fittings you might position against it; kitchen units, for instance are 900mm (2ft 11½in) high and as a result a widow sill in a kitchen should be a minimum of 1050mm (3ft 5¼in) above floor level. In living areas it is nice to be able to see out of the window when you are sitting down, and a height of 600mm (2ft) is about right for this. So mark on the various heights making sure that each of them is clearly marked. Finish off by drawing a thick line 150mm below the ground floor, this will be the outside ground level. Follow on by drawing the roof pitch on.

123

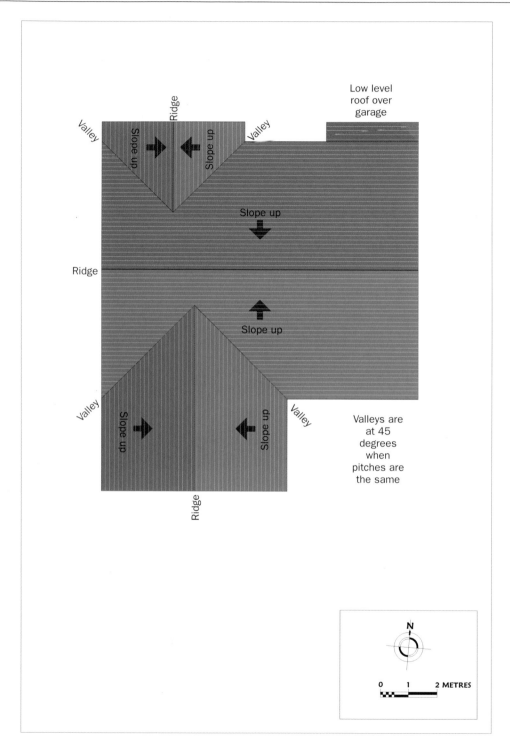

The roof plan.

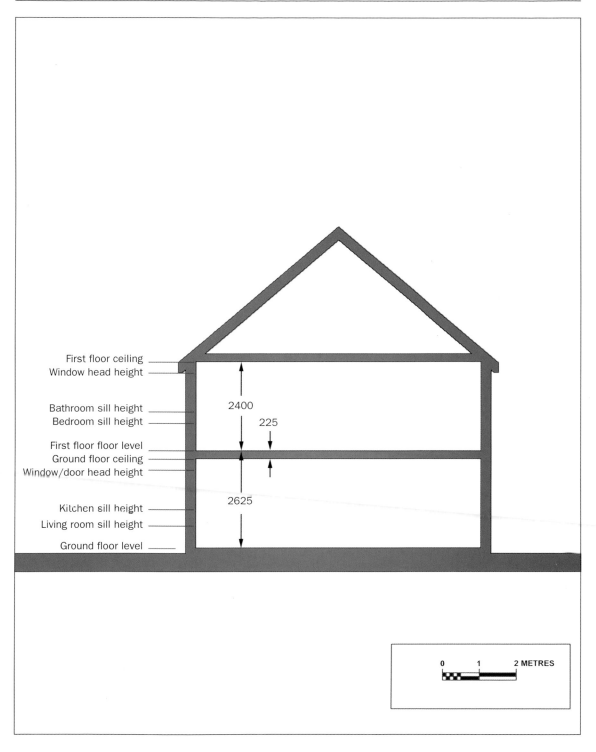

First floor ceiling
Window head height

Bathroom sill height
Bedroom sill height

First floor floor level
Ground floor ceiling
Window/door head height

Kitchen sill height
Living room sill height

Ground floor level

2400

225

2625

0   1   2 METRES

Coordinating dimensions allow you to set up the height of various building elements.

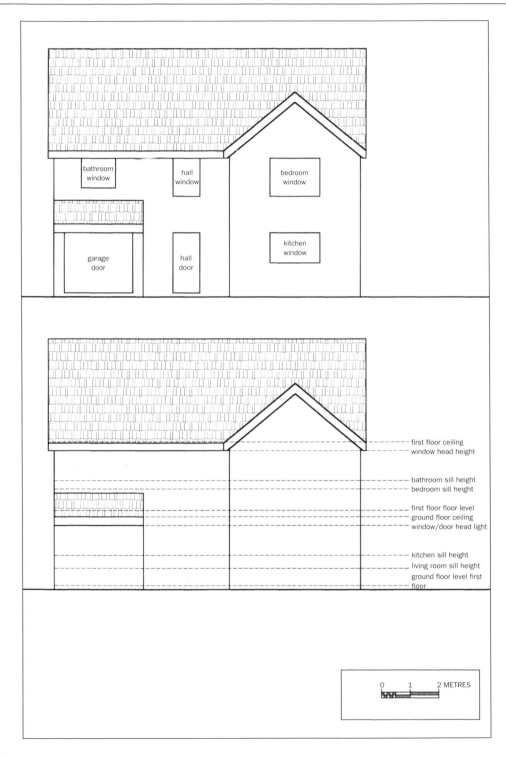

The elevation starts to emerge.

You are now in a position to start on the elevations. Start by taping the plan drawing on to the table or board with the side of the building you want to elevate pointing towards you. Tape the coordinating dimension diagram underneath and fairly close to it, and tape a new piece of tracing paper over the top of the coordinating dimension diagram. The idea is to project the corners of the building down so that they form the outline of the building.

When you have done this, draw in the roof by projecting the ridge(s) down to the coordinating dimension you have drawn and then draw in the slope of the roof.

You can see that you now have the outline of a house emerging onto the paper.

The next stage is to start positioning the windows and doors on the elevation. The best way to start this is to work from the inside out. Look at each room that is facing you on the plan and decide where the window(s) should be placed. It may be that the window would be best centred on a particular wall or that the furniture layout dictates it should be off set. It may even be that two windows would be more suitable. Quirky windows positioned in corners or niches can also add to the interest of a space. You will now have a diagram of the building with the windows marked on in haphazard fashion. The building will probably look a little arbitrary as a result and you will probably want to impose some order on it. The usual way of doing this is to line windows through with those above and below; this may mean a compromise or even a redesign of internal areas. It is also a good idea to start imposing some kind of hierarchy of windows at this stage, with the widows to lounges being emphasized by being bigger or possibly expressed as bay or French windows, and with other windows given an emphasis proportionate to their rank. Again you will need to refer back to the plan to ensure that the windows are sitting comfortably, and possibly make alterations to the plan as necessary.

You should now have a bare-bones diagram of the building with the roofs, walls, doors, and windows all marked on in outline. The next step is to flesh out the building with some detail. Mark out any porches, balconies, chimneys, roof features and the like, then mark in glazing bars and other detail on the windows.

With windows and doors you have two options; you can either have bespoke joinery made up to your own design, or you can use 'off-the-shelf' type joinery from a catalogue. If you go for the second option you will need a catalogue, which can be obtained by answering advertisements in the magazines or by ringing up one of the numbers supplied at the end of this book. Standard windows, it goes without saying, are cheaper than bespoke windows by a considerable margin.

It is also a good idea to consider detail of external materials; whether the walls will be brickwork, stone, render, tile hung, weatherboarding or even shingles.

In addition, you need to consider the details around openings and at the corners of the building. For each opening you need to think about the head (top), the jambs (sides) and the sill (bottom). Common head details are the stone lintel, the brick flat arch and the full stone surround. Common jamb details are brick quoins, stone or rendered quoins, the stone surround and just plain brickwork. Common sill details are the stone sill, brick on edge sill, plain tile sill and again the stone surround.

Corners can be decorated with quoins if the brick you are using is soft or you are using render.

When you have finished with the first elevation, rotate the plan and start on the next elevation, then the next one and so on. Remember to refer back to the plan and make any necessary changes as you go along. In this fashion you should be able to build up a complete image of the building in elevation. Once you have got the basics it is worth having a radical look at the elevation; you may not want simple windows in walls, but perhaps glazed screens, or you may want to add decorative items such as chimneys, weathercocks, bay windows and so on.

The next thing to do is to complete the plans by adding the door swings, windows and furniture, and add all the room names.

The final thing to do in the scheme design is to show the indicative landscape design. This is something that can be done in detail later on, but you will still need to show the hard and soft landscape areas,

The elevation.

lawns and planting beds, parking and boundary treatment.

The final touch with all the scheme-design drawings is to add the few touches that bring the scheme to life; this can include shadows, people, trees and bushes, cars and title blocks and references. It is also nice to colour a set of drawings to achieve the final result.

APPLYING FOR PLANNING PERMISSION

Now you have finished the scheme design drawings it is time to apply for planning permission. Planning permission, put simply, is the Local Authority's agreement to allow you to build your building. To apply for planning permission you need to have the scheme design drawings already described, an ordnance survey drawing showing the site location plan (as described in Chapter 1) a filled out application form as supplied by the Local Authority, a cheque for the planning fee and a written design statement.

The planning forms will be sent to you by the Local Authority if you telephone them. Be sure to ascertain whether or not your property is within a conservation area or is listed, since if either of these situations applies you will need special forms for that as well. The planning forms will lead you through a series of questions which are fairly straight forward; if you are unsure about any of the points contained, a telephone call to the planners should give you the information you need.

The design statement is always a good idea since it will give the planners an insight into what it is you are striving to achieve and make them less likely to try to impose their own ideas on you. It should state, in simple terms, your design philosophy, what you have done to mitigate the impact of your building on adjoining properties, why your building will make a positive contribution to the locality and anything else which you believe will help you to obtain planning permission. The design statement can be in the form of a letter or a report.

It is also helpful if you colour the drawings – the more seductive the drawing the more chance you stand of getting planning approval.

In addition you will need to pay the planning fee – the planning forms will inform you as to the exact amount.

It has to be recognized that the planning authorities are under severe pressure in the UK; the planning fee itself is a fairly paltry sum compared to the amount of work involved in processing your planning application and, like most local government departments, planning departments are starved of resources.

The national target for processing planning applications is eight weeks; in practice this programme is almost never achieved due to lack of time on the part of the planning officers, and the time spent on negotiations with other parties and any subsequent changes. As with any human interaction it is easier to ignore an anonymous person than someone you have met and who talks to you on a regular basis. It is important, therefore, to build up a relationship with your case officer and the earlier that you do this the better. A suggested timetable and list of actions post-scheme-design through a typical planning process is as follows:

Stage 1 – Pre-Application

Before you have coloured the drawings, try to arrange a preliminary meeting with the planner who is likely to be the case officer. The best way to go about this is to ring the planning department of your local authority, quote the address of your property and ask who the area planner for that location is. Most local authorities will have one or two planners who cover each area, with a senior planner to whom they answer. When you have found out the name of the planner, ring them up and ask for a preliminary meeting to discuss your scheme. At this stage it is common to get a voicemail and also, as a result of the pressure of work on some planners, quite common not to get a response. If this happens to you then find out if the planning department runs a rotation system with their duty planners. A duty planner is a system by which a local authority will keep a planner on duty to consult with members of the public who 'cold call' their offices with a planning query. If you can find the day that your area planner will be on duty, drop in then. If all this fails try dropping in anyway and asking for the area planner. If none of

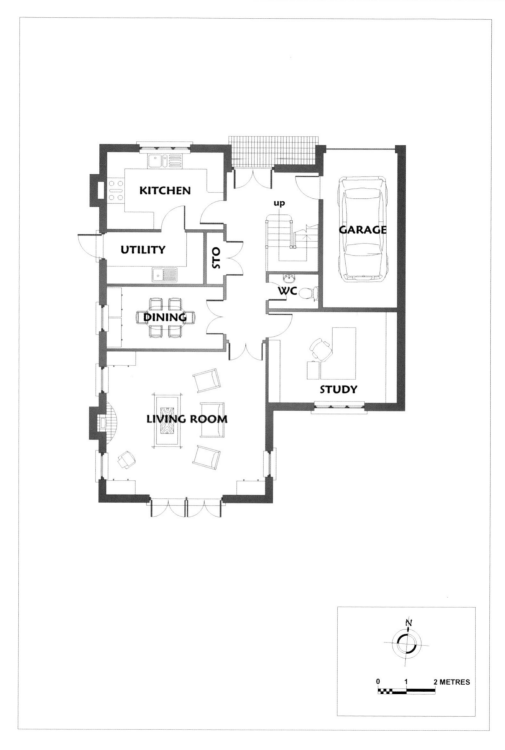

Completed floor plan – ground floor.

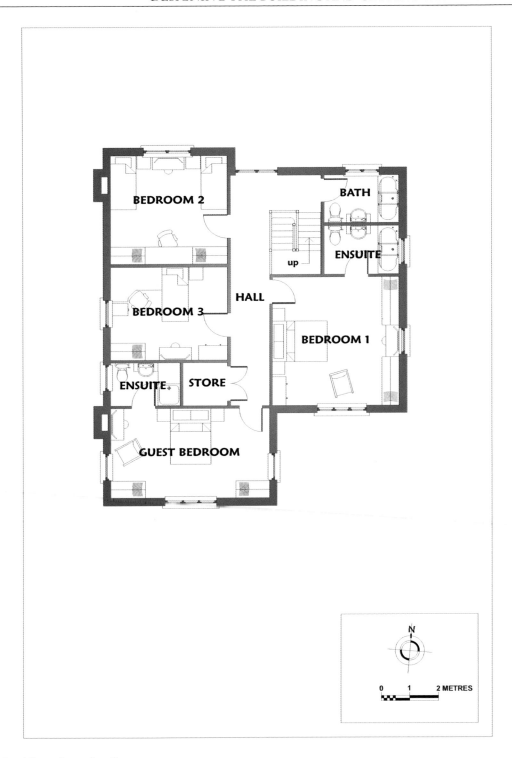

Completed floor plan – first floor.

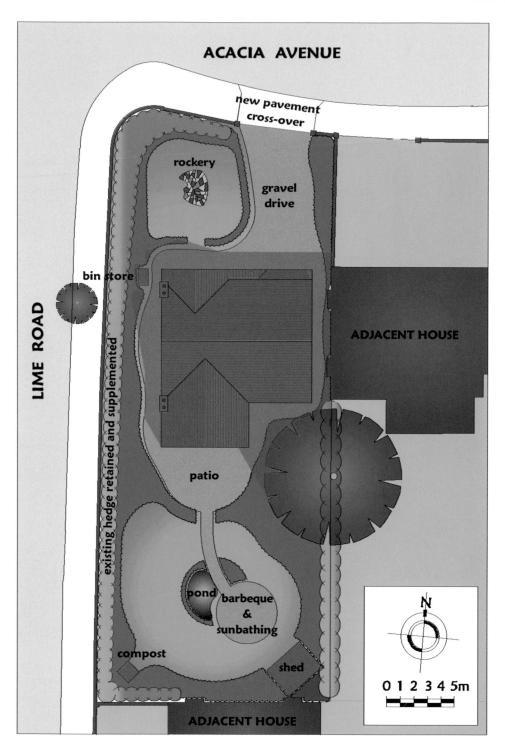

The site plan showing landscaping both 'hard' and 'soft'.

this works it is better to see the duty planner than no planner at all. Once you have got a meeting, a suggested agenda is as follows:

- Introductions – introduce yourself and tell the planner about your project. Try to be positive and excited about it; if the planner can be involved in the project and taken along with its 'spirit' you will get a better response.
- Description of Site – if the planner is not well acquainted with the site go through the location, the adjoining sites, the means of access and any physical objects of relevance on or around the site that might affect the design (trees, water, services etc).
- Description of Proposals – go through the scheme in detail and describe why you have arrived where you are. If you worked from a design philosophy, tell the planner all about it so that they understand where you are coming from. Make sure you discuss siting, massing, means of access (both vehicular and pedestrian), parking and materials of construction.
- Programme – let the planner know when you will be submitting the application, ask them how long they are currently taking to process applications and ask them about planning committee dates.
- Feedback – get any feedback from the planner.
- Next Meeting – try to set up a programme for your next meeting, post application.
- Consultees – get a list of who the Local Planning Authority will be consulting (see Stage 3 below).

It is a good idea to try to incorporate any ideas that the planner might have – they should be there to help you achieve an approval, but be clear about your intentions and true to them; this is your house, so do not let the planner design it for you.

Stage 2 – Registration

Once you have made the application, there will be a pause of a week or so and then you will receive a letter from the planning department telling you that either your application has been registered or that more information is required for registration. If the latter happens try to supply the information as promptly as possible, since the application will not go ahead without it. When you have got the scheme registered, the letter of registration will tell you the date of registration, the registration number and who the case officer is. It is possible that the case officer is different from the one you have already seen; if so, try to set up a meeting immediately, using the same devices as before so that you can get any feedback.

Stage 3 – Consultations

Once the application has been registered the planner will go through the consultation process. This is a mechanism for letting any interested parties know about the application and also getting feedback from them. Typical consulters will be:

- The immediate neighbours on all sides.
- The highways and refuse department.
- The design officer at the local authority (if there is one).
- Any local design groups/residents associations that the local authority recognizes as valid consultees.
- English Heritage and/or the listed building officer if there is a listed building on, or immediately adjacent to, the site.
- The Conservation Area Officer if the site is in a conservation area.

The consulters have a period of twenty-one days from the date of the consultation notice to respond, although, in practice, if they take longer their views will still be respected. For most of the consultees, the processing of the application will be a matter of procedure and you will not need to get involved, but for some of the consultees you may like to get in contact just to get your view across. These would be:

- Neighbours – getting notification of a planning application through the post can produce a knee-jerk reaction that leads to a letter of objection. Many people have a fear of anything new and, if they do object, their views (if relevant) will be respected. It is better, if possible, to get to them first, explain your proposals and emphasize any advantages to them that your scheme might have – increase in general property values by beautifying the area; upgrading of a derelict site; renewal of boundaries and so on. If you can get them to write a letter of support – even better. At the very least this exercise will give you a chance to meet your potential new neighbours.

- Conservation Area Officers – if your site is within a conservation area, then the conservation area officer will have a big say about the design and the choice of the materials, so it is better to talk to them direct rather than letting them make up their mind about the scheme without knowing your reasons for doing things.
- Listed Building Officers/English Heritage – if you have a listed building on the site or immediately adjacent to it, what these parties say about the proposals will be of particular importance. Again, it is worth making contact before the consultation notice reaches them.

As part of the consultation process, you might like to do your own canvassing to win over anyone who you think might support you. This might include any neighbours who might be close to the site but not directly adjacent to it – any letter of support will strengthen your case, but beware of involving someone who didn't know about the scheme, but might object.

The other people you might want to involve are local councillors. The way that the planning authorities work is that the planning officers do all the leg work and formulate the report, which is then referred, in most cases, to a planning committee who make the decision on whether the scheme should be granted approval or not. It is to your advantage, therefore, if you can get the local councillors on your side. The people who are of prime importance to you are the ward councillors, and the chair and deputy chair of the planning committee who will be considering your application. Councillors are essentially political creatures, since they rely on residents of their ward to vote them into their seats – this can be a disadvantage in that they will often take account of dissenting voices if it wins them votes, but also an advantage in that they might support you as a potential voter.

Stage 4 – Negotiations

Once the feedback from the scheme has got back to the case officer they will be ready to talk about any changes they think might need to be made. Bearing in mind the fact that the planning authorities are under severe pressure, it is a good idea if you instigate the negotiation stage.

Try to set up a meeting with the case officer about three weeks after registration. The purpose of the meeting is to take on board any comments from the consultees. The things to gauge at these sorts of meetings are, firstly, what changes the planning authorities want and, secondly, whether they are critical to the scheme getting planning approval. If you are in a situation where the changes demanded are such that you cannot accept them or even where there is no common ground at all, then this is not the end of the story (see appeals below), but generally it is much better to negotiate a solution if you feel that you can.

Like any negotiation, a discussion on a planning application will involve a certain amount of horse-trading. It is better to give way on the minor matters if it means that the major matters are intact; if you put your foot down on every issue you run the risk of being seen as intransigent and hence getting a refusal.

Stage 5 – Resubmission

Once you have made any changes, as negotiated with the planner, you can resubmit the drawings. It is a good idea to accompany the revised drawings with a letter explaining exactly what changes you have made and the reason why you have made them. You may even like to arrange (yet another) meeting to explain what you have done.

Stage 6 – Decision

The final stage is the decision of the planners. This can be made in two ways, either by the planning committee if the scheme is referred to them, or by the planning officers under delegated powers if there are no objections or if the scheme is to be refused outright. The decision will come in the form of a letter from the local authority. If it is an approval it will generally list the approved drawings and list any conditions that apply (generally materials, hours of working, landscaping and the like).

The planning decision does not mean the end of the design evolution, you can go on to make very minor external changes, or you can even make reasonably big changes so long as you obtain approval from the planners for them. Often, developers will use a permission as a platform to achieve something a bit closer to what they want and there is no reason why you cannot do the same.

If you are refused, you have the option of re-submitting the scheme (there is no additional fee if you are prompt), taking into account the reasons for refusal or of appealing the decision. An appeal is to the Secretary of State for the Environment and is based on the assertion that the Local Authority acted wrongly in refusing the scheme.

The planning decision notice will inform you as to how to obtain the appeal forms. The appeal forms will also explain how to make the appeal. There are three types of appeal. These are: written representations; informal hearing; and public enquiry.

An appeal based on written representations will allow you to make a case in writing as to why you believe the application should have been allowed and allow the Local Authority to make a case as to why it should not. The Planning Inspector will then review the scheme, the reasons for refusal and the statements for and against the scheme. There will be a site visit by the inspector and a representative of the council, and you (or your architect) can also attend. The Inspector can ask questions and any party can point out salient points, but there is no open debate. The advantage of this method is that it is the least time consuming and, if you are not confident of your (or your architect's) ability to debate the merits of your case, there is no exposure to a damaging slip-up in open forum.

An informal hearing will have written representations as before, but will then involve a meeting between the Inspector, the two concerned parties and any third parties who wish to speak, where a debate is encouraged on the salient points of the appeal. The advantage of this method is that it allows a second bite at the reasons for refusal, allows you to (potentially) destroy the council's case and allows a far more open situation on the site visit. The disadvantage is that, if you or your agent do not possess the necessary knowledge or ability to debate matters, you can end up harming your case.

A public enquiry involves barristers, cross-examination and a courtroom format. This method is generally only used for very large or important schemes and tends to be very expensive. The advantages and disadvantages are as for an informal hearing, but even more so. It is not a good idea to consider this option unless you have very deep pockets

If you are very confident about your case, you can apply for an award of costs – namely, any money that you have had to spend that you would not have spent had the scheme been allowed. Be warned, however, that if you lose the case the Council's costs can be awarded against you.

The purpose of an appeal is to examine whether planning policies, both national and local, have been correctly applied; it is not a debate about whether those policies are fair or correct. If a Planning Inspector believes that you are trying to argue that planning policies are wrong then they will, at best, ignore that part of your evidence and, at worst, believe that you are wasting appeal time and not listen to your other points with such keenness. It is essential, therefore, to look carefully at both the reasons for refusal and the policies they refer to, and then to argue why they have been incorrectly applied – also look for other policies that are in support of your case. To do this you will need to either buy, or look through at the Council's offices, the Local Authority's Unitary Development Plan (UDP) and refer to the policies therein. It is also worth referring to national policy, which is generally in the form of Planning Policy Guidelines that can be reviewed in some libraries, bought from Her Majesty's Stationary Office (HMSO) or read on the Internet.

You will receive an appeal decision in writing from the Secretary of State for the Environment. The decision will set out the reasons why the appeal is granted or refused. If the appeal is refused, but the Inspector believes that a permission is possible for a scheme of a similar nature, there will often be pointers in the decision as to what should be done to get the scheme through. If pointers of this sort are included then you can reapply, taking account of the Inspector's comments, and the Council would then be ill advised to refuse you.

After having gone through the processes described in this chapter you should now be in a position where you have a scheme that you are pleased with, that answers your needs and that has planning approval.

So far, however, this has been a paper exercise with nothing physical or tangible to show for it. The next stage, therefore, is to realize the dream and start the building process.

The Construction Process

When we build, let us think that we build for ever.
(John Ruskin *The Seven Lamps of Architecture*)

It might seem a bit strange that in a book of six chapters it takes until Chapter 6 to get round to describing what is the whole purpose of the exercise, actually building the house. The key to the construction process is, however, preparation; that is what everything has been focussed on so far and is what will continue to be the focus. More preparation will be still be needed before the first spade breaks ground.

If you get to this stage you will have a design that you are happy with and (hopefully) a planning approval. When starting to build, you will need to focus in by another order of magnitude and start looking at the nuts and bolts of the project.

DETAIL DESIGN AND PRODUCTION INFORMATION

Imagine yourself standing at some distance from a building, at this range you can see the size of the building the disposition of the openings in its façade and the general type of the materials it is constructed from, you cannot, however, see the detail of how the doors fit together, how they open and you cannot see the way the building works inside. Now imagine walking towards the building, as you do so the actual details of the construction spring to life, and the way it all fits together becomes apparent. Now imagine opening the front door and going in, you can now see what the internal materials of construction are, and how the building works in terms of detail, ironmongery, lighting and so on. The process of detail design emulates this focussing in exercise, concentrating on the detail of the building, and the

process of production information consists of recording this detail on paper. To some extent detail design and production information are inextricably linked, in that as detail design progresses you will be recording it on paper, but for the purpose of this exercise I have separated them slightly for clarity.

Detail Design

Structural Design

Since the way that the structure works will effect various of the elements you will be drawing, such as floor and wall thickness, roof design and foundation type, it is a good idea to start this process by calling a meeting with the structural engineer. This way you will not be involved in abortive work, whereby you draw something and then have to redraw it when it is sized up. Even if the engineer can only give you a preliminary idea, at least it will be something to work from.

Work through each internal wall with the engineer, agree whether it should be block work or lightweight studwork, and establish the thickness in each case.

Also work through each internal floor and decide how thick the structure will be and its direction of span.

It is possible, when the engineer gets down to doing the calculations, that certain of the sizes will change but at least this process will allow you to get started.

Internal Finishes/Decorations

Before you embark on the nitty-gritty plans sections

and elevations of the detail design, it is worth giving some more thought to what you are trying to achieve in terms of the feel of the interior. By its very nature the scheme design and planning application process is more concerned about the external form and appearance of the building than the way it is treated on the inside. The detailed design of a building means that you need to commit to the selection of doors, sanitary ware, skirting, flooring, tiling and general decorations, and if you know what it is that you are trying to achieve as a whole then you will find this selection process easier. If you have a design philosophy, then this will flow naturally.

The key thing to bear in mind is to think of the concept and then try to keep the integrity of the concept alive. If you have decided on a rustic cottage, then select the doors, fittings and fixtures on the same basis; if you are going for a hi-tech look then do the same thing. Even if you are going for differently themed rooms then be true to the concept within that room and do not let anything creep in that will compromise it.

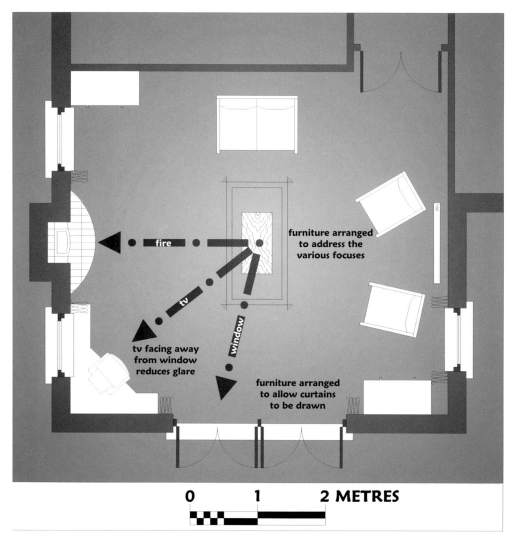

The living room – reconciling different focuses.

138

Plans

The best way to start is on the plans. Now is the time to really get into the detail of how the plans work. Firstly, get the plans you did for the scheme design blown up to 1:50 (twice the size of 1:100) or, even better, to 1:20 (five times the size); also get the furniture plans you have already done increased by the same margin. Arrange the furniture in a room and imagine using it, including entering the room and imagining what you will see. A few tips are as follows:

Living Rooms: The living rooms are public spaces, so generally you will want to open the door in such a way that the whole room is visible when you open it. Arrange the door to open so that you will see as much of the room as possible. A living room will generally have a focus or a series of focuses; these can be the view from the windows, a fire, the television, a dining table or even something like a piano or fish tank. What is more, these focuses can change depending on what time of day it is – the view may be the focus during the day, the television or the dining table the focus during the evening. The dynamism of these focuses should be kept in mind when arranging the furniture.

Bedrooms: A bedroom is generally perceived to be a private room, so the door should open against the room, that is to say, shield the room as much as possible until you actually step into it. This allows you to give someone a wake-up call without actually seeing them in bed. The focus of the room will clearly be the bed, but you also need to have secondary focuses, like the television, a dressing table or maybe a work desk for homework in the case of children. Care has to be taken that there is adequate space for dressing and undressing.

Kitchens: A well thought-out kitchen layout will make your culinary efforts much easier and it is certainly worth giving this a good deal of consideration. It might help if you think of cooking as a linear process when laying out a kitchen, so preparation, cooking, serving, storage of dirty plates and washing up should have their own zones, preferably next to the ones before and after in the sequence and, hopefully, with the storage appropriate to that activity beside it. Care should be taken to ensure that there is adequate space to crouch down and get things from cupboards; also be careful not to let the entrance door open against the oven – this can lead to fires or knocking pans off the range. If you are having a fully fitted kitchen there is generally a 'no extra charge' deal available from the supplier by which they will design the layout.

The bedroom – it should be attractive and interesting, not just a place to go and sleep.

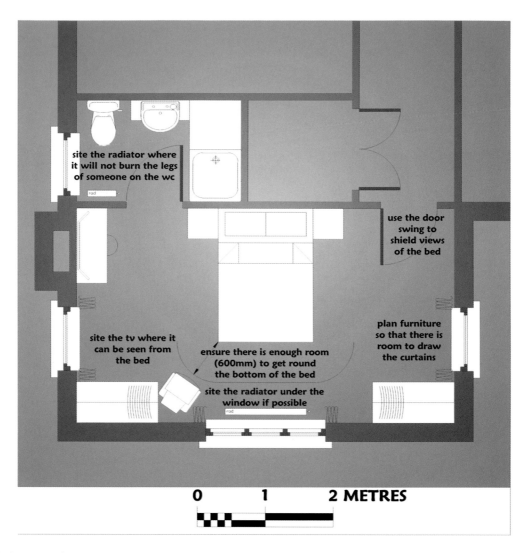

The bedroom needs to work functionally as well as being attractive.

Bathrooms: House builders traditionally design bathrooms to be the minimum size possible, but you may want to rethink this attitude; a bathroom can be somewhere to linger and siting the bath in such a way that you can enjoy a view or perhaps watch television can be a worthwhile exercise. As far as the disposition of the various bathroom fittings goes, you will need to take account of drainage, but also various other considerations. If you have (or are intending to have) small children, make sure that there is space by the bath for you to attend to the baby, or even space for you to get into the bath with the baby. If you are intending to use the house well into retirement or have regular visits from elderly relatives, you need to consider how someone with mobility problems can get in and out of the bath, and perhaps leave room for the eventual installation of a hoist. Similarly, it is a good idea to position a WC against a side wall so that you can, if necessary, install a 'grab rail' to assist people to get on and off.

140

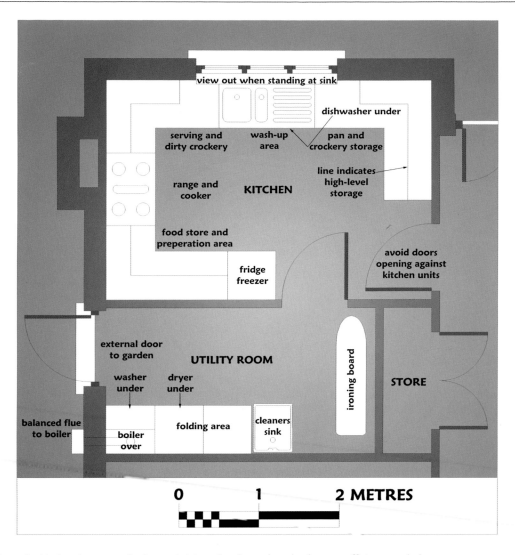

Thinking of a kitchen in terms of what activities take place where leads to an efficient workplace.

Once you have arranged the furniture to your liking and got all the doors positioned and swinging in the right direction, it is time to position the fittings. These will be items such as heating fittings, electrical fittings, lights and the like. In doing this the best thing to do is to start by creating a menu of fittings in graphic terms, so that you can represent them as you go along. A suggested legend is shown.

Take each room in turn and, again, imagine how you will use it and try to position the fittings. Some things will be obvious – for instance, you will need to

have a TV point next to the television – but some, like lighting, will be less obvious. Here are a few ideas for the various items:

Lighting: There are three types of lighting: these are background or mood lighting; task lighting; and decorative lighting (see page 145).

- Background or mood lighting – can be wall or ceiling lights controlled by dimmers, or with a low level of light. With background lighting it is sometimes best to have it indirect, such that it

The kitchen can be both functional and easy on the eye.

bounces off some other surface before it gets to your eye, or is muted by a lampshade or the like; up-lighters are useful for this, as are recessed down-lighters, since they wash the ceiling or wall with light rather than directing it straight into your eyes.

- Task lighting – designed so that you have enough light to see what you are doing. This could be a bedside light, study angle-poise light, wall or ceiling-mounted spotlights, or pelmet lighting below the high-level cupboards in the kitchen. Whatever the task lighting is, it needs to be fairly direct and easy to control from where you are undertaking the task.

- Decorative lighting – is about creating a point of interest. This could be coloured light washing a

wall, a light illuminating an object of interest such as a picture or sculpture, or even just a light fitting which is intrinsically decorative.

Light switches: It is important that the various types of lighting are separated from each other in the way that they are controlled or switched. It is also well worth having a good think about where you put the switches. It is very irritating and possibly dangerous to walk around in the dark trying to find the light switch, so locate them by the doorway in such a position that they are immediately to hand as you open the door. With bathroom switches it is best to locate them outside the room entirely, to avoid the possibility of touching them with wet hands – unless you are a fan of the slightly quaint look of pull-cord switches, which can be located in the room. It is also worth considering two-way switches in certain locations. For instance, it is an advantage to be able to switch the upstairs-hall lights on from downstairs and vice versa, but you also need to have control on the same level. Similarly, it is nice to control the bedroom lights from the doorway and from beside the bed, so that if you forget to turn the main lights out you do not have to get out of bed to switch them off.

Power Points: Power points are a necessary evil; the modern home can never have enough of them, but they are a visually intrusive item with a multitude of plugs and trailing wires. Power points come in three types: those that are for permanent appliances;

illustration 81

Background lighting should be easy on the eye and non-direct.

A bathroom can be somewhere to linger.

those that are for temporary appliances but do not need to have regular access; and those that are for temporary appliances and need regular access.

Power points for permanent fixtures, such as fridges, washing machines, cookers and the like, are best sited out of the way behind the appliance in question and then switched remotely by a simple switch – these are known as spurred outlets. Those that are for temporary appliances but which require little access, for equipment such as TV, Hi-fi, bedside lights and the like, are best tucked away discreetly out of sight behind items of furniture, or the appliance itself, at low level.

Power points that need regular access, for vacuum cleaners and such, need to be sited in positions where they can cover a wide are, so they should be near doors and in hallways. If you or any of your house-

hold have problems bending down you can consider siting regularly used sockets at higher level.

TV Sockets: It may seem self-evident that a TV point should be located next to the TV, however it is worth thinking about where else you might want to put a TV; perhaps in one of the secondary bedrooms, or even the kitchen or bathroom. It is much cheaper to install these things now than later.

It is also worth thinking about what sort of cable you want. With the advent of cable and broadband TV, you need to ensure that you do not get saddled with old technology before you have even started – so consult a TV provider.

Telephone Points: The same things apply as to the TV point.

Hi-Fi: When you are creating a new electrical layout it is well worth considering the possibility of wiring your new house for sound. It is easy to create speaker points to other rooms from your central stereo so that you can, for instance, listen to music in the kitchen or the bath. Take care to create a way of switching these speakers off so that you do not have to listen to the music if you do not want to.

Radiators: It is generally considered to be good practice to site radiators under the windows, since the hot air 'curtain' that they create helps to eliminate draughts and cut down on the radiated cold from the glass. With modern standards of double glazing and draught stripping this is no longer as necessary as it used to be and the under window location can be inconvenient if you want to use long curtains. In recent years there has also been a growth in, what you might term, radiators as 'art form' so now you can get brightly coloured, glass, elaborately shaped and unusually proportioned radiators. If you are taking this approach then you will want to site your radiator somewhere on display, but be warned, these kind of radiators are wickedly expensive when compared to normal panel ones. Whichever approach you adopt, try to site your radiators away from furniture, since if they are behind it their efficiency will be compromised and there is the possibility of damage to the furniture.

Entry System: It may be that you want an entryphone system. If so, you need to think where you will want to answer it; many people opt for the entryphone in the hall, but you may want to go to the

⚇	external double power point
⊕	downlighter
dis board	distribution board
⌀	one way toggle light switch
⌀	two way toggle light switch
●	dimmer light switch
⌂	external bulkhead light
⌒	double power point
△	telephone point
▲	television point
⅄	spot light
⌒	spurred switch to appliance
(sd)	mains powered smoke detector
⌒	5 amp outlet
rad	radiator
⊕	spotlight ladder
⚇	data cable outlet

An electrical and fittings menu – add any of your own additional items.

extra expense of having extra sets in the living or bedroom. If you are just opting for the doorbell system you need to consider where you are putting the sounder, since you will probably want to hear it from all parts of the house; it can also be worth considering a sounder on the external wall in the garden.

Computer Points: We are in the middle of a revolution in the world of information technology and it is important that you take account of this in your design. Even if you are not computer orientated now, you might find that you will want to be in the near future; it will be much more expensive to gear up in then than when you are actually constructing the house. It is suggested that you choose a location in each of the major rooms where the computer might be and then wire from there back to a central 'server' point using the latest category of data cabling. This will give you the flexibility to cope with changes in telecommunications technology at the same time.

Task lighting illuminates the job you are doing.

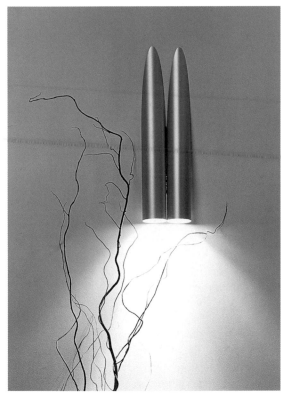

Lighting can be decorative in its own right.

Radiators do not have to be simple rectangles.

Consumer Unit/Fuse Board: You will need to put this in a discrete position (they are not pretty) but somewhere where they are accessible, so that you can get at them with the minimum of fuss.

Boiler: Boiler design is now quite advanced and they are commonly disguised as high-level cupboards in kitchens or utility rooms. It is important, however, to consider where the flue goes when siting the boiler. Boiler flues come in two basic types; balanced and conventional. Balanced flues mix the flue gases with fresh air so that they are less noxious and therefore can go straight through a wall. They are not, however, a decorative item and you need to think about the outside of the building when positioning the boiler. With a conventional flue the flue will rise up through the building and discharge above the highest opening window, but this may mean that it has to be boxed in through another room or encased in a chimney.

Hot-water Cylinder: It is perfectly possible to use a 'combi' boiler that heats the water directly without the need for any storage; these are now very efficient. The problem with this method, however, is that if you have more than two points drawing off water at the same time the flow to each point is generally reduced. This is really irritating if someone is showering and someone else turns on a hot tap, since the shower will suddenly go cold. So if you have a family or take a lot of showers it might be prudent to have a hot-water cylinder. A hot-water cylinder is traditionally mounted in a linen cupboard at the first floor, but there is no reason why you cannot put it anywhere you like. You should be aware that they give out a fair amount of heat and some noise, and their presence in a living room or bedroom can be quite disruptive in the summer and at night.

Smoke Detectors: Good practice and building regulations dictate that all bedrooms and the living room should have a mains smoke-detector. It is also a good idea to put a heat detector in the kitchen; these should be on the ceiling but can be placed more or less anywhere. It is well worth thinking about the position of smoke detectors at this stage, since they are not the most decorative items. You can place them in a discreet place – if you leave it to an electrician you can guarantee that it will end up just where you don't want it to be.

Extract Fans: The Building Regulations dictate that all bathrooms and kitchens should be equipped with an extract fan. The bathroom fans are generally linked to the light switch so that when you enter the room the fan goes on and then 'runs on' afterwards for a while after you switch the light off. The kitchen fans can be a simple on/off switch and are often related to the cooker hood. Whatever the method, you should bear in mind the position of the grill both internally and externally. Internally it should be placed in some kind of relationship with the light fittings so that it looks thought about; externally the terminal will come through the roof or wall and needs to be placed somewhere where it will not show too much.

Meters: In the past meters would be located inside the property, now, due to difficulties with access, this is a rarity. Water meters (where fitted) will be located in the road or other hard landscape area. Gas and electricity meters are generally fitted in flush cupboards, which slot into a prepared niche in the external wall. This means that meter readers can gain access to them without having to bother the resident of the house. Although this is a very practical solution, these cupboards are not particularly nice to look at and a bit of thought at this stage can avoid a potential eyesore. A possible solution is to locate the meters around the corner from the front elevation, so they do not hit you straight away, or within a properly designed cupboard of their own (this has to be kept unlocked).

You will now have plans that show the position of the fittings and all furniture. The next step is to reference any items that are not apparent from the menu so far. First of all, the various forms of construction need to be referenced; to do this you will need to refer back to the structural engineer to tell you what density block-work the various walls will be. In addition, you will need to decide the construction of the various internal studwork partitions. You have the choice of metal studs or timber ones. Metal studs will generally be 50mm metal with plasterboard either side making a total of 75mm, or 81mm if you skim the plasterboard with plaster rather than just taping the joints. Timber studs will generally be 75mm with plasterboard either side, making a total of 100mm, or 106mm if you skim the plasterboard. The timber studs are more traditional and you will find most small builders more comfortable with them, the metal studs are usually associated with bigger projects and are quite a specialized art.

It is a requirement to incorporate an insulation quilt in partitions that are between a living room and a bathroom so that you lessen bathroom sounds percolating through.

When all this is decided you need to reference them on the plan, a suggested convention for doing so follows.

The final thing to do with the plans at this stage is to set the opening dimensions. The crucial choice at this stage is to make the final decision on whether you want to use standard or bespoke windows and doors – if you decide on the latter you can end up spending thousands of pounds more, but will probably end up with a more unusual and more luxury effect. Bespoke doors are often worth considering for fitted wardrobes, since standard doors are often too repetitious when they are multiple. There are a great variety of standard windows and doors, and you may well have already obtained some catalogues of these as suggested in the last chapter.

Standard doors are still saddled with the legacy of imperial measurement and come in imperial and metric sizes; for ease of explanation I will use metric sizes, but if you prefer imperial they can be obtained readily. Doors are generally 2040mm high and come in widths of 526, 626, 726, 826 and sometimes 926mm wide, which gives a frame coordinating size of 2100mm high by 620, 720, 820, 920 and 1020mm wide. Conventionally, door widths are generally 826 mm, with the 726mm sometimes used for bathrooms and the other sizes restricted, usually, to stores and the like. If you are looking for a 'cottage' feeling, you may like to use the 726mm width throughout. If you are looking for wheelchair friendliness you should go for the 926mm width.

You will probably have already selected windows as part of the scheme design process, but you will need to firm up on these now. Standard windows generally come in brick coordinating heights (multiples of 75mm) and in a plethora of widths too extensive to mention here. They also come in a great variety of different shapes – bowed, bay, circular, arched and

You can opt for off-the-shelf doors, but a bespoke drawing can lead to a feeling of greater quality – note the way that the en suite door is concealed as one of the run of wardrobe doors.

the like. Bespoke windows, of course, can come in any shape you want.

The various opening sizes need to be shown to scale on the plans.

Sections

When you have completed the detail design of the plans, you can move onto the sections. You have already considered the floor-to-floor height as part of the scheme design stage and, providing the engineer has not given you any unpleasant surprises about the depth of the floor structure, you should be able to go ahead on that basis. If you are using masonry construction then it is sensible to use coursing height dimensions – a standard brick is 65mm high with a 10mm joint making an overall coordinating dimension of 75mm, a standard block is three courses of brickwork or 225mm, so an overall floor height might be 2625 mm, which would be thirty-five courses. If you use a coordinating dimension then it means the window sills can bear the same relation to the floor level whichever floor they are on. If you are using non-masonry construction then you can set the floor-to-floor dimension at any height that is convenient.

Having set the floor-to-floor height finally, the next thing to do is to set the window, door sill and head heights. For standard doors and windows the head height will generally be 2100mm above finished

Bespoke windows come in a variety of shapes and sizes.

Bespoke windows can form free shapes, but at a cost.

floor level; in the case of windows this can be varied, but you should take care that you don't end up with a random 'higgledy piggledy' effect. The sill height of the windows will be set by the overall height of the window you have selected.

At this stage you will also need to set the height at which the roof springs relative to the top floor ceiling. If you are using a flat roof then the roof joists will double as the ceiling joists. If you are using a 'vaulted' type of ceiling then the underside of the rafters will form the ceiling. In most other cases the ceiling will be attached to ceiling joists, which act as ties stopping the rafter from spreading.

Staircases

You will, at this stage, also need to design the staircase in more detail. There are various standard staircases available and the catalogues will list various of them. If you do decide to use a standard staircase the manufacturers will generally supply you with data sheets showing the exact dimensions, widths, headroom and so on. If you decide that the expense of a bespoke staircase is worth it, then it is still useful to obtain some of these standard layouts so that you can base your design on them. Staircase design requires a lot of three-dimensional thinking and the classic staircase mistake is to design one with insufficient headroom. You need to ensure that there is sufficient room under the floor you are climbing towards and also the flight above if it comes over. For this reason you should always consider a staircase in sections.

When designing a staircase you will need to think in three dimensions.

149

Elevations

You will already have a set of elevations from the planning process, but you now need to look at them in a bit more detail. Check that they accord with the sections, mark them up with the position of any of the services you have positioned on the plans and add the windows and doors on in more detail. You also need to check that the each habitable room has a minimum area of opening window that equates to one twentieth of the floor area.

Drainage

Drainage falls into two categories, foul and surface water, with foul drainage being that from bathrooms, kitchens and the like, and surface water being the disposal of rainwater. You will have, hopefully, obtained information on the sewers as part of the feasibility study and the site survey.

Foul Drainage: Unless there are no public sewers available and you are using a septic tank, you will have, hopefully, the position and depth below ground of the nearest public sewer to your site. Foul drainage design will consist of getting all the drainage from your house to that manhole, usually at a minimum fall of 1 in 60 and at a minimum depth below ground level of 600mm. There are a lot of standard drainage products on the market and it is suggested that you obtain one of the catalogues, which will give you guidance as to what fittings you should use and general layouts. The keys to good drainage design are to ensure that no sewer gases escape into habitable areas; that the sewer is, as much as is possible, self cleansing (there is sufficient flow to wash the pipe out); and that if any blockages occur they can be readily cleared.

In principle, foul drainage involves collecting together the outflow from several sanitary fittings above floor level and then linking them to the public sewer. The above-ground drainage usually consists of a vertical pipe or 'stack' with a pipe from each fitting going into it. You need to ensure that this stack is located in such a position that the distance from each fitting to it is fairly short (a couple of metres is ideal), that the pipes follow a wall and that they do not cross any doorways and so on. Also, the vertical stack needs to be carefully positioned to respect any rooms below it. It is common to have two or three stacks in

a reasonably sized house. When the stack hits the lowest floor it will penetrate it and go below ground; it then needs to follow a fairly direct route to the outside where it will connect into an inspection chamber or manhole. You can have several stacks connecting into one inspection chamber. The inspection chamber needs to be connected to the public sewer by a pipe falling a minimum of 1 in 60 and at a minimum depth of 600mm to avoid frost heave. Any change in direction or new connections will need to have an inspection chamber.

If there is an existing connection to the road on site you might be able to utilize it (although a video survey is recommended) otherwise a new connection to the road sewer will be required. The Local Authority will generally carry out this work and charge you for it.

Surface Water Drainage: In concept, surface-water drainage is similar to foul drainage. From the item being drained (the roof), drainage is moved horizontally (by gutters) to horizontal stacks (rainwater pipes) and from there into the sewer system. The main difference between the two is that rainwater is less likely to block (especially if you fit leaf guards to gutters or rainwater pipes), so inspection chambers are really only required at changes of direction providing that you provide access points (gulleys) that can be rodded at the base of each rainwater pipe. Gutters can generally be sized by using the manufacturer's literature.

Public rainwater drainage is generally via combined systems, where the rainwater flows into the foul system, or sometimes dedicated surface-water sewers. Many systems are working at capacity, however, and the authorities will often not allow additional rainwater drainage into the system. As a result of this, a common way to dispose of rainwater is via what are known as soakaways. These are essentially chambers that are sunk into the ground that collect the water and then allow it to percolate away into the surrounding soil. Soakaways used to be simple pits filled with rubble, but these were prone to silting up and have been superseded by purpose-built chambers made from perforated concrete rings. Sizing the soakaway can be done using the manufacturer's literature and is something that is dependent on the porosity of the ground (the less porous the ground the bigger the chamber must be). You can gauge the porosity of the ground by digging a hole down through the topsoil to about one metre in depth and filling it with water. If the water disappears immediately then you have porous ground; if it lingers for a few minutes but then goes, you have ground of medium porosity; if it stays any longer then you have non-porous ground. It is also worth asking your local Building Regulations department how well drained the local ground is.

External Works

When considering the external areas you need to think in the same detail as for the internal areas about how you will use the space; you need to study the garden for areas of light and shade, for openness and privacy, and for views out. In addition, you need to decide what activities and uses you will have in external areas and allocate areas for them.

Typical uses are: access on and off site; parking; deliveries; playing; sunbathing; entertaining; storage; growing crops; decorative planting; eating; relaxing; exercising; creating views; clothes drying; refuse storage.

As part of the detailed design you will also need to decide on the nature and disposition of the external materials. These will break down into four categories:

Hard Landscape: This will consist of hard surfaces such as drives, paths, patios and the like. Generally there are a great deal of different materials to choose from here and your personal choice will be governed by aesthetics and budget. From the aesthetics point of view you need to think of what 'feel' you are trying to create; for a more rural feel, typical materials might be gravel (or gravel-dressed tarmac) and random or 'crazy' paving; for a more urban feeling you might consider undressed tarmac, interlocking paviors, regular paving and the like.

A guide to costs (with the least expensive at the top) might be as follows:

- Gravel.
- Undressed tarmacadam.
- Dressed tarmacadam.
- Concrete or reconstituted stone paving.
- Interlocking concrete paviors.
- Clay paviors.

- Natural stone paving.
- Granite sets and cobbles.

You can also think of more natural, softer materials, such as tree bark or seashells, for areas not subject to vehicular traffic.

Soft Landscaping: This may consist of areas laid to lawn, planting beds and planted features like trees and hedges. It is worth considering the edge between the hard and soft, and the various types of soft landscaping. If you do not delineate the edge properly you might find that one material creeps into another and you get a blurred boundary – if this is the effect you want, fine, otherwise you might find that your carefully designed boundaries gradually move over time and that you create yourself a maintenance problem. Common edge treatments might be: kerbs; walls; gravel boards; proprietary edging strips; and sleepers. When designing deep beds consider maintenance; if you plant the beds with anything too impenetrable you might have trouble getting into the farthest-flung areas of the beds, so it is a good idea to provide paths winding through the deeper beds.

The choice of planting obviously relies on not just your taste, but also position, the area you are in and how much maintenance you are prepared to carry out. The success of your soft planting relies heavily on your knowledge or how much you are prepared to find out, so if you do not employ a landscape architect, it is strongly recommended that you do your homework – there are many books to choose from.

Landscape Features: As well as planted features you may like to consider built features that will provide focal points to the garden, typical of these are: ponds; statues; birdbaths/tables/feeders; pergolas; summer houses; garden furniture; barbecue pits; sheds.

Boundaries: Boundaries are a much neglected feature of the external areas of a house and the reason why has a lot to do with the confused nature of the legal ownership of boundaries. Boundaries can belong to the property on one side or the other, or they can be party (shared) structures. This often means that you will get a mish-mash of different boundary treatments on one plot and they can be less than decorative. The construction of a new house can prove an ideal opportunity to rectify this situation.

If the ownership of a boundary is not clear, or the boundary belongs to another property, it does not mean that you cannot do anything about upgrading it – your neighbour might be glad to have it replaced and might even be prepared to pay for some of it. If all else fails, you can always erect a different boundary on your side of the one which is in question. If you do this, it is prudent to send a recorded letter to your neighbour noting what you have done and also keeping a weather eye open for the removal of the boundary treatment on their side; conveyancing and land registry plans are not all that accurate and you can find that boundaries gradually 'creep' over the years, and your neighbour might gain an extra bit of site by simply reducing the fence or wall on their side.

Typical boundary treatments rely on both budget and the effect you are trying to create. A softer feel can be created by planted boundaries or a rusticated fencing; more urban locations might call for walls, railings or close-boarded fencing.

One of the boundary treatments will be how you access your property from the public road. This may require liaison with the Local Authority, especially if you have to form a new crossing over an existing pavement. When laying out the access it is prudent to consider sight lines, to think about where you will be sitting in your car when you turn out and to try to maximize the view up and down the street.

You will now have made most of the detailed decisions about what is going where, what it will be made of and so on, but you need to get this down on paper in a form that you and a potential contractor and sub-contractor can understand. To do this you will need to move onto the production information stage.

Production Information

You will have been recording a lot of the production information on the drawings as you go along, but now is the time to formalize it. There are three primary ways of imparting and/or recording information at the production information stage; these have been touched on in Chapter 4 and are basically the drawings, the schedules and the specification, as follows:

The Drawings

Start by looking at the plans. You will already have a drawing with the position of all the furniture and the fittings on it; the next thing to do is to reference the windows and doors so that they can be referred back to a schedule as part of the production information. With the windows, reference them first with 'W', then with the floor number and then a sequential number – 'G' for ground, '1' for first and so on. Thus, WG1, WG2, WG3 and so on. With doors do the same thing, but using a 'D' prefix instead of 'W', thus, DG1, DG2, DG3 and so on.

You will also need to give all the rooms a distinctive name, so that when you are referencing the finishes and sanitary ware people will understand what it is that you are talking about. With a house it is generally enough to do this without assigning numbers to the rooms, except where you have rooms whose function repeats; so you can label them Living Room, Dining Room, Study, Bedroom 1, Bedroom 2, Bedroom 3, Bathroom 1, Bathroom 2, Store 1, Store 2 and so on.

There may also be something unusual about a room or wall that cannot be picked up by standard references or conventions; this might be a change in level, a hearth or something of that ilk. If this is the case, then make a note on the plan referring specifically to that item.

You will also need to dimension the plans so that they can be used as the basis for setting out the building. The convention is to always dimension to the structure since this will be built first, never to the plaster face. Always dimension the door and the frame, never just the door. The right way is to do overall dimensions for each room and each wall, and then do running dimensions, which pick up the position of each opening in the wall. Any detail references (see later on in this section) should also be added, circling the area of construction detailed. You should now have all the information you need on the plan of each room. An example of a general arrangement drawing can be found in Chapter 4.

Turning now to the sections, you need to impart the relevant information on them. Sections should be at a minimum scale of 1:50. The first thing to do is to add the construction notes, which can pick out specific items as per the plans but can also give general constructional information such as make up of the walls, roofs and floors. When you have done this, move onto the vertical dimensions, again using only structural dimensions, picking up the sill and head of any windows, the floor-to-floor and floor-to-ceiling heights, and the height and angle of the roof. Any detail references (see later on in this section) should also be added, circling the area of construction detailed. Be sure to mark on the plans where any sections have been taken.

The elevations should be at a minimum scale of 1:50 and should bring together the information given on the plans and sections. The windows and doors should be shown in detail, together with any opening areas and with their reference numbers marked. Service terminals should be marked on, and meter positions and so on. If you are using masonry then the coursing heights should be accurately marked on – similarly with the roof tiling. Any elevational features, such as widow surrounds, quoins, porches, chimneys and the like, should be accurately marked. Again, any detail references (see later on in this section) should also be added, circling the area of construction detailed.

The external-works drawing or site plan should show the areas of hard landscaping, together with a key to show what they are. Edgings and boundaries should be shown, together with a key to indicate what they are. Areas of soft landscaping need to be shown, together with what area is laid to lawn and what is planting bed. In addition, levels should be indicated at a maximum 5m grid and it should be ensured that, for hard landscape areas, these fall towards drainage points. Any landscaping features and the position of any trees should be indicated. Underneath all this, detail the position of the foul and surface water drainage. This should include the position of stacks, rainwater points, gulleys, rodding eyes, manholes and soakaways. Manholes should show their cover level and invert (depth of bottom of inside of pipe) level. Once more, any detail references (see later on in this section) should also be added, circling the area of construction detailed.

Staircase drawings should be at a minimum of 1:20 and should show the plans and sections. The drawing should list the height of the risers, the depth of the treads and the general pitch line. Unless a standard stair is being used there should be details of construction. The height and position of any handrails and balustrades should be shown, including around any open stairwells.

The final part of the drawing process is to zoom in on the typical and special details; these should be at 1:5 or 1:10. Each situation and boundary should be shown – if you leave them to the builder they might end up being sloppily done. Typical details should include the following:

External Envelope:
- Ground – wall base details.
- Windows – sills, heads, jambs, details of any bespoke joinery.
- Doors – thresholds, heads, jambs, details of any bespoke joinery.
- Roof – eaves, ridges, abutments, valleys, verges, parapets, roof widows, roof features.
- Features – porches, chimneys, balconies, verandas, any bespoke joinery.

Internal Construction:
- Doors – heads, jambs, details of any bespoke joinery.
- Partitions – ceiling/wall junction, wall/floor junction, ducts, any other apertures such as kitchen hatches or internal glazed screens.
- Ceilings – details of any sloped, dropped or featured sections of ceiling including beams and the like.
- Features – fireplaces, fixed furniture, columns

External Works:
- Details for the junctions of one material and another.
- Details of specialist drainage features, such as specially built soakaways or inspection chambers.
- Details of boundary features, such as walls gates and railings.
- Details of any features.

Having completed the drawing package, the next step is to schedule the various items that are indicated on them. Things to schedule include doors, windows, sanitary ware, kitchen fittings, and decorations. Each schedule should set out clearly the information required to order the item, its location and any special features about it, thus:

Doors should be scheduled by reference, location, manufacturer, ironmongery and fire resistance (see below).

Windows should be scheduled by reference, location, manufacturer and ironmongery (see below).

Sanitary ware should be scheduled by location, manufacturer, colour and fittings as detailed in Chapter 4.

Kitchen fittings should only be scheduled if you are planning to order them as off-the-shelf items from a DIY centre or similar, rather than having a kitchen supplier schedule them. They should be scheduled by location, base unit, door and any special fittings.

Decorations should be scheduled by location,

element (wall, ceiling etc) finish, colour and any special details (see opposite).

The Specification
The specification consists of three sections: the preliminaries, the preambles and the works section as covered in the 'Briefing Your Contractor' section in Chapter 4.

TENDER ACTION

When the production information has been prepared, you will be in a position to go out to tender. How you do this is somewhat reliant on the form of contract. If you are doing a design-and-build or a conventional contract then the entire package, consisting of drawings, specification and schedules,

Door scheduling									
Door Ref	Location	Wall Type	Size of Door	Overall Size	Thickness	Fire Rating	Ironmongery	Manufacturing
DF 6	Guest En Suite	105mm Partition	826 × 2040	886 × 2100	44mm	None	SET 2	23438

Window scheduling					
Window Ref	Location	Wall Type	Size of Doors	Ironmongery	Manufacture Ref
WF 4	Guest Bed	275mm Cavity Wall	860 × 1350	SET 7	2VS0813

Room	Walls	Ceiling	Floor	IR Timberwork	Tiling
Decoration scheduling					
Guest En Suite	Matt Vinyl Emulsion Soft Apricot 527.III	Matt Vinyl Emulsion Light Apricot 517.IV	300 × 300 Slate Tiles to Spec	White Gloss 700.III	HR Johnson 100 × 100 White HR 372

can be handed over to the one contractor for pricing. If you are managing the contract yourself and sub-contracting the work out, then you will need to break the specification down into its constituent parts, together with the relevant drawings, and then send them out to each of the sub-contractors for pricing.

As has been mentioned in Chapter 3, the trick with tendering is to allow sufficient time to do it. If you try to force the contractor(s) into preparing a tender in next to no time they will either gloss over some items and insert provisional sums, or possibly have a 'punt' and put in an unrealistic price in the hope that it will be accepted.

CONSTRUCTION

This chapter does not aspire to give you a comprehensive run down on the construction process; there have been many larger volumes than this dedicated exclusively to that. What I will seek to do here is give you an overview of the various processes, the way that they interact and what to watch out for.

The construction process is an interesting one, in many ways it is similar to the manufacture of larger factory-made components, in that it is essentially linear, with one process relying on the completion of the previous one, and it also relies on the supply of components sourced elsewhere arriving at the right time. To extend the metaphor, as a factory relies on the production line to keep on rolling, so the

construction process relies on the various trades arriving in a managed and coordinated fashion. Both the manufacturing and the construction industry rely on good management and coordination to keep things rolling along, and if there is anything you can do to increase the efficiency of the job, whether you are managing the contract yourself or whether you are employing a main contractor, then you should o it.

Coordination and Management

There are a number of key activities to management and coordination, and whether you are managing the contract or whether you are just an active part of the design team there will be many things you can do to assist.

Information
'Information' is the name that the industry gives to any material required to inform a contractor or sub-contractor about the building.

From day one, the construction of your house will rely on the arrival of information. You will need to provide sufficient information for:

- Costing.
- Ordering.
- Construction.

If the information does not arrive on time for this, then at best you will get delay and at worst you will get claims for additional expense. It is recognized within the industry that, generally, all information will not be available on day one, but will be needed in good time. It is important, therefore, that you ensure that any required pieces of information arrive in an orderly manner and that you prevent a logjam of required information building up or a panic situation setting in.

It is a good idea from your first meeting with a contractor or sub-contractor to set down the timetable for the arrival of information. The best way to do this is to assemble an *information required schedule*. This is a document that can be constantly updated, showing the latest date that various pieces of information have to arrive.

As well as the arrival of the information in good time, it is important that this information is legible, that it does not contradict other pieces of information and that it is complete. It is a common mistake made by the design team to assume that, because they have discussed something or believe something to be true, the contractor will know what they are thinking. Remember that a contractor has not necessarily been present at earlier discussions and also that they will generally take the easiest or simplest path – so if you want something special make it very clear.

Decisions

Of equal importance to the information flow is that decisions are made in good time. Due to the complexity of construction and the fact that it will turn up unexpected situations (especially at the earlier stages), it tends to be somewhat 'seat-of-the-pants' at times. When you have a fluid and fast-moving situation you have to be prepared to make speedy decisions; you may have got used to spending weeks over decisions pre-construction, but once work has started that luxury will not be available to you if you want to avoid delay.

As employer you will be called on to make decisions and you will need to make them promptly. When asked to make a decision, firstly try to establish what the timetable for that decision is, then what effect it will have down the line, then what other options there might be, and only then what the reason is for the need to make a decision.

Programme

A programme is the framework on which hangs the coordination of the whole project. A good programme should be: *predictive*, in that it anticipates what the next processes will be and ensures there is plenty of warning to all concerned; *reactive*, in that it will adapt to changing circumstances during the construction process; and *instructional*, in that it should act as a catalyst to the instruction of various key parties.

You should ensure that a master programme is prepared and that this programme is consulted on a daily basis, updated on a weekly basis and reviewed on a monthly basis. If you are employing a main contractor, make sure that you keep a copy of the original contract and of the reasons for any delays – if you have a damages clause whereby you can penalize the contractor for delay then you will need a good record of what has gone on.

Cash Flow

Money greases the wheels of industry and, in this case, the particular industry is building. The end of the construction industry you are operating in is notorious for bad debt and cessation of work, and as a result all the people connected with it are paranoid about payment. If there is any suggestion that the job is running out of money you will find that the site becomes a lonely place as the workmen take up their tools and go elsewhere.

It is important that you ensure that sufficient funds are available, that you can demonstrate to others that they are available and that they arrive on time. The best way of doing this is to prepare, or have prepared, a cash-flow forecast that should set out clearly the month-on-month requirement for cash and which should be updated on a monthly basis. If you have funders you should give them the cash-flow forecast so that they can make funds available and, if you are using capital, then make sure these funds are unlocked and ready to go. In addition, make sure good records of any additional expenses are kept so that you don't get any nasty surprises and that, if you are going to need additional funds, you have plenty of warning so that you can arrange them.

Procedure

A well-managed contract should involve a number of people who know what they have to do and when they have to do it, and should make sure that uncertainty is, as much as possible, reduced to a minimum. The way to do this is to ensure that there are procedures in place that provide a framework for the smooth transferral of decisions, variations and instructions as follows:

Meetings: Right from the start, regular meetings with the design and construction team will ensure that all issues are aired, processes are gone over, finances are sorted, programmes are monitored and instructions are given. Meetings should work to an agenda, with all parties reporting, and should be minuted with actions and who must act clearly shown.

Instructions: If an instruction is given it can be verbal, but it should always be confirmed in writing – the construction will take months, and it is easy to forget something that was said ages ago.

Updating Information: When an instruction is given, it is given to a specific person or persons, and may not be given to other people down the line. It is important, therefore, to keep drawings and schedules updated and to signify any revision with a revision letter. It is also important to make sure everyone has a copy of a record of the latest drawings and schedules, so that they can refer to them before acting to ensure they are working to the latest information.

Valuation: To ensure the efficient flow of money to the contractor and to ensure that money is released in a way that reflects progress on site, it is important to set up a valuation procedure. This involves a formal assessment of progress, on a two-weekly or monthly basis, against the priced specification. If the price for a certain item is x and it is your or your architect's view that on a certain day they have done half of that work, you should pay 50 per cent of x (subject to retention as covered later on in this chapter), no more no less.

Safeguards

Construction can be a risky process, from the point of view of both physical and financial dangers, so you need to put in place as many safeguards as possible to protect against these risks, as follows:

Health and Safety

This has been covered in some detail in Chapter 3 but, basically, it is important to bear in mind that the Construction and Design Management (CDM) Regulations are there to give the people who construct the building and those who will use it in the future a measure of protection, so it is well worth going through the provisions as thoroughly as possible and then implementing them in full. Just thinking about this will ensure that your site and building is a safer place to be. If you have told people about procedure – such as safety clothing and working methods – then if they choose to ignore your instructions you are less likely to get any blame.

Insurances

I have touched on insurance in Chapter 4, but it is worth reiterating that you need to make sure that any contractor or sub-contractor carries the correct insurances and that you are correctly insured yourself. If in any doubt at all always check with your insurer; the amounts involved can be huge and it is better to be safe than sorry. There are four types of insurance that are needed:

- Employers Liability – this insurance is to protect anyone employed on the building site. If you are employing a main contractor you do not need to take it out yourself, but if you are managing the contract yourself and are employing sub-contractors you will need it.
- Public Liability – this is to cover people who are not working on your site but who are damaged by it in some way, possibly by falling materials or even by trespassing and hurting themselves! The same applies as for employer's liability with the main contractor/managed contract situation.
- Contract Works Insurance – this is often known as 'Contractors All Risks' insurance and covers theft of plant or materials, fire and structural damage caused by the work. Again, if you are employing a main contractor you shouldn't need this unless your work involves the conversion of an existing structure, which is generally not covered.
- Building Insurance – if you are dealing with existing structures then you need to make sure

33 ACACIA AVE

DRAWING ISSUE REGISTER

General Arrangements amd Schedules					1.1.2004																		
				DATE OF ISSUE																			
NO.		SCALE	SIZE	REVISIONS																			
33 AC GA 01	GROUND FLOOR PLAN	1:50	A1	A																			
DISTRIBUTION				**NUMBER OF COURSES**																			
	BODGITT & SCARPER LTD			2																			
ISSUED FOR	INFORMATION=I TENDER=T CONSTR=C PLANNING=P BREGS=B																						

A drawing issue record keeps tabs on what has been issued and to whom.

Interim Certificate

Architect address: Camp & Flattery
No 1 Paper Chase, Scale Rule, Wessex

Job reference: 33 AC

Certificate No: 8

Employer address: Mr J Bloggs
33 Acacia Avenue, Pastures New, Wessex

Issue date: 1st April 2004

Contractor address: Bodgitt & Scarper Ltd
Last Chance Saloon
Dodge City USA

Valuation date: 1st April 2004

Contract Sum: £145,323.00

Works situated at: 33 Acacia Avenue, Pastures New

This Interim Certificate is issued under the terms of the above mentioned Contract.

Gross valuation inclusive of the value of works by Nominated Sub-Contractors... £120,320.00

Less Retention which may be retained by the Employer as detailed on the Statement of Retention £6,016.00

£114,304.00

Less total amount stated as due in Interim Certificates previously issued up to and including Interim Certificate No.7... £83,151.83

Net amount for payment £31,152.17

I/We hereby certify that the amount for payment by the Employer to the Contractor on this Certificate is

THIRTY ONE THOUSAND ONE HUNDRED AND FIFTY TWO POUNDS AND 17 PENCE

We hereby direct the Contractor that this amount includes

All amounts are exclusive of VAT

Signed_____

(1) The Contractor has given notice that the rate of VAT chargeable on the supply of goods and services to which the Contract relates is 0%

(2) 0% of the amount certified above is... £

(3) Total of net amount and VAT amount (for information)......................... £31,152.17

This is not a Tax Invoice

Valuations should be recorded on a certificate.

that they are insured even during the works. You also need to ensure that you take out the correct insurance as soon as you take possession.

Performance Bonds

In the building industry, companies go into receivership with monotonous regularity and if you have employed a main contractor and they go 'belly up' during the contract it will be very inconvenient, and possibly very expensive, for you to restart the contract with someone else at the helm. It is possible to insure against this eventuality with what is known as a performance bond, by which an amount will be paid to you if your contractor defaults. The contractor will put the performance bond in place themselves and then pass the cost on to you. Performance bonds are quite expensive and if you have satisfied yourself as to your contractor's stability in the way discussed in Chapter 4 you may think this to be an unnecessary expense.

Retention

It is common practice in the building industry to keep back a percentage of payment to guard against latent defects and only release it when you are satisfied that the work is not faulty in any way, this is called the *retention*.

The usual way of doing this is to keep back 5 per cent of the value of any interim valuations. If a contractor or sub-contractor has completed 50 per cent of a certain work stage which is valued at £x you would pay them 50 per cent of £x less 5 per cent of the figure owing or 47.5 per cent of £x.

On completion of a task it is usual to keep 2.5 per cent of the final valuation for a period of up to a year and then to release this when the contractor or sub-contractor has rectified any defects.

Building Trades

Demolition

If you are in a hurry to get on to site it may be worth getting quotes for the demolition works in isolation, since they are very much a stand-alone item.

Make sure that the demolition contract includes for the complete removal of all existing structures that you don't want; this should include roadways, services and foundations, since it is quite common to leave things that are not actually sticking above ground in place on the basis that the site will still look cleared. Also make sure that all demolished structures are cleared away – tipping prices can be expensive and demolition contractors will often leave materials piled on site if given half a chance. It's simple really; do not pay the last instalment until everything has been removed.

Foundations

The type of foundations will depend on the ground conditions. There are many different types of ground in the UK and each will have different 'bearing' characteristics. For most types of ground a simple 'strip' footing will be enough. A strip footing involves digging a trench through the topsoil to a level where the ground is firm and below the level where frost can

Foundations – the sooner you are out of the ground, the better.

penetrate, and then filling it with concrete so that you can build your building off it. This sounds simple but there are many factors that need to be taken into account when deciding on the foundations:

Unstable Ground: There are situations whereby, unless you want to keep digging until you get to Australia, you will be unable to find stable ground; this can be as a result of natural geology or of man-made conditions such as fill. In this situation you can use columns of concrete or other material, which go down to solid ground or support the weight of the building by their length and friction against the surrounding material; these columns are known as 'piles'. Piled foundations can be bored (screwed or drilled) or driven (hammered) into the ground; driving piles is noisy and can literally make the ground shake, so drilled piles are generally the preferred option when there are other buildings close by.

When the piles have been inserted, the foundation trenches are dug between them, then a 'cage' of reinforcement bars is put into the trench before the concrete is poured, so that you get, in essence, a concrete beam spanning between the piles that puts no weight on the ground.

Piling is obviously a more expensive option than ordinary strip foundations since you are paying extra for not only the piles, but also the reinforcement. Piling is more expensive the more 'ins and outs' you have in the building, since you normally need a pile at each change in direction of the wall.

Another option for unstable ground is to use a 'raft'. This is, as the name suggests, a solid structure, which literally floats on the surface of unstable ground. This sounds a little disconcerting, since you might think the building would float away or sink, and it is true that this method is unsuitable for sloping sites or where the ground is too soft or of uneven bearing ability, but in the right circumstances correct design will make this a cost effective method.

Whatever happens, if you have unstable ground, you will need an engineer to design your foundations.

Elastic Ground: There are various ground conditions where the ground is constantly on the move, swelling when it is wet and contracting when it is dry

– these are generally what is known as 'shrinkable clay' soils. To combat this ground movement you need to, firstly, excavate to a level where this is no longer happening (if you can't you need to use piles) and, secondly, guard the foundation against being damaged by the movement of the soil. To guard the foundations you have to install a compressible layer against the foundations to take up any lateral movement at right angles to the foundation and sometimes a slippage layer to take up any movement parallel to the foundation. These provisions will, obviously, cost more than a standard strip foundation.

Trees: If there are trees close to the building they can cause damage directly, through their roots trying to grow into or under the building, or indirectly, by affecting the level of ground water locally by their thirst. To ensure that you do not get problems with trees you need to ensure that your foundations go deep enough to be below the lowest of the tree roots and also below the level of soil that will be subject to shrinking and expansion caused by the tree sucking moisture out of the ground. Generally, the closer you are to a tree the deeper the foundation needs to be. The NHBC publishes tables to show how deep a foundation should be according to the proximity and type of tree, and the type of ground. It should be noted that you cannot necessarily get over this problem by cutting down the offending tree, even if it is not protected by the Local Authority, since when a tree is cut down it will stop taking water and the ground will swell or 'heave', so it will need a good long time, perhaps a few seasons, to settle down before you build.

Inclement Weather: Foundations are probably the building process that is most effected by adverse weather. If it is raining heavily when you are excavating you will get trenches crumbling and flooding, and if it is freezing you should not pour concrete since it will not set properly and will be too weak. You can mitigate the effect of inclement weather by starting at a time of year when you are less likely to get extreme weather, but generally delays caused by inclement weather are temporary and you can soldier on. If you are employing a main contractor, inclement weather is a valid reason for an extension of time.

Sulphate Attack: Concrete foundations are constantly wet (or at least damp) from naturally occurring groundwater. In some areas this ground water will contain high levels of soluble salts, some of which will be sulphates. Concrete can be attacked and weakened by high levels of sulphates and if you are in a high sulphate area you will need to specify sulphate-resistant concrete. A telephone call to your local Building Inspector will tell you if this is the case.

It is quite probable that you will not encounter any of the above problems but, if you do, the last thing you want is to be presented with a change when you are already on site. It is prudent, therefore, to check with the Local Building Inspector at the Council's offices whether the ground is likely to be unstable or highly elastic and, if it is, have a soil survey done – this involves testing the ground conditions to see whether they need to have specially designed foundations and is carried out by a specialist firm (your structural engineer will give you some names). At the very least, a good while before you start building, you should dig a trial pit to what you believe to be the foundation depth and get the Building Inspector to come and look at it so that you can agree what the foundation depth should be.

Ground-Floor Slab

The ground-floor slab is generally installed when the foundations have been poured and the walls built up to ground level. At its simplest, a ground floor is a simple slab of concrete sitting on a bed of ground-up bricks or rocks, which in turn is sitting on the ground, but, as with the foundation, there are factors that you need to be aware of before starting on the slab.

Unstable and Shrinkable Ground: As with foundations the ground-floor slab needs to bear onto secure ground; if it doesn't and the ground moves under it you will get settlement and cracking. If you do have unstable ground you need to span the floor between foundations or walls as you would with upper floors. You can do this by making a reinforced-concrete slab, by using a proprietary precast concrete floor system, or by having a traditional suspended timber floor. Of these, the second option is usually the favoured one, since it is less expensive than an

in situ reinforced-concrete slab and lasts longer than a suspended timber floor, but it does take a few weeks to arrive so you must make the decision in plenty of time. Whichever sort of suspended floor you have, you will have a void under the floor that needs to be ventilated via airbricks in the external wall to prevent build up of gas.

Inclement Weather: Concrete floors are subject to the same problems with bad weather as foundations.

Gas: There are some areas where the ground contains and releases injurious gases such as radon or methane; your local Building Inspector will tell you if this is the case in your area. If such gases are present in sufficient quantities, you will need to take measures to stop them from entering the building or building up to sufficient concentrations to pose a threat. Such measures can range from laying an impervious sheet over the ground so that any gases are kept in the ground, to ventilating the floor void so that gases do not build up. The local Building Inspector will inform you as to the preferred method.

Sulphate Attack: A ground-bearing slab will be subject to the same provisions as the foundations when you are in a high sulphate area.

Any ground slab will also need to be insulated, damp proofed and finished. If you are using a ground bearing slab this can be done right at the beginning when the slab is being constructed, or later on when the building is weather tight. With a suspended slab you do not really have a choice, although any precast floor should sit on a damp-proof course where it is supported, to stop ground water being absorbed and rusting the reinforcement. Finishing the slab after the building has been made weather tight will be dealt with later, since it comes much later in the building process. If you are damp proofing and insulating a ground-bearing slab right at the start this involves installing insulation and a damp-proof membrane underneath the slab before it is poured. If you opt for this method, make sure that the insulation and the damp-proof membrane turn up at the slab edge, and that the damp-proof membrane laps over any damp-proof membrane in the wall.

External Walls

There are many treatments to choose from when constructing external walls, and such is their variety that there is no point in going into them here. There are a few points that are worth mentioning, however, as follows:

Below Ground: Even if you have selected one of the system-built options that involve timber-frame or steel-studwork construction, this is obviously not suitable for below ground where the wall will be permanently wet. So, for almost all situations, the construction will be in masonry below ground. In this situation it is important that a sulphate-resistant brick or block is used, together with resistant mortar, if the ground contains high levels of sulphates.

Damp Proofing: Any wall construction will need to prevent the penetration of water both horizontally, from rain falling on it, and vertically, from ground water rising up the wall from capillary reaction. To prevent water coming in horizontally it is usual to have a physical separation between the inner layer and the outer layer – this void is known as the cavity. When you have openings for windows and doors this cavity needs to be bridged, so you need to ensure that a means of stopping water travelling from outside to inside is incorporated. This is known as a vertical damp-proof course. It is common these days to incorporate the vertical damp-proof course as a thermal break (see below). In masonry construction the outer layer is permeable and you will get water penetration to the inside face of the outer leaf of the cavity wall. When an opening is formed, therefore, it is important that this water is diverted to the outside; for this reason a stepped damp-proof course should be incorporated over openings; it is common to incorporate these into lintels.

Insulation: Standards for insulation are quite high these days and you will need to ensure that your walls conform to these standards. When you are using a timber-frame type of construction the timber frame will include insulation, but if you are using masonry construction you will need additional insulation, either in the cavity or as an insulation board applied to the inside of the wall. The trouble with the latter option is that you are cutting down on the useable space within the building, so the former option is usually the preferred one. If you do insulate the

Pouring the slab.

cavity, make sure that the insulation does not sag down into the cavity or you will create cold spots on the wall.

Batching/Samples: When you are using masonry construction you may find that the bricks vary slightly in appearance from each other and that different lorry loads may also vary from each other. This is known as 'batching' and is caused by variations or impurities in the clay from which the bricks are made. For this reason it is better, if you can, to buy all your bricks at the same time and also to mix up the bricks from different palettes before laying them. If you are employing a bricklaying contractor it is a good idea to ask for a sample panel and agree the quality of the brickwork so that there can be no disputes later.

163

Quality detailing of external walls is important to make a quality building.

Building In: It is common practice to build-in windows and door frames as work proceeds, but this can result in damage to them. You can opt for the building in of timber templates of the windows and doors, which will then be replaced at a later date, but this can result in a poor fit, so building in is acceptable but do look out for damage and ensure that built-in elements are protected as much as possible.

Movement Joints: Masonry construction is essentially making one big element (a wall) out of lots of little ones (bricks or blocks). The wall, when built, will act as a single entity structurally and also thermally. The wall will expand and contract infinitesimally with fluctuations in temperature and when it is over a certain length (generally 15m (49ft) horizontally or 7.5m (24ft 6in) from a corner) it needs to incorporate movement joints to prevent cracking. These movement joints are just a continuous vertical break in the brickwork, packed with a compressible material. Your structural engineer will advise whether movement joints are necessary and where they should go; they are not the most decorative items so it is a good idea, if you can, to site them unobtrusively or to hide them behind rainwater pipes.

Internal Load-Bearing Walls
It is likely that you will have a few load-bearing walls internally. These are walls that are designed to take some of the load of the intermediate floors and the roof. Because of their structural purpose they will need to have their own foundations and will need proper lintels over any openings formed in them.

Load-bearing internal walls should be constructed at the same time as the external ones and should rise as they rise. It is usual that load-bearing walls will be bonded in with the external ones so that they interact together, but they also sometimes have a movement joint (see above) to prevent cracking.

Intermediate Floor Structure

Intermediate floors can be constructed in a number of ways, but the two most common are timber and precast concrete. The advantage of precast concrete is that it has good sound insulation so that noise generated by children in upper rooms, for instance, will be lessened, but it is generally more expensive to use.

It is usual to construct or build-in the floors as work proceeds; this means that the walls are properly braced and also gives a working platform on the inside of the building to assist with their construction. Do not, however, allow the floorboards to be installed until the building is weather tight, since they will warp if they are exposed to damp.

Make sure that openings through the floor for staircase and the like are properly trimmed and in the correct place. It is also a good idea to check the floor joists or beams against the place where your drainage stacks will go, since wrongly positioned joists can mean that a drainage pipe has to be moved to a much more obtrusive place than was originally planned.

Roof Structure

It is likely that you will be constructing your roof, be it flat or pitched, in timber, the only exception to this being where you are planning to take large loads – perhaps when you are planning a roof garden, or where you plan to use a flat-roof terrace for sunbathing, barbecues or the like – in these cases it is common to use concrete (precast or in-situ).

If you have a flat roof then it will generally be constructed from timber joists spanning between load-bearing walls. It is a good idea to have some form of access onto a flat roof, either via a roof hatch or via an adjoining window if the flat roof is over a portion of the building that is lower than the rest; this is for the purpose of maintenance, since flat roofs are more prone to failure than pitched ones.

A relatively recent innovation in the construction of timber roofs has been the introduction of trussed rafters. A traditional roof is built up of loose timbers with inclined rafters restrained by ceiling joists and supported by purlins; this type of roof can be slow to build and needs a good measure of skill on the part of the builder. Trussed rafters are lightweight trusses that are prefabricated off site and then simply dropped into place. The advantage of trussed rafters is their speed of erection and their cost, the disadvantages with them are that they only really work with simple roof shapes and the fact that they fill the roof with a web of criss-crossing timbers, making the loft space unsuitable for storage or future conversion, unless you opt for more expensive 'attic' trusses.

Roof Coverings

Installing the roof covering is a crucial point in the construction process. The project is suddenly virtually watertight and is no longer subject to the vagaries of the UK weather. This will trigger all the internal efforts and finishing trades.

Again, with the number of different finishes available there is little point in going into this in great detail, but there are a few points, which are worth being aware of.

Insulation: As part of the drive to conserve resources the government has introduced increasingly stringent regulations to insulate buildings. This has been particularly focussed on the roofs where a lot of the heat is lost. Heavy insulation has increased the chance of condensation on the cold side of the insulation and this condensation can be particularly damaging, since it is in out of the way places, against timber and you can get wet rot developing over a period of time. To get over this problem you have two options; you can either put the insulation on top of the roof timbers or you can make sure the roof void is well insulated. The trouble with the first option is that it is more expensive, since the insulation must be in board form rather than the cheaper glass fibre quilt and the overall thickness (and hence the height) of the building is greater. If you go for the cheaper option you need to make sure that there is at least a 50mm (2in) ventilation gap over the insulation, that the roof is well ventilated by specialist ventilation fittings at the eaves and possibly ridge, and that any tanks and pipes within the (cold) roof void are well lagged.

Insect Infestation: The roof space is a secluded area and hence things can go on there that you may not be aware of. One of the most common problems is unwanted tenants such as wasps. It is important, therefore, to check and ensure that all the ventilation gaps are protected by insect mesh, and that there are no gaps or tears in the sarking felt (the waterproof layer under the tiles).

Penetration of the Roof Covering: There will be various points where the roof coverings will be penetrated by ventilation pipes, flues, drainage stacks and the like. It is clearly important that these points are properly protected so that they don't let water or pests back into the roof space. Most types of roof covering will come with proprietary systems to get over this, such as ridge vents and ventilation tiles, and it is generally better to use these products rather than go for more traditional methods like forming a lead collar round pipes where they penetrate the roof.

Drainage: Roofs are the worst source of leaks and problems with water penetration, and special care should be taken with them. It is obvious that you need to ensure that the covering is continuous and well sealed at its perimeters. Also of prime importance is the way that the roof is drained – rainwater pipes and gutters are notorious for blocking. With flat roofs it is common to have a parapet detail with a concealed gutter behind it. If you do have this arrangement and there is a blockage, you can get water build-up and sometimes it will flow back into the building. It is important to detail the roof in such a way that this cannot happen, by making sure that the water will flow outwards first. This can be achieved by detailing a 'weir', which is a hole in the parapet through which water can flow, alternatively an overflow pipe installed 50mm (2in) above the surface of the roof and projecting through the parapet will give warning that water is building up. Whatever the situation, it is good practice to provide two different drainage points from any roof and also to install leaf guards on gutters and down pipes to prevent blockage.

Screeding and Damp-Proof Membranes

Concrete floors will generally have a rough finish and it is common practice to finish them with a smooth screed. If you have not opted for insulation and damp-proof membrane (DPM) under the slab, it is common to install a DPM and insulation over the slab and under the screed. When installing the DPM, care must be taken that it laps and seals with the damp-proof course at the base of load-bearing walls, since you are, in effect, forming a continuous water-proof liner to the building.

A screed can also be subject to movement in the same way as brickwork, so it is important to control that movement to prevent random cracking. The screed will be installed in batches and, to prevent cracking, you can install movement joints at the boundary between the batches.

It should be noted that a screed is not the only way of finishing a concrete slab. If you are going for a timber-effect finish rather than a carpeted floor, you can install levelling battens and insulation straight onto the slab, and the floor over that.

Floor Deck

Having got the building watertight the floor can be boarded over to give a secure platform to work from. What the deck will be rather depends on what the floor finish is going to be. If you are intending to install carpets throughout, the cheapest deck to use is tongue and groove chipboard (water resistant in bathrooms and kitchens); if you are planning on tiling the floor you will want to use a more stable deck such as water-resistant (WBP) plywood; or if you are thinking of a timber floor, it is worth thinking about combining the deck and the finish by installing timber floor-boards – if you do this, however, you should ensure that the floor is protected with sheets of hardboard securely taped down for the rest of the job.

Internal Partitions

The next process is the installation of the framework of the internal partitions; it is likely that these will be in the form of timber studs rather than the more unusual metal ones.

The studs will generally be constructed at 600mm (2ft) horizontal centres to conform to standard plasterboard widths. Crosspieces, or 'noggins', are also installed to restrain the end of the plasterboard. It is also important to fix noggins anywhere where

There is an increasing use of metal studs to construct partitions ...

... but the effect is still the same at the end.

there are likely to be heavy objects, such as cisterns, hung on the wall.

It is a good idea to build doorframes in as work proceeds, to ensure a good fit.

Electrical First Fix

The 'first fix' is basically the process by which all the electrical wiring and back boxes, which will be hidden from sight, are fixed, thus allowing the plasterboard to be fitted. Care should be taken to position the cabling away from areas where it might suffer physical damage from the tacks that are used to fix the plasterboard.

When the cables are buried in the wall and plastered over it is good practice to protect them with 'capping'; this is PVC or galvanized steel, which fits over the wires to give them some measure of protection in the future.

Where the electrical back boxes are set in partitions, make sure that they are securely fixed to studwork or noggins since, if they are not, they will work loose as you plug and unplug electrical equipment.

Plumbing First Fix

First fix for plumbing is similar to that for the electrical works; this time it is the pipe work for heating, hot and cold water, and drainage. Again, it is of prime importance to try to keep the pipes away from areas where they will be damaged by nails.

Pipe work will need to drop down from one floor to another and it will often not be possible to site it within partitions. A plumber is likely to site the vertical ducts in the place that is the easiest, not necessarily the most aesthetically pleasing. It is a good idea, therefore, to allocate specific locations for vertical pipe work and to make sure that this is conformed to.

Pipe work will have various key points that will need access for maintenance purposes; these are rodding eyes in the case of drainage, and valves and drainage points in the case of hot and cold water pipes. These can be concealed, as long as access traps are provided to get access. It is a good idea to fit 'ball-o-fix' valves at each sanitary fitting, so that they can be isolated when necessary for maintenance or

replacement without having to drain the whole system.

Before covering up it is a good idea to bring the pipework up to full operating pressure to check for leaks, since it will be much more difficult and expensive to find any leaks once everything has been sealed up. In addition, it is suggested that the drawings are brought up to date so that all the pipe runs are marked on them – in the event of a problem you will find them much easier to locate. It is also very important to ensure that all pipe work is properly lagged where it is in areas that might be prone to freezing.

It is a good idea before covering up the pipes to offer up the radiators and the sanitary appliances, and even connect them loosely so that you can ensure that connections are correctly positioned.

Fitting the Staircase(s)

It is the usual practice to fit the staircase and the balustrade before beginning the plastering, so that you can get a good finish to the soffit and the top. The staircase will also act as a useful means of vertical circulation and a guard against any of the workmen falling down the stairwell, but care should be taken to ensure that the balustrade and the treads are protected with hardboard to protect them from damage.

Any wall handrails should not be fitted until the plasterwork has been finished.

Plasterboard/Plastering

Traditional plastering consisted of a thick layer of wet plaster spread over walls and partitions. This is still an option, although you should be careful to put expanded metal lath (EML) on studwork partitions and ceilings to give the plaster a 'key' to hold on to. You will get a good finish this way, but it will be expensive and it will take a long time to dry.

There has, in the last few decades, been an increasing trend towards a plasterboard-based technology for creating a plastered finish; this is known as 'dry lining'. Dry lining involves the use of plasterboard throughout, stuck to masonry with spots of special plaster known as 'dabs' and tacked to ceilings and partitions. This can be finished by either taping the joints between the boards with a special tape and then putting a filler across them, or by putting a thin

Wet plastering on expanded metal lath gives an opportunity for unusual shapes.

'skim' coat of plaster over the whole board; the second option will give you a better finish, since the joints always show through with the first, however hard you try. You can go for a hybrid solution where you plaster the masonry walls and dry line the partitions.

When you do use conventional plaster it is worth trying to minimize cracking. The way to do this is to install reinforcement at the junction between different materials and at external corners. This is usually done with expanded metal lath (a sort of mesh). In addition, you should use plaster beads where the plaster stops but is not covered with an architrave, for instance at the junction with a window frame; this ensures that the plaster ends with a nice even line instead of an unsightly crack. Another

way of minimizing cracking at the wall-to-ceiling junction is to install a plaster cornice or coving to cover it up.

Carpentry Second Fix

After the plaster has been finished you can do the second fix on the carpentry items; these are skirtings, architraves, doors and the like. Architraves cover up the junction between the plaster and the door frames, but there has been an increasing trend of late to do without an architrave and to install instead a plaster stop that incorporates a shadow gap; this will give a less complicated more modern approach.

Similarly the skirting has evolved to cover the junction of the wall and the floor, and to prevent the plaster from being scuffed or marked by brooms or vacuums, but you can employ a similar shadow-gap detail at the base of the wall, or recess the skirting with a shadow gap over for that modern look.

When hanging the doors you will need to take account of the thickness of the floor covering. If you are laying carpet you need to plane enough off the door to clear the carpet; this will avoid you having to hang the door twice.

It is a good idea to install a window board on the inside of the sill to avoid damage to the reveal; if you are in a bathroom or kitchen it is usually better to tile the sill instead.

Plumbing Second Fix

Before commencing the decorating it is a good idea to fix the sanitary ware and the radiators, and run the system for a while. That way, if there are any problem, or any minor adjustments required, they can be made without ruining the decorations. You can always drain the system and temporarily disconnect so that you can paint behind the radiators and other appliances.

Make sure the protective film on the sanitary ware, where provided, is in place to minimize damage.

Electrical Second Fix

For the same reason as above, the electrical second fix should be completed before decoration. When it has been done you need to check carefully that all the points are there – it is common for plasterers to inadvertently loose them behind the plasterboard and it is also only at this stage that it becomes apparent what the various wires emerging through walls actually are.

Decorations

Before allowing decorations to proceed you should ensure that the electrical points are loosened from the wall, so that they can be 'cut in' behind, and that radiators and so on are off the wall, so that you can paint behind – even if you have to try hard to see it, that bare patch behind the radiator will really irritate after a while.

External Works

Finishing off the external works traditionally gets left to the very end, so that contractors can store materials and park their vehicles on site to the very last minute. It is good policy, however, to finish off the externals before you complete the decorations and certainly before you lay the floor coverings – you do not want contractors grinding site debris into your nice new carpets!

You have to be careful what time you do the planting, since planting or laying turf at the wrong time of year can end up being time and money wasted. Again, a good gardening book is a sound investment.

Completion

It is easy, when the building is virtually complete, to let impatience and frustration take over and to move into your house prematurely. If you do this you will find that the uncompleted parts of your building will become an irritation, spoiling your enjoyment of your new home. You may also find that if you do not complete various procedural matters they will return to haunt you later. Of particular note are the following:

Snagging: At the end of each of the work stages listed above, make a list of any items you believe have not been completed or include defective work. The best way to ensure that the contractor or subcontractor completes the work is to withhold payment on that item until it is properly finished. The building will inevitably settle down a little as it dries out and you will get cracks appearing at the junctions of different materials. It is pointless to repair these as they arise, since they will open up again; it is better to repair them after a period of time – usually six months – once they have finished moving. Hopefully you will have put in place a defects liability period as mentioned in the 'safeguards' section above.

Guarantees: A building is a complex machine and has various systems that function separately and together to make the building work. You will find that, over the first few months after completion, various of these systems will have malfunctions, mostly of a minor nature. During the defects liability period you can get the contractor to come back and repair any problems that arise, but once you have released all the money you will have more difficulty; this is why it is important to obtain the relevant guarantees. You will have fitted various complex pieces of electrical and mechanical equipment as part of the contract that, had you brought from a shop, you would have ensured were covered by warrantee; it is important, therefore, to ensure that any guarantees are handed to you at the end of the job and it is also worth contacting the supplier or manufacture with a view to taking out an extended warrantee.

NHBC: If you have gone for an NHBC warrantee, make sure that everything is signed off – do not get the inspector in too early since your ten-year guarantee will run from the time the final inspection is made, but do get them in while the job is still fresh in their mind.

Planning Approval: Any scheme that has been the subject of a planning application will have a number of conditions attached to any approval. It is well worth ensuring that all these conditions are discharged, even if the planning authority is not particularly proactive in enforcing them, since, if you sell the property in the future, you may find that the purchaser's Local Authority search turns up the fact that the conditions have not been discharged and delay your sale.

Building Regulations: For the same reason as above, it is important to ensure that the Building Inspector signs the building off, and issues a completion certificate.

Moving In

It is not particularly easy to point at what exactly constitutes completion, but completion will trigger several different processes so a date must be set.

Practical Completion

If you are employing a main contractor the end of the contract works will be triggered by 'Practical Completion'; this is an acknowledgement by you or your agent that the building is, to all intents and purposes, complete. This will trigger, in return, the start of the defects liability period. It is an accepted precedent that, if you move in, you have accepted the building as practically complete, so be wary of moving in too early – even moving furniture into the building can be construed as moving in.

Insurances

If you have employed a main contractor, practical completion will signify that responsibility for insurance has passed to you, so make sure that you have the building insured. Similarly, if you are running the project as a managed contract with subcontractors coming in, your occupation signifies the end of the need for your contractor's all-risk insurance. The golden rule of all this, however, is to keep your insurers informed at all times as to the state of progress.

Council Tax

The imposition of council tax will be triggered by the completion of your house and when you move in, but you might have to be prepared to prove it. Often it will be enough to simply state when you have moved in and you will be billed accordingly, but suitable proof, if required, can be the Certificate of Practical Completion or the Building Regulations completion certificate.

Conclusion

We may our ends by our beginnings know.
(John Denham *Of Prudence*)

It is difficult to write a conclusion to a book such as this, since in a sense, the end is the beginning. As diverting and interesting as the process of building a house is, the target must always be the finished product and the way that it is used, and this is really where the whole thing starts – your future in your new home.

So there we have it, you have come through it all and you are now the proud owner (or part owner) of your own home. Hopefully, you have found the whole thing exciting and, perhaps, you have found it a little too exciting at times, but the fact is you will have achieved something that most people only dream about; you have joined the elite and become a self-builder, but be careful – this business is addictive.

Useful Contacts

HELPFUL ORGANIZATIONS

Advisory Conciliation and Arbitration Service	020 7210 3894
Architects Registration Board	020 7580 5861
ASBA (Association of Self-Build Architects)	0800 387310
Association of Consulting Engineers	020 7222 6557
Association of Self-builders	0704 1544126
BIAT (British Institute of Architectural Technologists)	020 7278 2206
Community Self-build Agency	020 7415 7092
Constructive Individuals	020 7515 9299
Federation of Master Builders	0207 242 7583
RIBA (Royal Institute of British Architects)	020 7580 5533
Joseph Rowntree Foundation	01904 629241
Segal Trust	020 7831 5696
The Building Centre	0906 516 1136

LAND SOURCES

BuildStore	01506417130
Landbank Services	0118 9626022
Plotfinder	09065 575400

COMMERCIAL ORGANIZATIONS

Border Oak (timber-frame houses)	01568 708752
Bradford & Bingley (self-build mortgages)	0800 570 800
DMS Services (self-build insurance)	01909 591652
Ecology Building Society (self-build mortgages)	08457 697758
First Direct (self-build mortgages)	01132 766100
Halifax (self-build mortgages)	01422 333333
Huf House (prefabricated houses)	01932 828502
NHBC(warranties, building control)	01494 434477
Norwich & Peterborough (self-build mortgages)	0800 883322
Project Builder (warranties, insurance)	01227 367245

Self-build Advisory Service (mortgages and legal insurance)   01968 678989
Trenwick Willis Coroon (warranties)   0151 625 3883
Wolsey Securities (finance)   020 8481 7676
Zurich Municipal (warranties)   01252 522000

GREEN ORGANIZATIONS AND COMPANIES

Association for Environmentally Conscious Building   01559 370908
Association for the Conservation of Energy   020 7359 8000
Centre for Alternative Technology   01654 705950
Construction Resources (green builders' merchant)   020 7450 2211
The Green Shop   01452 770629
National Energy Services Energy Ratings   01908 672787

FURTHER READING

Blackberry Books (a range of self-build titles)   01983 840310
Building Bookshop   020 7692 4040
Build It (self-build magazine)   020 7772 8307
Home Building and Renovating (self-build magazine)   01527 834400
HMSO (building regulations, planning legislation, etc)   0870 600 5522
HSE Books (health and safety books)   01787 881165
JCT (various forms of contract)   020 7637 8650
Joseph Rowntree Foundation   01904 629241
RIBA Mail Order Books   020 72519911
RICS Mail Order Books   020 7222 7000
Ryton Books (a range of self-build titles)   01909 591652
Selfbuild & Design Magazine (self-build magazine)   01283 742950
Stonepound Books (a range of self-build titles)   01273 842155

Index